Children and Dramatics

RICHARD CROSSCUP

Children
and
Dramatics

Charles Scribner's Sons   New York

To my wife

Acknowledgments

THERE ARE NUMEROUS DEBTS of gratitude which I owe in connection with this book. I am grateful, first of all, to my wife for enduring all the extra burdens which a working wife must endure when her husband's nose is to the typewriter and his attention in the clouds. I am much in debt to her also, and to Dr. Frank Horne, for important criticisms while the book was in progress, especially for their penetrating discussions of the treatment of some of the social implications of the subject. I am also deeply indebted to two others, Miss Muriel Sharon of the 92nd Street Y.M.H.A. in New York and Miss Eleanor Sullivan of Scribners, who read the manuscript and made many valuable suggestions.

There are older debts than these, debts which lie in the area of the substance of the book—that is, in the area of creative work with children. When I first came to the Walden School in 1940, Miss Berta Ranz, who was the English teacher in the high school, set up a course in creative dramatics, and this course was my initiation into this activity. For a number of years, too, I benefited from her candid evaluations of the work in dramatics which I did with eighth graders. At that time, Miss Hazel Welch was teaching the seventh grade, and it is to her, perhaps, more than to any other adult, that I owe such understanding as I have of the creative potential of children. Her insights were transmitted to others only in small measure by what she said, but in very great measure by what she did. In my case, they were transmitted most significantly by the creativity, already released, of the children who came from her to me. It is to these children, and to hundreds and hundreds of others in schools and camps and centers in many parts of the country, that I owe the greatest debt of all.

—*Richard Crosscup*

Introduction

THE FULL FINE MEANING of this book will sweep over you like
a sunburst only when you have laid it down. Then you will
see that Mr. Crosscup has shaped a kind of technical poem,
throbbing with impulses of purest dedication. The title *Children and Dramatics* is modest, exact, and a little misleading
until you realize that in Mr. Crosscup's construction it is almost
a hallowed phrase. He is literally an "educator." There is a
word whose meaning we take in our casual stride unless we
remind ourselves of its original Latin energy—*educere*, "to lead
out." For the children of Israel it was what Moses did—the
first great e*duc*ator.

The pathos of some of our most venerable phrases. "As

the twig is bent"—"the child is father of the man"—"trailing clouds of glory"—"shades of the prison-house . . . growing boy." I thought of this as I finished reading Mr. Crosscup's final chapter—in a not dissimilar connection. Our very first play in the Group Theatre, *The House of Connelly*, held within itself a meaning which for us transcended the play itself. It had to do with the pathos—even the tragedy—of *beginning*. Even of being born. The play was about that—and in its way it provided us with our annunciation.

That forward impetus, generated out of the obscure needs of the maturing twenties, gave the Group Theatre not only its form but also its pioneering élan. Everything was ours to investigate, test, discard, or preserve; our search as actors was extended to all the possibilities of a craft committed to the exposition of truth in the living transaction between performer and audience. But primarily, sustaining this process, there was the faith, all too fragile in a world whose bent was cynicism and destruction, in the enlargement of Man himself. The combination of Actor-Man was held in mind as a heroic possibility for the enrichment of theatrical culture. The slogan of the Moscow Art Theatre, "the justification of Man," and Gorki's "Man—it has a proud sound!"—these words animated our spirits even as we retaught ourselves to look, to listen, to absorb, to relax, to concentrate, to connect, and to act.

This is why I speak of Mr. Crosscup's book as a *technical* poem. My look at the beginnings of the Group Theatre is a long, backward one. Dealing with the young as he does, Mr. Crosscup's look is a perpetually forward one. Where our regards mingle is in that area where the learning process (the *how*) is interpenetrated with the *quality* of the young man and woman who absorb it (the *what*). Our interests, differing in emphasis, are fundamentally the same. For the practicing actor, with his responsibility to author and audience, a lifelong dedication to learning his craft will inure him to the act of nightly repetition, of reproducing in performance those values which were planned in rehearsal. For Mr. Crosscup's youngster the rehearsal period is probably the most fruitful, while the actual performance may be fringed with a kind of mystery, for the full act of facing an audience waits upon years of yet unexplored experience of life. The author says it all when he writes:

> For the performance itself is unimportant, except as it may give momentary pleasure to adults or as it may lend new insights or a sense of standards and creative possibilities to an audience of the players' peers. It is the process which is important because it shapes the players' sensitivities, their human understanding, their creative potential, and, hence, the course of their lives.

This can be said as well of the sensitive professional actor's development, though in a less poignant sense. In addition to "Live and learn," his motto must also be "Stand and deliver!" But the truly sensitive and growing actor will always remember his roots. He will check what he is and does now with what he once aspired to, remembering and treasuring its untried sweetness as though he still carries a space within him that once housed some kind of vessel of vision and desire. From this point of view, Mr. Crosscup's book is something more than a *Lehrstück*. It is a tactful reminder to all of us more-or-less mystified adults, in and out of the theater, that in a profound spiritual sense we may have lost our way and that there's really no point in our looking back. As someone I know is fond of quoting: "If you don't act as you believe, you end up by believing as you act."

A pessimistic conclusion. "I hate it," says Sir Toby, "as an unfilled can!" To fill the void, I remind myself that there's a perpetual vigor in the very act of succession, of handing on the torch. I remind myself that the double idea of "technique of acting—technique of living," "tragically" undertaken by the Group Theatre, was inherited from the great Stanislavski and has been passed on into the bloodstream of American theater. The idea is immortal—and in this book we find it informing the work of an educator with passion and understanding. From Make-Believe into Expanded Communication, Mr. Crosscup has examined the principal stations of his quest with more than sympathy, with love, love for the deed and for the doer.

We make ourselves over from within. Acting has taught me the power of the inner Image to transform the outer Reality. The imagination is teased into believing that such a conception, properly used, might open our lives to undreamed-of fulfilments. Mr. Crosscup has felt this in his work, and has said as much in many ways. Never so movingly, however, as in the finale of this book, where he tells how one young student, dedicated to seeking *his* Image, found it in the pursuit of one of the grimmest Realities of our world, even to the sacrifice of his life. Let the last chapter describe the beauty of this young man's pilgrimage and pronounce his name.

—Morris Carnovsky

Contents

Children and Dramatics

1
ooooooooo
Activity and Meaning

A SMALL FARM CAMP in Pennsylvania had two ping-pong tables, and during the camp's first summer these tables were in constant use. Boys managed somehow to get in a game or two between wash-up and breakfast, the girls insisted on their rights to the tables at certain times during the day, and the counselors played at night after the campers were in bed. There were other activities—arts and crafts, hiking, field games, sports and even the beginnings of a dramatics program which later became part of the camp's distinction—but nothing towards which the campers turned with the spontaneous enthusiasm they devoted to ping-pong. Thus, at whatever time of day a camper could make a free choice of what he would do, more than half the camp's population could be found at the ping-pong tables, either playing or waiting a chance to play. Because the camp was new, there were no traditions, no established tone, no remembered gratifications from prior summers for the campers to renew, children and adults were largely new to each other and had not yet established a mutual trust. The proprietor-director's philosophy was such that he did not wish to regiment or over-schedule. He wanted the children to have time to find things to do on their own. But his heart was heavy, and during that first season the incessant *ping* and *pong* which formed a background for all the other camp sounds seemed to him like the drum-beat of a death march, the death march of his aspirations, which were to make valuable contributions to the lives of the boys and girls.

By the middle of the second summer, however, what he had hoped for came to pass. The ping-pong tables went unused and stood folded under a tarpaulin against the wall of the stone barn that was used as a recreation hall. The children were now too active to bother with ping-pong. They were busy walking, seeing, talking casually, holding discussions, planning events and carrying out their plans, dancing, singing, writing poetry, putting on plays, lying on their backs in stubble fields and watching the sweep of clouds and soaring hawks, tending kittens, making jelly, building dams in the brook, painting, learning to understand and like each other and each learning to understand and accept himself. They had forgotten the easy pleasures of ping-pong in favor of things which touched in more gratifying ways on their lives.

The needs of children for activity are subtle and extensive, and it is a misconception to assume that these needs are met if children are provided with physical outlets. Children have an equal need for social, cultural and intellectual outlets. The need for activity is a need of the psyche and extends to every aspect of the child's growth. In long-range terms, the child who is terrified of strenuous physical exertion is no more unfortunate than the one who commits too much of his emotional force to physical action and does not know how to be contemplative and still.

The validity of an activity does not reside in the activity itself, but in the meaning it has for the child. Swimming, reading, doing arithmetic, listening to a teacher, washing dishes, acting in a play, lacing a pair of shoes—under certain conditions any one of these can be thwarting, humiliating or even frightening; under other conditions, gratifying and fulfilling. Does dishwashing seem to be inherently thwarting? Consider the enormous sense of enlargement felt by the four year old who is first permitted to share in this familial act—or the hilarious comradery of teen-agers on a camping trip experimenting with assembly-line efficiency at drainboard and sink. What exaltation a little child feels when he laces his own shoes for the first time! But for the child whose parents have pushed him unwisely, repeated frustrations in such matters become a lasting measure of his sense of self-defeat. It might be said that the meaning of an activity in the life of a child consists of the pleasure he feels in sensing an enlargement of himself.

· For an activity to be meaningful to a child, he must commit emotion to it. It is for this reason that activities which are called "fun" or "play" are more easily taken hold of. However, the distinction between fun and work is often purely semantic. Children who have had extensive experiences, most of them gratifying, begin by nine or ten years to realize that some forms of play are all right as far as they go, but are not really much fun; that there are forms of work which are no fun at all, but which have to be done; that there are forms of work which are very satisfying, but which couldn't be called play; and that there are forms of work which are the most gratifying, the most fun of all. Children are ardent, and they commit their ardor to fun and play. But their ardors often compel them to undertake the arduous.

Is arithmetic fun, or is it hard work? Two eighth-grade girls, not particularly fond of arithmetic, spent more than a month solving an arithmetic problem, an activity they undertook on their own volition. It had started in the sixth grade when they had studied the freedom struggles of American history. Discussions and reading assignments had been supplemented by a considerable variety of activity. The group had filled the four walls of the classroom with wrapping-paper murals depicting Bacon's Rebellion, the Boston Tea Party, an incident of the Underground Railroad, the suffragette movement, etc. They had dramatized the story of the struggle of conscience of a young boy during the Revolution, who learned that the itinerant book peddler to whom he had become deeply attached was a British officer and a spy. The group had set this story in Valley Forge and in the process of dramatizing it had incorporated elements of their own making into the plot—for example, General Von Steuben drilling the ragged and undisciplined mechanics and farmers:

> VON STEUBEN (*Very softly*): Would you be so good as to take the pipe out of your mouth?
>
> SOLDIER: Why, General, sir, I smoked this pipe through the whole battle of Trenton!
>
> VON STEUBEN (*Even more softly but with withering acidity*): I'm sure it contributed to General Washington's victory! (*Bellowing*) TAKE IT OUT!

Later the group visited Valley Forge. Wearing jeans and T-shirts—for they were camping out not far away—they listened while the guide told them of the rigorous winter of 1775, pointed out scattered graves of Revolutionary soldiers and described the amputations performed by Dr. Bodo Otto. (Meantime gangs of children from other schools, the girls in pretty dresses, the boys in jackets and ties, as befitted a visit to a national shrine, swarmed wildly through the groves of rhododendron and dogwood, rooting up shrubbery.) At one point the group stopped by one of the Continental Army's bake-ovens, a mound of stones in the ground, and one of the boys asked, "Is this original or is it a reproduction?"

"We poured cement over it to preserve it," answered the guide. "Otherwise it is original. The iron door is original." At this point, one boy was squatting down, peering into the gloom of the bake-oven, one hand on the iron door. He gave the door a few shakes, crying: "I'm shaking hands with someone out of the past! I'm shaking hands with someone out of the past!" One after the other, each boy and girl in the group dropped to the ground and gave the door a shake. In the bus, as they travelled between one historic point and another—especially as they passed a farmhouse and thought that it was here that the boy of their story might have lived—they would pick up snatches of their play. The boy who had played Von Steuben had a tendency to loiter at each stop for one last look at a fort or a hut, and the guide, who had caught the spirit, would call, "Hey, Von Steuben! Hurry it up!"

During seventh grade the two girls concerned in our story continued to play soldier. Each was an officer of the Continental Army and various teachers, without their own knowledge, were generals—the school director General Washington and the sixth-grade teacher Anthony Wayne, etc. In eighth grade they had a very inspiring teacher, but very different from their sixth-grade teacher—no plays, no aesthetics, but earth-history, sky-history, man's pre-history and the science and mathematics of man's growing knowledge of his world. The students learned to make simple astronomical devices for measuring the degrees above the horizon of sun and stars and moon; they wrote monthly reports called "lunar reports" and often came back to school at night to observe astronomical phenomena from the roof.

The two girls were as involved in this program as they had been in the American Revolution. One day, while thumbing through a magazine, they saw an advertisement which showed Paul Revere setting out on his ride under a full moon. The girls knew that Longfellow had likened the yardarms of the British ships in Charlestown harbor to prison bars across the moon. But now they were very moon-conscious. They decided to find out whether the moon had really been full on that April night in 1775. The mathematical process was long and complex. They had to calculate backwards from a full moon sometime in 1960 to a full moon in April 1775. There were leap years, even changes in the calendar. Their teacher helped them refine their mathematical method and finally, in about a month's time, their computations were complete. Their data indicated that the moon, on the night of Revere's ride, had not been full, but gibbous—a phase which did not invalidate Longfellow's simile, but which did raise questions about the historical accuracy of the advertisement. The girls wrote to the advertiser and received a courteous but self-assured reply. The advertiser had actually been very scrupulous—he had had the phase of the moon checked by the astronomical mathematician at the Museum of Natural History. The girls checked their figures again, found no flaw and proceeded to the Museum. The mathematician was away and would be gone for about two weeks, but their data would be submitted to him when he returned. On his return, he studied the data, rechecked his own and wrote the girls a most respectful letter. It was not their computations that were in error, but his. The moon had, in fact, been gibbous on the night of Paul Revere's ride.

Thus is illustrated the interplay of activities by which a bridge between the adult world and the child's world can be built. The remote material of history books is humanized through discussion and through visits to museums and historical societies. It is given further realization through literature— through stories and poems about the people involved in the Revolutionary struggle—young people about the age of the students themselves or their older brothers and sisters or their parents—about artisans and farmers whose hearths, furniture and tools the children have already seen and touched—people raw and inexperienced (as the children, being raw and inexperienced, feel themselves to be) but growing and changing (as the children feel themselves to be growing and changing). The children are ready to express this identification in creative forms—in paintings, poems and stories of their own—and to pool their insights and creative forces in their own group play. In this instance, the visit to Valley Forge completed the process by which a paragraph from a history book ceased to be abstruse and remote and became a meaningful statement charged with the vision of the human condition. George Washington loses his patina as a public monument and becomes for the children a human figure—a man, deep and determined and often angry. And when he says, reacting bitterly to criticism, that it is "a much easier and less distressing thing to draw remonstrances in a comfortable room by a good fireside than to occupy a cold, bleak hill and sleep under frost and snow, without clothes or blankets," the children know what he means.

Yet the process is never complete, and this dynamic interplay of experiences and activities remains part of the child's functioning two years later—or ten, or twenty. In short, the validity of an activity resides not in its vigorousness or stillness but in its meaning; and that meaning is made up of a number of elements which relate a human being to his world in a number of ways. As Thoreau perceived, people lead lives of "quiet desperation" not because they don't have enough to do—quite the contrary, they do far more than they need—but because they do not establish for themselves that relationship between *doing* and *meaning*, and between *meaning* and *being*, through which life —however racked by inescapable sorrows and problems—is deeply fulfilled.

It is, of course, the role of adults to establish, where they can, the forms of activity in which children will engage, and to provide, as best they can, a content for such activities which is potentially rich in meanings, and to guide the activity in such ways that the meanings unfold for the child and become *his* meanings. This process presents a polarity. On one side, there is the adult—whether parent, school teacher, religious teacher, camp counselor, group worker or any adult whose role is to influence the child's development. This adult has certain purposes for the child—certain designs on the child, so to speak—certain attitudes, certain controls, certain facts and concepts and skills which he wants the child to acquire. On the other side, there is the child with his active inner life, with his attachments and scars, his evaluations and desires. Adults are often afraid of this active inner life of the child and tend to curb it. But the wise adult will love the child precisely for this inner life; he will not want to curb it, but to draw on it, to help the child channel it and find those more complex and postponed gratifications which growing up demands. He will find the forms by which a bridge can be built between his educational purposes for the child and the child's own inner life.

It would be a very profound mistake, but a mistake often made, to conclude that such activities as those described in this chapter are devices by which the adult helps children to stomach facts and concepts which would otherwise be dry, difficult and unpalatable. For the facts are themselves, in such instances, only the raw material of the activities, whose goal is the development of an historical vision, an interpretation of the human condition, a broadened and deepened humanity. It would be a further mistake, though a subtler one, to conclude that creative activity is justifiable primarily as a means to some other end. For creative activity has its own position; it stands at a point where any discussion of means and ends is semantic and worthless. An act of creation is both means and end. For the person who performs it, it is a probing, an expression, an extension of the self.

The need for creative self-expression is a need shared by all children. In slums and ghettoes, the world of young people, both their inner world and their outer world, is hurtful, intense, baffling, often turbulent; and, lacking other forms of expression, they often express their hurt and bafflement and turbulence in dangerous and harmful ways. On the other hand, children from sheltered homes in middle-class communities often have a problem of a different kind. Their outer world is orderly enough, but it lacks inward meaning. All too often these children find the schools arid, the camp program silly, the community center pretentious, the home without values, the church or temple without passion, so that the inner life goes its own way, and by the time the child is thirteen or fourteen his inner life may be almost beyond adult influence.

The cynicism of the "advantaged" child who has not really had advantages—who has been pampered and pandered to on one hand, and condescended to and stifled on the other—is often more impenetrable than the hurt of the "disadvantaged" child, who apparently can tell the difference between an advantage and a disadvantage. For such children exhibit a compelling thirst for the creative act. This is a truth which can be extensively documented in terms of little centers which devoted people have managed to establish in slum communities in the hope of attracting dozens, only to find that they have had to turn away hundreds. In both camp and urban situations, in large cities and in small mining patches throughout the East and Midwest, this writer has seen over and over again the avidity with which the children of poorer communities take to those human situations in which loving adults help them to explore their values and meanings and to express those values and meanings in creative forms. A similar eagerness for creativity among older boys and girls in slums and ghettoes—young people in their late teens and early twenties—has been documented by others; for example, by Dr. Kenneth Clark in *Dark Ghetto*. Dr. Clark's documentation also cites the constructive changes which creative activities—particularly dramatics—have brought about in the lives of those who were involved. Enrollment figures for the Harlem Community Art Center, which flourished during the WPA period, and for other similar centers in similar areas, support the assertion that creative activities meet deep needs. This writer has taught creative writing to Harlem adults and to Puerto Rican veterans of the Korean War. The response of these adults was deeply moving in every case. The need and the response are evident. The tragic fact is that the centers and institutions that are set up to meet these needs flourish for a year or so and then go out of existence for economic reasons, so that there are no permanent establishments which give the people in such communities the dignity that comes from self-expression.

The greatest part of this writer's experience, however, has been with truly advantaged children—children who have had the chance to go to schools and camps which promote the child's fullest development in every way, especially the development of conscious values which the child takes hold of and makes his own through productive and creative activity. Children growing up in such situations do not show the impenetrable cynicism which characterizes other "advantaged" children who grow up with no clear idea of what their meanings are. Sometimes a young person who has reached this characteristic stage of withdrawal, in changing schools, or even, in some cases, in changing camps, finds himself in a situation in which the probing and expression of meanings and values is part of the new air he now breathes. Little by little, in this new situation—or sometimes very swiftly, as if by an act of "conversion"—such a child throws off his cynicism and begins to take hold of life in more invigorated ways. We are not saying, of course, that children who attend schools and camps of a more vital and dynamic kind will grow up with a radiantly optimistic view of life. They will more likely grow up with a very critical view of life and will find a great many things not at all to their liking, for they will see life *consciously*. It is, of course, this critical spirit, this consciousness of the disparity between values and realities, that makes human betterment possible. This is to say, such young people will know better what use they want to put their lives to and why.

In this regard, the state of young people seems at the same time much better and much worse than it was a generation ago. Never before, it would sometimes seem, have so many young people been growing up with such scope of understanding, with such active commitments and interests, with such clear values. And never before have so many been growing up so lost. It is this contradiction, perhaps, which gives urgency to the question of the kinds of things which home, school, camp, settlement house, center, church and temple provide for young people to do.

2

○○○○○○○○○
Why Dramatics?

ADULTS WHO ARE CONCERNED with the problems of children and are in a position to influence what program of activities an organization will offer should give serious thought to the importance of including dramatics. It is an activity children frequently (young children almost constantly) indulge in without adult support. A leader from a social-work agency met with a large group of Negro parents and children to discuss the setting up of a program of children's activities in a center which the adults had acquired on Chicago's south side. He addressed himself primarily to the children, asking them about the kinds of activities they would be interested in. Dancing? They liked the idea. Painting? They were enthusiastic. Dramatics? They did not seem to know whether this was something they wanted or not. After talking awhile, the group worker led some games—party games of various kinds. After a number of these games, a girl put up her hand. "May we play our own game now?" she asked. Thereupon a group of boys and girls, ranging in age from eight to twelve, acted out a fairy tale—*Rumpelstiltskin*, perhaps— adlibbing the dialogue as they went along. "That," said the social worker when they had finished, "is what I meant when I asked you if you would like to have dramatics." Yes, indeed, they did want dramatics—now that they understood this strange new word.

These children, in their own play, had been creating values for themselves. But, of course, they would be able to go only so far without adult help. Under good adult leadership, dramatic activity offers rich contributions to the development of children, richer perhaps than those offered by any other activity.

Dramatics offers, as do reading or a good unit of study, an extensive subject matter. It offers, as good discussions and heart-to-heart talks do, an examination of life, but rendered more concrete by the setting up of a replica-of-life situation.

The subject matter of dramatics is as broad as the world of literature, of the poetry and stories which children read or write. It is as broad as the world of the senses, as various as the objects of thought, as intimate as the family, as remote as the heavenly bodies, as deep, as touching, as absurd as the human condition. The subject matter of dramatics is also, unfortunately, as shallow and tawdry as the surrounding adult culture, the commercialized culture, which children will all too easily absorb and emulate unless they are offered something better. "For who," says Socrates in reference to young people, "if offered the choice between poorer and better, would choose the poorer and eschew the better?" It is the leader's responsibility to offer them the choice, to offer them many choices. And to make a choice, children must, under the adult leader's guidance, probe the slice of life or the element of sensory experience which they will enact. So important, in fact, are these two things—the matter to be dramatized and the discussions through which the dramatization is to be developed—that neither can be treated adequately at this point. Each has a chapter to itself—"Communication and Values" for one, and "The Adult Leader's Role" for the other.

Putting on a play, like playing basketball, involves teamwork and, as an aspect of teamwork, the subordination of self to group. It is this subordination, perhaps, which creates for the individual a most gratifying sense of belonging, of sharing in purposes and goals. But it must also be admitted that dramatics activity often shares some of the liabilities of team sports—rivalry for position and the ego inflation of performing exceptionally well and receiving excessive recognition. The dramatization of standard plays, especially, involves much of this rivalry. If the number of parts is limited, a number of children may—like the boy or girl who doesn't make the team—have to retire and lick their wounds. In an original play, however, much of this rivalry will be eliminated, though not altogether, since even in the original play one part may be more desirable than another. But when children make up their own play, they can make up as many parts as they need and parts of such a kind that every child will have a chance to play a role which is challenging and satisfying to him. Furthermore, dramatics activity is free from that central characteristic of team sports as a form of human relationships— the determination to clobber an adversary. For when a group puts on a play there is no adversary, but only an audience, usually well disposed, an audience of whom the performers may feel a little wary, whom they may occasionally like to pique a little, but whom their central purpose is to stir and delight. Finally, the greatest and perhaps the most important part of dramatics activity will take place informally, for the pleasure of the group itself, without outsiders, and in such a way that there will be satisfactions for everybody and no rivalries at all.

Far more than in the case of team sports, but like other group undertakings, such as planning a trip or a party, the processes of creative dramatics are inherently democratic and provide for children an intense experience in democratic practice. For unless a play put on by children is to be, not their creative product, but the product of the adult who is "directing" them, who is using them, so to speak, as the raw material of his own creative expression, the process must necessarily involve that most democratic of all procedures—free discussion, free give-and-take, free expression of attitude, of point of view, so that decisions will be, in the deepest sense, collective, arrived at more often by consensus than by vote. Few activities involve so much free discussion, so much liberation of attitude and point of view. Yet in dramatics, perhaps, more than in any other activity, the widest diversity of individual attitude is least often an obstacle to unity and most often the very substance out of which the final unification is composed.

Dramatics also forwards the social growth of the child in other ways. Winifred Ward, in *Playmaking with Children,* has a chapter on the use of dramatics as therapy, in which she cites examples of children who have overcome stammering, of deeply withdrawn children who have come out of themselves and established relationships with others through dramatic activity. The adult working with children's dramatics must distinguish therapy of this kind from the use of psychodrama, a kind of dramatic activity which is to be employed only by people trained in psycho-therapeutic technique. But the kind of therapy of which Miss Ward writes is inherent in the process of creative playmaking, and the sensitive adult will handle things in such a way as to benefit individual children in very specific ways. For in any group of children some will be timid or introspective and will need to be strengthened. Others will be aggressively outgoing and will need to learn to look a little more deeply inside themselves. Some will move awkwardly, some will speak poorly, and in many cases the very process of being a new person or animal or natural force—of being something other than one's usual self —will free the child and help him to move and speak better. In other cases, the perceptive attention of the adult will help the child work on his awkward movements and poor speech, so that he can play, with satisfaction to himself, the role he is eager to play.

Dramatics also has for children the advantage, not of one activity, but of many. Although it is the point of view of this book that the process in creative dramatics is more important than the product, and that a rich and varied program of informal dramatics and dramatizations is more valuable than putting on plays, nevertheless performance has its own importance and its time and place in the growing up of boys and girls. And a group of children, eleven or twelve years old, who have something to say and are preparing to say it to an audience through a play will find themselves involved in reading, discussion, painting, designing, sewing, carpentry, rigging, furniture moving, electrical wiring, the aesthetics of lighting, cosmetics and make-up, various crafts such as wood carving and papier-mâché, writing, mimeographing and/or printing, silk screening, music and dance, poster painting and business management.

Through this wealth of activity, each child will find ways to contribute his skills or learn new ones. And if for some reason there is a child so shy that the adult has felt it wiser not to insist on his having a part in the play at this time, then the child can still find plenty to do and can share in the excitement. (One high school girl came to every rehearsal and during the rehearsals upholstered two chairs to be used in the play, though upholstering is perhaps too unusual an item to be included in our list.) Anyway, it is this headiness, this esprit de corps, this marvelous sense of accomplishment, of important culmination and significant experience which are among the growth-giving elements for children in putting on plays.

In creative terms, however, it is the dramatic process and not the collateral activities which is important. If a child paints a horse, he translates onto a piece of paper or canvas or wood panel, by means of tempera, water color or oils, his vision of grace or fire or pathos. But if a child *acts* a horse, he becomes a horse; his medium is his own organism; he translates his vision into a visible and audible image composed, so to speak, of his own flesh. As in writing poetry, he uses his own words, his own ability to find words suited to his vision. As in reading poetry aloud, he uses his own voice to project words and give them the force or the stillness, the tones and cadences characteristic of the beast whose words they are supposed to be. As in creative dance, he uses the resources of his own body—whether the large muscles of thigh or back, or the small muscles around the eyes—to make him be that beast. Thus in creative dramatics, as in no other art except dance, not only the vision, the image to be created, but the media for its creation, lie in the self.

And another dynamic enters which is not present when a child paints or models with clay or writes. These are activities which, even when surrounded by others, a child does alone. But in dramatics the child's creative vision is subject to change and modification through the vision of others. For if the child is playing a part in a group dramatization, then his individuality, his image of what he is being and the movements, words and cadences by which he creates that image are an element of the total composition. Whatever one child does helps or hurts, not only on the level of competence, as in sports, but on the level of appropriateness. If the child's insight is inadequate, he must think harder. If his vision is forceful and effective, but inappropriate, he must re-see his vision. Such inadequacy or inappropriateness will become a matter of group discussion and criticism —very objective criticism if the leadership is good. This evaluative process is perhaps the most inseparable part of making a play. In this way the individual's vision will be shaped as much by the group's vision as by the first germinal movement inside himself. And yet, in the end, the vision must be his own, or else it will lack creative validity. The child must learn the most important lesson of creativity—that is, that one must go beyond spontaneity and must learn to work at creating.

A performance by a high school class of Dylan Thomas's *Under Milk Wood* furnishes an excellent example of this point. The boy whom the casting committee chose for the part of blind Captain Cat had a great deal of natural but shapeless dramatic talent. In early rehearsals, the group began to despair of his carrying the role, though there seemed to be no one else suited for it. His pantomimic ingenuity in regard to the blindness was excellent on a realistic level, but his vision of the emotional depths of the character and, more importantly, of the poet's intent in regard to the character seemed shallow. His attempts to express these depths consisted too often of clever tricks of voice and rashly experimental pantomimic devices. The group and the teacher were candid in their discontent and their criticism. Gradually, as this criticism forced him to think and rethink, he began to drop deeper and deeper into the character, his vision spiralling down into himself and the buried resources of his own subjectivity. The role—both the character and the poet's intent, which is deeper than the character—emerged at last, beautiful and deeply moving. In the last few rehearsals, the whole group was rendered taut, like a bow string. All the comicality, absurdity and bawdry of the dramatic poem became lyricized, as the characters and their episodic snatches of drama moved around the pivotal form of Captain Cat. It was real vision, it was the boy's own vision, his own act of creation, and no one could have told him to do what he did. But it is also the case that this boy could not have achieved his vision without having his vision forced by the vision of others.

But there is yet another dynamic, even more important than this. Assume for a moment that a nine-year-old girl and boy are working on a dramatization together. Each knows what he is to represent and the general direction to be taken by the story.

Each seeks in his own imagination for the stance, the gesture, which will express what he represents. On this creative level, the two meet each other. The boy, for example, in his aspect of the wind blows on the girl in her aspect of fire. Fire reacts to wind —wavers and dies, or perhaps wavers, then expands and rages. And now wind must seek to cope with the force he has kindled and set in motion. Thus the creative image of the fire-ness of fire and the wind-ness of wind interact on each other, force each other in the very act of creation to new and greater visions of fire and wind. No purpose is served by philosophizing this point. It is an exciting and beautiful phenomenon. It is the essence of the creative element in dramatics when two or more children are working together.

These are some of the reasons why dramatics activity supports, deepens and illuminates for the young person the search for the self. We live in an era of scientific revolution, an era when the material world seems all important, and we seem to have forgotten that matter is important only to the extent that human consciousness assigns importance to it. In such an era we see increasingly that the inner life tends to become strident, to stagnate, to wallow in its own preoccupations, to become alienated—and this is the paradox of our times—from reality. Young men seek expression in violence because they do not know what they are. "What in God's name am I?" asks the Harlem youth of seventeen, feeling inside himself the surge of great forces, but forces which cannot find release in learning, for the schools have stunted him, nor in wholesome pleasures, for the streets have debauched him, nor in constructive, manly work, for there is no such work for him to do.

To claim that programs of children's dramatics are the answer to these profound problems would be absurd. On the other hand, it is very apparent that good activity programs, dramatics included, are an element in the answer. The Head Start program for pre-school children and the Haryou Act for youth are examples of steps which are being taken in this direction. It is also apparent that among such programs, many must be reality programs—that is, activities which relate the young person directly to the circumstances of his life and involve him in the bettering of those circumstances. But it should also be apparent that many of these programs must be creative, charged with strong psycho-emotional elements.

In this serious context, dramatics recommends itself to the attention of adults who want to help young people structure their inner experience. From their earliest years, young people should have extensive opportunity to participate in a process which over many centuries has provided for mankind some of the deepest symbols of his condition and of his relationship to the universal. It would not seem to be a chance thing that drama began in the rites of renewal—in Greece in the mysteries of the rebirth of Dionysius and in Western Europe in the mysteries of the Resurrection. For young people—particularly perhaps for pre-adolescents—creative dramatics provides much of what was provided, in primitive societies, by the rites of passage at puberty. It provides the opportunity for the youngster to move toward the new thing, at a time when, for a complex of reasons, he cannot or dare not actually become the new thing. Thus a twelve-year-old girl, dramatizing Ezra Pound's translation of Li Tai-po's "The River Merchant's Wife, A Letter," foretastes the quality of a profoundly self-contained but all-consuming love which is still a long way off. And a twelve-year-old boy, acting out, in *The Yearling*, Jody's flight from the hard conditions of reality and his return to them, tests himself against the stern demands of maturation.

Serious as these considerations are—and however soberly children will approach dramatics when the content of what they are doing is serious—it is not surprising that dramatics should be such tremendous fun. For drama is not only representation and symbol; it is also laughter and mockery, it is magic, it is manipulation of illusion, it is hoax and hocum—and hoax and hocum seem to be important elements in the nature of children, especially boys.

On a limited stage a group of sixth-grade boys create the deck of a privateersman in the War of 1812. Her sail can be hoisted or lowered; it can be turned on the yardarm and can be cleated down to starboard or port. And, illusion of illusions, it actually bellies, wind-filled, as the graceful privateersman plays cat and mouse with the lumbering British frigate in a light breeze! But now it hangs limp in the dreadful calm during which the frigate will send over wave after wave of long boats thronged with armed men in an effort to board and take the under-manned privateersman. The boys know perfectly well that what *they* do in breeze or calm, how they walk, talk, hold themselves, scan the sea (in which the audience is sitting), is far more important to dramatic realization than the bellying of their sail. But the sail is fun—and as long as the electric fan remains unseen the audience will be hoaxed, and this hoax creates a sense of wonder and delight.

Another year these same boys will play an old circus trick on their audience in a dramatization of Sholom Aleichem's *Mottel, the Cantor's Son.* One of Mottel's brother's get-rich-quick schemes is the making of ink. "Everyone," says the brother, "needs ink." When the ink is made—tubs and crocks of it—the brother finds out that not everybody needs ink and that those who need it already have it. The tubs and crocks of ink have to be disposed of, and the brother and Mottel carry out this disposal under cover of darkness. In the morning the village is in a state of uproar. The river is contaminated, the drayman's white horse and the milkman's white goat have turned black overnight. Now at the time that Mottel and his brother are disposing of the ink, the audience sees them pour black ink into a bucket; they see the bucket is full, for a little of the ink slops over the edge; they also see Mottel take this bucket up and throw its contents into their faces. When their screams subside, they realize that somehow or other it was not the same bucket, for they have been showered, not with ink, but with black confetti.

It is a preposterous thing to do, but very much in keeping

with the spirit of the play. For Sholom Aleichem is a writer in whose work deep tenderness is the inner and hidden content of the preposterous. The children know this, and this more than anything else is what they express. In short, the seriousness which this book attaches to children's dramatics is not at all incompatible with a joyous sense of mischief and fun.

3

ooooooooo

Make-Believe

ONE IS RIDING through the tree-shaded residential section of an unfamiliar city. From a doorway a little figure emerges, swathed in an enormous dress that almost entangles her; she clomps down the front stoop in shoes so big for her that the high heels wag behind in a kind of independent existence. The image is fleeting but familiar. It is somewhat more alarming to look from a taxicab window in Central Park and see a helmeted soldier emerge, sub-machine gun in hand, from behind a piece of shrubbery and run squatting in the manner of soldiers under fire. As he runs he keeps his steely eyes fixed on a wooded knoll on the other side of the road, from which, as one passes, one expects a burst of musket fire. Alarm quickly passes, however, as one sees that this resolute figure is an eleven- or twelve-year-old boy. Whether he plays alone and the enemy whom he both stalks and avoids is only in his imagination, or whether, hidden on the knoll, are other boys, his boon companions in the aspect of enemies, there is not enough time for one in a moving taxicab to determine. Anyway, we have recognized him—he is one of Tom Sawyer's brotherhood.

The hours and days of children, especially of children who are blessed without too much adult supervision, are spent largely in "acting." Or is it acting? The little girl is not acting Mother —she is *being* Mother. The boy is not acting a combat soldier— he is *being* a combat soldier. Human inwardness is capable of this process—of becoming whatever it has seen, or even of becoming what it has been told about but has not experienced. One can become mother or nurse or the wicked stepmother or the bad wolf or a combat soldier or a steamboat—or Beauty or the Beast, or Prospero, Miranda, Caliban, Hamlet, King Lear— or the tempest itself, or lightning or fire. This capacity for make-believe is inherent in the human organism. It is perhaps the human capacity which underlies all creative activity—it is certainly the capacity which underlies all creative expression in dramatics. It is a capacity which children make more use of than adults, but which many adults retain—which perhaps *all* adults retain, though it is often deeply buried and they no longer know how to make use of it.

Yet many adults do make use of this capacity, though infrequently, and not just actors and artists and writers, but people in everyday life. Years ago this writer looked from a window of a house in one of the suburbs of Boston and saw a charming pantomime being enacted by two ash men. (In New York they would be called garbage collectors, but in Massachusetts—at least at that time—the garbage men took away table scraps and the ash men took away furnace ashes and dry rubbish.) Anyway, the ash men had found, among some of the rubbish put out for them to take away, two tall silk hats, and these they were wearing. As the ash truck rolled along from house to house, the two silk-hatted gentlemen accompanied it on foot. Before each ash barrel they would stop, one on either side of the barrel, then they would bow low to each other, sweeping their hats from their heads in a courtly gesture, and with the same courtly grace, almost indeed as part of the same sweeping gesture, they would swing the ash barrel up and dump its contents in the truck, return the barrel to the sidewalk, bow and doff their hats again and move on. To paraphrase Huck Finn, "No English swell couldn't have done it better."

Adults do have some redeeming qualities and can sometimes, if given a chance, recover some of the gifts of children inside themselves. In courses in creative dramatics given to adults who are preparing to work with children, the things the adults come up with are often very charming. In one such course, given out of doors in a camp situation, it became the custom to take a make-believe coffee break during a recess from intensive dramatic exercises, much as "hunting for Sonya's purse" filled the recesses in Stanislavski's class lessons. This practice of taking a coffee break came about on the first morning of the course, when, during a brief recess, one of the men students quite spontaneously transmuted a tree into a coffee urn and began drawing and serving coffee. One of the women helped him pass the cups. Cream, sugar and coffee cake made their invisible appearance, together, of course, with spoons. One student found a very ingenious way of disposing of the soiled dishes. He picked up the cake plates; on these he piled the saucers, and on top of the saucers he stacked the cups, so that he held in his hands a tower of invisible pottery four or five feet high. This tower of pottery he balanced precariously for a few moments, while everyone waited expectantly for it to fall. Then, seeing nothing else to do with it, he tossed it high, brushing his hands together in a gesture of finality and looking up, as everyone else did, to see plates, saucers, spoons and cups vanish on the summer air. One rather elderly Ukrainian woman delicately brushed crumbs from her lap. It was characteristic of this impalpable coffee break to be marvelously refreshing.

But not all such adult make-believe is so innocent. Looking from an apartment-house window in Manhattan, a window that gave on a small, rocky park, this writer one day saw a terrifying and lonely pantomime. A lean young man, perhaps nineteen, perhaps twenty-five, wearing an ugly brown overcoat, was mounting the stone stairs that spiralled to the top of the rock. On a landing of these stairs, the young man swung around suddenly, flashed out a switchblade knife, and began to make murderous passes with it, first in one direction and then another. This kind of adult make-believe is unhappily not uncommon. How often on the streets or in subways one sees people who mutter to themselves, or whose silent but vigorous lip-movements adlib the burning psycho-dramas of their lives! Such behavior on the part of adults is frightening, for it expresses a lack of control over their impulses and an unnatural relationship between fantasy and reality. On the other hand, the make-believe of young children is similarly intense and the lines between fantasy and reality similarly indistinct. For the child, however, the acting out of his fantasies is wholesome and natural. It is a means for dealing with the turbulent wishes which reality does not permit him to fulfill in other ways.

It is also natural that, as children grow older, the intense subjective content of their make-believe tends to become recessive. Dramatic play becomes a pleasant routine, or it moves in the direction of the cultural and the humanistic, if the adult world provides opportunity for this movement. The distinction between the image and the reality becomes more precise. The intense subjective content remains inward as fantasy or daydream; or its latency provides the force behind rational, purposeful drives, or irrational, neurotic drives; or it gratifies itself vicariously through books or other works of art in which it sees itself expressed; or it expresses itself through creative activity.

Given the importance of make-believe in the life of the child, what contact can the adult make with this make-believe world? The camp group which goes out on a hike with one counselor returns tired and mean and homesick. The man has taken his work too seriously, has alternated between indulgence and harshness, or resignation and asperity—he has, in short, "kept on their tail" and made them trudge. The same group returns from a hike with another counselor tired but exalted—the physical arduousness having been transmuted by some kind of magic into spiritual attainment. Perhaps, little by little, as they walk along, a piece of make-believe has developed, embracing them all—they have pushed through the jungle growths and have looked on the Pacific. Or perhaps the counselor has achieved the result in less obvious ways—by a few imaginative touches, by a spicing of make-believe in retort to this boy or that girl, so that the hike has become for this boy or that girl a personal quest.

This kind of deftness at touching things with momentary make-believe is often a means by which a skillful adult can simultaneously enforce disciplines and establish a companionable rapport. "Come here," says the camp business manager sternly. "Let me see what kind of stones you are throwing." The boy, who has been throwing stones in perilous proximity to cabin roofs and passing campers, approaches timidly, carrying a stone. The business manager takes it and hefts it. "This is a hard stone," he says, with no relaxation in his sternness. "We've got two kinds of stones here—hard stones and soft stones. If you want to throw stones, throw soft stones!" So the adult sternness is make-believe—the business manager is an affable and companionable man making believe he is a Dutch uncle. The boy runs off, whether to do something else, or—if he is imaginatively suggestible and the fantasy pleases him—to look for soft stones.

There is the story of a teacher who had struggled through a

year with an enormously difficult eighth-grade group. He felt he
had done a valuable job of bringing the group together and establishing attitudes of respect and concern for each other, the
school and the content of their studies. But at the end of the
school year at a graduation party in the school gymnasium, they
began to go wild, to revert to all their harsh and rowdy and over-
stimulated ways. The teacher was angry—genuinely so, for he
was disappointed that after all he had achieved with them they
should again have come apart at the seams. He roared at them to
line up against the wall. It was a silly directive, but they were
ashamed, so they lined up awkwardly and felt silly. The teacher
looked at them and loved them and felt himself relax. Their own
eyes and mouths relaxed, and they looked back at the teacher
and loved *him*, though they still felt foolish and very uncertain
as to what he was going to say or do. Bending, he took up his
sub-machine gun and, making a machine-gun noise with his
mouth, he mowed them all down. They writhed and fell and
laughed and were chastened and got up and went back to their
party and had a better time than they had been having, because
they were filled with their unity and took pleasure in each other.

These are slight examples, but valid. What these adults have
conveyed wordlessly is this: "I am on your side and I understand. However, I am also part of an adult world which can't
quite put up with some of the things you do." Or, in the case of
the machine-gunning teacher: "I could kill you, I could absolutely kill every one of you, and would, too, if I didn't love you
so much."

For an adult working with children to lose himself, however, in their make-believe would be wrong and dangerous. A
high school girl wrote a disturbingly beautiful short play about
this matter. A little boy is playing, for his own reasons, the story
of King Arthur and the sword Excalibur. An adult man, a bystander, watches for a time and then joins in. The boy becomes
frightened and runs away, for the bystander has intruded the
highly charged symbolic content of his own fantasies. Nevertheless, an adult who knows how to be unobtrusive, who can bring

a sense of simple pleasure to the process, who has no neurotic axe of his own to grind, who can keep his inner and outer eyes open at the same time, can sometimes participate with children in their make-believe world. Whether or not through such participation he can subtly open up for the children aspects of the content of their make-believe world which gives this world cultural extension is not important, and any consciousness of doing so on the part of the adult might break the spell. But such participation would not hurt the children, could bring the children and the adult closer together and could offer to the adult drafts of deep refreshment.

One group of seven and eight year olds spent a whole evening being driven about by a camp director in the camp station wagon. They were looking for the town of Hutchenclutch, which one of the little girls had come upon one day, or so she said, while returning (all alone, it would seem!) from a hike. It was a beautiful town. It had no king—only a mayor. Fruits, meats, raw carrots, ice cream and chocolates grew from the trees year round. From time to time as they turned down this country road or that, someone—even the camp director—would catch glimpses of the towers of Hutchenclutch in the distance, but on closer approach these towers would prove to be only the formations of clouds or of mountains in the late dusk. In their search they drove by error into private lanes and were greeted suspiciously by farmers and barked at by farmers' dogs. So pleasant was this search that from time to time, over several seasons, groups of children, even teenagers, would take it up. But Hutchenclutch was never seen again.

These examples of adult participation in children's make-believe lead to another question: What part does the child's spontaneous make-believe play in an organized program of children's dramatics? What responsibilities do adults have to encourage it and give it direction? The pure Montessorians, apparently, give it no place and orient the programs of their schools completely on reality experiences. Other schools, however, many of them having at least one leg in the Montessori tradition and originating from the same educational upheaval of half a century ago, incorporate children's make-believe into the programs of nursery and primary groups—for children from three to about seven. In the nursery and kindergarten groups it is called "dramatic play"—or simply "play." And the inclusion of this play period in the program constitutes the first step in a dramatics program which will develop from grade to grade. The adults provide the time, and in many cases they also provide the materiel—a play corner, perhaps, stocked with dresses and jackets, pots and pans and dishes, shoes and hats—but especially hats, since the hat seems the most universal magic wand for transforming a person from one thing into another.

When children play with blocks, there is often a strong element of make-believe in what they do. And while the dominant element in this form of activity is not *being* something, but *making* something, the things which three, four and five year olds make with big blocks are "dramatic" in another sense of the word—that is, architecturally magnificent! Yet there is a further connection, for a little later on it may be that experiental activity, constructive activity and dramatics activity—still in the form of make-believe—meet at a common point. In one school, for example, the second-grade unit of study is the city. The group visits police station, fire station, fish market and waterfront, airport, zoo, etc. They see the things that make up their city, meet the people who do important things, discuss these things and these people, read about them and write about them—or, more frequently, dictate stories about them to the teacher or the student teacher. The culminating project is a vast construction, vast enough for a number of children to get into. One year it will be a fire engine, another a locomotive, or a tugboat, or an airplane or a supermarket—made of wood or of a wooden frame covered with cardboard or corrugated paper. It is when this construction is finished that the dramatizations begin. Bells clang; steam whistles toot; there are women and children to be rescued, liners to be docked, the clap-trap and baggage of the adult world to be mimicked, the strange patterns of adult attitude and behavior to be noted and explored.

Is this an example of "creative dramatics?" Or is it merely an example of the spontaneous make-believe, the capacity for which underlies all dramatic activity? It is, of course, both. It is children's spontaneous make-believe because there has been no defined goal towards which the dramatization is working, it is altogether "free." Yet if one defines creative dramatics as the extension of the child's make-believe, through adult help, to a content which expands the child's horizon in cultural and human terms, then it is creative dramatics. The adult's role has been oblique, but it has been present in the organization of the experiences on which the children have drawn for this new phase of make-believe, and it has guided the construction project that has stimulated the dramatic play through which these new experiences are savored, inter-related and assimilated by the child. Parents can play this role, too—and many do. For example, a parent who builds a playhouse in the back yard is providing the stimulus but is probably not extending the experience, for the playhouse will re-enforce the acting out of familial situations. This is not wrong—quite the contrary, for the playing out of Father and Mother and children is the first and most basic and perhaps psychologically most important phase of children's make-believe. However, at a certain time in the child's development a tree house might be better. Or the construction of a pilot house or an old rowboat on the lawn will stimulate a somewhat older child to invent all manner of dramatizations through which to absorb his expanding world.

Good toys also represent an extension of the child's resources for dramatic play. To provide a boy with a toy tractor or a girl with dolls in various national costumes might serve this purpose. The problem of representational toys, however, is that they limit as much as they expand—they tend to re-enforce repetitive patterns of fantasy. On the other hand, large blocks, cardboard cartons, sand piles and non-representational constructions such as one sees set up for children on the grounds of many housing projects—such things can become anything that the child wants them to become. Whether these things will be used, day after day, for the same old make-believe or inspired, when the child is a little older, by TV, or whether they will be used imaginatively, to transport the child to new worlds or to open up new phases of the real world, will depend almost entirely on whether adults have given the child anything to work with. For it is not the materiel which represents an expansion in the content of the child's make-believe, but it is where he has been and what he has seen and handled, and what things have stirred his thoughts and feelings through stories told him or read to him from books.

Even so, perversely enough, the unsupervised dramatic play of children will often fix itself and become repetitive—become merely a pleasant habit, like eight-year-old girls playing house or ten-year-old boys playing soldier or detective. We adults have very little understanding of the meaning and importance of those neutral preoccupations which children indulge in— counting Cadillac convertibles or bouncing a ball and counting the bounces—things which are neither good nor bad, but which often annoy adults and in which they see no value.

In short, the adult should have no preconceived ideas as to the form or direction which the child's make-believe should take. What is at issue is the child's imagery, whether that imagery releases itself in dramatic play or in other fashions. The child from three or four years should go places, see things, become acquainted with firemen and mailmen, with dogs and cats, with fish markets, wild animals, barnyard animals, woods, lakes, waterfalls and beaches. And these experiences should be supported by the child's being read aloud to, and by good talk in the home, so that experiences are remembered, understood and related in a natural and easygoing way to the values of the home. In these ways children will have something to work with, whatever they do.

4

°°°°°°°°°
Dramatic Fun and Games

THE GROUP WORKER in Chicago who found the youngsters were doing dramatics under the impression they were playing games was not too surprised for, as a boy of eleven, he and another boy had formed their own theater company. They would send to Baker for plays—any plays as long as they were short and funny and had only two characters (men or women)—or three characters if they seemed funny enough, since there was another boy whom they kept on call. The living room of one of the boys constituted the stage. The parlor, which had big double doors which slid into the wall, was where the audience sat. The boys built themselves a set that served for any kind of play—a sort of house made with a framework of wood covered by heavy blue paper of a kind used by builders. This house stood as a permanent fixture in the living room throughout the life of the theatrical company—a period of about half a year.

Of the two boys, one did not do very well in school and did not go beyond high school. He became a millionaire within five years of graduation. The other developed intellectual and cultural interests in high school, went on to college, graduating magna cum laude, and took a graduate degree in social work. By his mid-fifties he found himself in a position for the first time to buy a new car. From this one cannot, of course, draw any firm conclusions about the correlation between children's dramatic activities and future adult income. One can, however, conclude that very different children will often undertake rather advanced forms of dramatization, in the case of these boys, taking a story and making it into a play of their own through improvisation. "For," says the group worker, "the stories told in the play scripts were pretty perspicuous, so we never bothered to memorize—simply read them over a couple of times, purloined whatever we needed for costumes and let the neighborhood know that a performance would be given on such and such a night."

Between the free make-believe of children and the dramatization of actual story material, there are many forms of children's fun with a varying degree of dramatic content. There are—or used to be—the so-called Play Party Games—singing games usually, lovely things with a very strong emotional-dramatic content just beneath the surface. Some of these still persist as games for little children—"London Bridge Is Falling Down," "Farmer in the Dell," etc. But the loveliest of this form of children's folk lore were the pre-courtship games of pre-adolescents—"There Came Three Dukes A-Riding," or "King William," with its refrain: *"Turn to the east, turn to the west, choose the one that you love best.*" These games were already forgotten by the time this writer grew up in a suburban town in Massachusetts, but his wife, when she was young, played them on the streets and in the vacant lots of Washington, D.C. and Harrisburg, Pennsylvania. Not so many years ago, the writer attended a children's party in Philadelphia where a Croatian-American working man led a dozen or so of these characteristically Anglo-American games with Croatian-American boys and girls ranging in age from seven or eight to fifteen. Whether these games were still played in the neighborhood or whether the parent who was leading them had researched them, the writer doesn't know. Recreational workers, especially those interested in folk lore, revive these games sometimes, but today's children will play them self-consciously unless there is a strong rapport between the adult and the group and a great feeling of at-easeness among the children themselves. In the old days, when these games were played spontaneously by children, they were none of an adult's business.

There are other forms of play, however, which involve a lot of dramatic content, and for which children will usually welcome adult organizational help. These are good starting points for an adult who would like to work with children's dramatics, and has had some experience in mobilizing children but none in leading dramatics as such. Working with these forms, such an adult can begin to develop insight into the dramatic expression of children. He can then begin to try other forms of dramatic activity with an increasing assurance.

In a less graceful and more rowdy direction than the Play Party Games are some competitive forms of dramatization which can be recommended—with reservations. One of these is Bean Bag Dramatics, which is played as follows:

The person running the game prepares in advance as many bags as there are to be teams, placing in each bag from five to ten items, such as a piece of string, a comb, a fountain pen, a walnut shell, a piece of broken crockery, a bird whistle—anything at all. Usually each team's bag contains the same items. Teams are chosen and should be as equal as possible in regard to age, sex, talent. Each team is given its bag of small properties and goes apart to work out a skit utilizing each of the properties in the bag. After the agreed-upon time allowance (from ten minutes to half an hour), the teams come back and each in turn acts out its skit. If there are judges and prizes, and if the same children play the game more than once with the same judges, the trend of the judging will tend to establish the trend of the skits. Thus, if the judges lean toward approval of skits which handle the bean bag properties more loosely in order to make a freer and more imaginative skit, then the children will tend to work in that way, but if the judges tend to favor skits in which the use of the items is more germane to the story or plot of the skit, then the children will work in that way. If the children get enough fun out of making the skits so that judging and prizes can be eliminated altogether, then there need be no competitive factor at all, though the adult in charge can express approval in ways that will help to establish standards of imaginative treatment and taste. There is nothing in this game to encourage creative expression and much to hamper it. Nevertheless, when the game is played by imaginative children, or when imaginative leaders can be assigned to work with the team, or in schools or camps whose traditions have encouraged creativity, the results are often quite charming. Anyway, it is fun.

In one camp the Scavenger Hunt evolved into a dramatic game, and can easily be so adapted. In a Scavenger Hunt, each team is given a list of items to locate and bring in, the winning team being the one that first returns with all the items. For example, if the game is played at a party in a suburban community, lists that contain such items as a hub cap, a window pane, a kitchen faucet, a door knocker, etc., could lead to a general community ravage. In the old days when most camps housed their campers in tents, there was a mythical piece of apparatus called a sky hook, which was used to hang the tent temporarily on the air so it wouldn't fall down while you were getting it up. Green campers—and even green counselors and maintenance men—were always being sent to fetch one of these things. And though tenting is largely a thing of the past in children's camps, the sky hook has remained a piece of camping folk lore. In this particular camp, the head counselor included a sky hook among the items which the Scavenger Hunt teams were to locate and borrow or anything short of steal. One team produced a sky hook—that is, they produced a purely pantomimic sky hook, and demonstrated its utility by hanging a purely pantomimic tent to the air with it. From that evening on, in this particular camp, all lists of items to be scavenged contained things beyond the possibility of actual acquisition—planets, lakes, historical characters, abstractions, etc.—and more and more the teams stopped trying to fetch actual items and depended on dramatic tom-foolery.

It is also possible to make dramatics a team game by picking teams and assigning skits. Many camps have "bunk nights," in which bunks compete with each other in this way. There is nothing inherent in such a situation to encourage creativity and nothing inherent to discourage it, except possibly the competitive element, though if boys and girls are having a good time with this kind of thing they don't care much whether anyone wins or loses. Whether, therefore, the results are moving, beautiful and delightful or whether they are trite, sloppy and monstrous will depend in a large measure on the traditions of the camp, on what it encourages and discourages, on what its values are and on the degree to which it has instilled its values in its campers and staff. Children have inside themselves imagination and creativity—that is, any group of children will have it, though one individual child may have more or less of it than another. But children will often fail to draw on these resources unless they are given standards and encouragement. In some camps

the announcement on the bulletin board TONIGHT—BUNK
SKITS means "Let's see how asinine we can be." In other camps
it is a creative challenge.

There is another area of activity which involves more spontaneous, and therefore more honest, dramatic content for children and for which an adult needs no more skill than the ability
to help children pool their efforts. This area includes costume
parties, masquerades, carnivals, fairs and circuses.

A children's circus is really wonderful, a fun-loaded business which gives children a chance to be all kinds of things—
barkers, ring masters, tightrope walkers (on chalk lines on the
ground), clowns, animal tamers, the animals themselves—the
savage beasts as well as giraffes, seals and elephants. It is a kind of
mass dramatization with sequence but no plot. The dramatic content will tend to be free and imaginative—untrammeled, so to
speak, operating out of the child's natural resources for make-
believe. A circus is the kind of thing which a generation or two
ago would have been organized and carried out with alacrity by
children as old as twelve or thirteen. Today its appeal is more to
younger children. Older children are too sophisticated—except
that the more deeply sophisticated children like to do childlike
things.

A carnival or a fair has similar, if somewhat thinner, dramatic possibilities. Still, there are barkers, clowns, fortune tellers,
midway characters. The children running the various carnival
games—ringing bottles with mason-jar rings, sinking a nail into a
4 x 4 with three wallops, tossing pennies into a pan floating in a
tub of water, etc.—can be carnival characters. The people who
attend the carnival, too, can be drawn into impromptu dramatics. For example, there can be a weight-lifting contest with a
purely pantomimic weight, the winner being the one who makes
himself seem strongest or makes the weight seem heaviest, as the
case may be.

Of course, a carnival is a lot more fun if it is frankly dishonest. That is, a group of children putting on a carnival to raise money for a charitable purpose or to finance a group trip can print their own money. When a person enters the carnival, he pays admission in hard cash—10¢, 25¢ or whatever. He also buys a sheet of mimeographed carnival money. This he can spend on games. If he loses, he will have to go and buy more fake money with real money. If he wins, he can go on playing games with his winnings. If refreshments are served, they should be paid for in hard cash, otherwise the big winners of paper money will eat and drink up the profits. Another way of conning the public is to curtain off an exit—preferably one with an exit sign. The exit sign should be concealed by the curtain and from the outside the curtained booth should look mysterious and intriguing. There should be a sign saying, SEE THE EGRESS—ONLY 10¢ (or $1,000, or whatever the thing is worth in paper money). A boy or girl in charge of the booth will entice people—"Hey, sis, don't you want to see the egress?" And when the customer responds and enters the booth, he will be shown the exit. Of course, the con-man or con-woman should have a dictionary on hand to prove his or her point.

Naturally, to give a carnival in this spirit, the children will need a better rapport with their community than one sixth-grade class had with the high school students in their own school. The games were ridiculously easy for some of the big high school boys, and some of them made millions in paper money and practically tore the carnival apart, booth by booth, when they were told they couldn't cash it in.

Masquerades and costume parties are full of the same dramatic spirit—but freer, since no one is concerned with any business, and people react and relate to each other in such ways as the personalities which they have put on with their costumes impel them to do, for the putting on of a costume opens the door on the world of make-believe for almost all children, and probably for almost all adults. Competitive elements which stress the costume as such—i.e., a prize for the most beautiful or most original—instead of giving attention to the person or animal or natural force which the wearer of the costume is being—will tend to inhibit the dramatic spirit. But if no prizes are given, or if everyone is given a prize, the award taking cognizance of the personality represented by the costume and not of the quality of the costume itself, then the children will *be* what their costumes induce them to be and will interact on each other in their imaginary aspects. The results may be a little riotous, and sometimes it is a good idea to organize things in such a way that, one by one, or in small related groups, the children act out whatever they are while the others sit and watch. At many such parties two children, or three or four, etc., may decide together what they are going to come as and will be prepared to act something out together. Thus seven boys may come as the Seven Dwarfs. Or a boy and girl may come as Romeo and Juliet. Or there may be the Three Bears, or the Three Little Kittens, depending on age and sophistication.

Two ten-year-old girls came to a camp costume party as Roman patricians. They had looped sheets about themselves as togas. They carried scrolls of poetry and had plaited green leaves as laurel crowns. They wore sandals but no stockings, and one side of their legs, up to the knee, gleamed through the slits of their togas. They wore the laurel crowns a little askew, a little rakishly. As they moved around, one became aware that they were a little rakish altogether, that they were, in fact, a little tipsy. Now, children—boys especially—often play at being drunk, but they have no real notion of what they are doing and do it very badly. But these girls were patricianly, Epicureanly, lyrically, ever so delicately and divinely "oiled." It seemed as though they had just stepped—with only a slightly faltering grace—from the odes of Horace. Now, where would two ten year olds get such a concept? Had they seen something like it at an adult costume party? Or in a movie? But even so—whence the understatement, the self-containment, the restraint? The costumes, as such, were nice for improvisations, but not startling, and their little "act" was so subtle as to go unnoticed by all but a few of the more perceptive older boys and girls and some adults, so that they got no particular praise or credit for what they did. Whence, then, their glow? Not from any real vintage, certainly, but from an imaginary draught.

Requiring less time and organization are the guessing games which children play while sitting in a circle, many of which have a high degree of dramatic content—word games, for example, in which the watchers try to guess what the player is acting out. Charades is, perhaps, the first such game to come to mind. It is, however, a very poor game for our purposes. In Charades, in fact, good dramatization, as against a repertory of communicative tricks and gestures, can be a distinct liability. One young woman of this writer's acquaintance had to act out "The quality of mercy is not strained." She began with "quality," using the word in the rather unfamiliar sense which it has in the sentence, "She was a person of quality." She was herself a person of quality, and the word in this sense apparently had some subjective content for her. So all that she did was to *be* a person of quality —very sensitively, beautifully and creatively—but with total rout and disaster for her team, who never got the faintest glimmer of what she was trying to communicate. Charades is actually anti-dramatic, anti-creative, and its only use in the present context would be as an ice-breaker, as a means of getting young people to get up and do something in front of others.

There is another word game, sometimes called Adverbs and sometimes called Adjectives, in which the dramatic content is rather good. When it is played with little children it is, of course, better called just Words. Little children can be given such words as "hot," "cold," "good," "bad," "funny," "old," "smooth," "bumpy," and "silly." Older children can be given more difficult adjectives, such as "dangerous," "flighty," "absent-minded," "dreamy," and "disgusted." A greater subtlety in dramatization can be expected if paired words are used. Thus "stealthy" (the physical aspect) and "crafty" (the character aspect) could be given to two children, each child acting out his word before any guessing is permitted. If the watchers know beforehand what the two words are, but don't know which child is to act out which, then they must put their attention very closely on the differences in the pantomime. However, in such cases the more subtle the acting problem, the more subtle, too, the semantics, and there is a danger that discussion will involve too much argument about the shades of meaning of words. For most purposes, then, simple adjectives with relatively strong meanings are best.

Better than these word games is the adaptation as guessing games of some of the rudimentary dramatics exercises, such as Being Something or Doing Something. These are played in the same way as the word games. Unless the adult is faced with children who can't enjoy anything that isn't highly competitive, he will not make up teams, but will let the simple act of guessing constitute the game "problem." He will prepare in advance little slips of paper or index cards, each with the word or thing on it that the child is to act out. If the game is Being Something, the slips would contain such things as a bear, a horse, a mother, an old man, a tree, a fire, a cat, a waiter, a machine, a tin soldier, a sightseer, a nurse, a blacksmith, etc., depending on the age and experience of the children. Or if the game is Doing Something, then the slips would contain such things as brushing teeth, cooking, washing clothes, ironing, reading an exciting book, pitching a tent, building a fire, giving baby his formula, waiting for a bus, watching a movie, eating supper, etc.—again, anything within the experience and competence of the group. The leader will give the child one of these slips and the child will read it, think about it for a moment and then act it out. The watchers will then guess what the child has acted out—and so on, one after another, until each child has had a turn, or, if the group is too large, until they have had enough of this particular game. If the game is to have any valuable dramatic content, then three rules must be established: 1. No watcher is to make a guess or to say anything until the player is through acting out; 2. The player is not to use any words or make any sounds; 3. He is not to use any properties.

Only the first rule needs to be used if the game is being played with little children. Little children will tend to be much less inhibited about being animals or natural phenomena than older boys and girls. To a little child, the movements of the wind, the crouching and rearing of a lion, the flight of a bird are perfectly natural things to be. Besides, little children will tend to be much more interested in the act of being something than in guessing. With little children, in short, this kind of game tends to be a true form of dramatic play:

ADULT: What were you, Linda?
LINDA: A bee.
ADULT: Then Bobby and Sally were right. How did you know Linda was a bee, Bobby?
BOBBY: She flew around and buzzed.
ADULT: Does anything else fly around and buzz?
SEVERAL: A mosquito! A fly!
ADULT: What does a bee do that a fly and a mosquito don't do?
TOMMY: It flies from flower to flower and sucks honey.
ADULT: Why don't you show us, Tommy? And maybe some of you would like to be flowers.

With older children, too, the guessing aspect will often get lost sight of in the almost instinctual predominance of the dramatic and the game will evolve into a true dramatics activity. There is a variation of the Doing Something game in which the children are told that the area formed by their circle is any kind of terrain or surface which any one of them in turn wants it to be, field or forest, or just plain floor. Each is to imagine an object lying in this space. When his turn comes, he is to approach this object and pick it up. The watchers are to guess what it was that he has picked up. One bad boy, when his turn came, picked up a snake, dangled it in the girls' faces and made them scream. He had bypassed the game phase altogether in favor of direct dramatic communication!

On another occasion, a teenage girl picked up a fallen bird and returned it to its nest. It took her as much as five minutes to complete her pantomime. First she saw the little bird lying in the grass and emoted over its sad fate; then, mastering her anguish, she approached tremulously, stooped low, took the bird up uneasily in both hands, emoted over it some more, pressed it to her cheek, and, at long last, standing on tiptoe, put it back in its nest in the imaginary tree. This was a city girl, and it has to be admitted that her "acting" was good—as one must admit that a certain book is well written, even when it is hard for one to stomach the attitude. A real nature girl among the watchers was outraged. "That's not the way you pick up a bird!" she cried. "You do it like this!" And in one fluid, unbroken and competent movement she got up from the bench she was sitting on, saw the bird on the ground, scooped it up in a single cupped hand, inverted the hand, and, reaching, placed the bird in its nest (without, if one will excuse the expression in this context, emotional fuss or feathers). At such a point the game has swept rapidly into the area of dramatic exercises and the evaluative discussions which give them meaning and direction—and beyond dramatics altogether into philosophy, into the on-going dialogue about man and his relationship to the universe. For the fact is that the distinction between dramatics and games is an adult distinction—though as children grow older and learn that some forms of work are more engrossing than play, the distinction will take on meaning for them, too. A skilled kindergarten teacher who provides a play period for the children, who gets them into a circle and has them be something or do something, who reads them poems and little stories which she encourages them to act out then and there or who plays the piano for them while they move about being things the music suggests to them—such an adult is conducting an articulated dramatics program, though the children may have only the words "fun" and "play" and "games" to describe the things they do.

On the other hand, a child a little older may be having exactly the same kind of fun and yet be under the sober impression that she is attending a dramatics class. In a small camp—small enough so that activities often cut across a wide age range—a dramatics class was established, and one little eight year old chose this as her activity, even though most of the members of the class were bigger boys and girls. In one of the early sessions, the exercise used was "looking for something." Each student, as his turn came, was to try to convey to the watchers what he was looking for, who he was being, the importance of finding what he was looking for, etc. When the eight-year-old girl's turn came, she bolted out of the barn and didn't return for twenty minutes. While the exercises continued with others, a junior counselor would take a look outside from time to time and report on her progress. Now she was skirting the edges of the pond, poking in the margin grass. Now she was breasting her way through field corn taller than herself and had reached the oak tree and was hunting about its roots. Now she was searching through the tall grass behind the backstop on the ball field, and now had dropped out of sight down the bank behind the backstop and was presumably wading across the brook to look for whatever it was in the undergrowth of the woods on the other side. She returned at last, very satisfied with herself. Apparently she had found what she was looking for and was proud to be a big girl and attend a real dramatics class, and proud that she had done a good job with her "exercise"—as, indeed, she had!

For parents who can unbend a little, these Being Something and Doing Something games are beautiful games for a family to play together. A stack of cards can be developed with things printed on them. When the game is played, these cards can be shuffled, and each in turn can draw a card from the deck, no one "leading" and everyone playing. "Mommy's a dog! Mommy's a dog!" cries Eric, the baby of the family. "Oh, Eric," says Cynthia, "can't you tell the difference between a dog and a seal? Mommy's a seal. Dogs don't have flippers!" "She barked like a dog," Eric insists, unconvinced. "Silly! She didn't bark like a dog, she barked like a seal!" Sobered by this disconcerting development, Eric draws his own card and, since he can't read, he shows it to Father, who whispers in his ear. Soberly he cranes his neck as high as he can, swells out his chest, struts about, flaps his wings and crows.

5

.oooooooo

Pantomime

IT IS NOT SURPRISING, as we have seen, that in regard to dramatics children cannot see much distinction between work and play— to the extent, perhaps, that an earnest group of eleven or twelve year olds, who have something earnest to say and who have worked their heads off for six to seven weeks on a dramatization as a vehicle for saying it, will sometimes feel a little guilty in the end because they have spent so much time having so much fun. And yet, on the part of the adult who has been working with these children, what he has been doing has been a serious business and the play that they have just put on has been the outcome of a much longer process. It is a process in which he will have "taught" dramatics, in the same way that an English teacher or an art teacher will "teach" creative writing or painting.

In a good art program, the children, over a period of time, will learn various techniques and the use of various media. Nevertheless, the techniques and the media will not be presented to children as the elements out of which creative expression will eventually emerge, but these techniques and media will have been introduced in what on the surface may seem a more or less random way, so that each technique and each medium will present the child with a complete, self-contained vehicle for his creative expression at the moment. So, too, with creative writing. At one time the children will look at the visible world around them and write down what they see; or they will look at people and write down what they perceive or what people do or might say in certain situations. At another time they will go inside themselves or inside of imaginary people and try to find ways of saying what people feel. Sometimes they will think about words and what words can do, for example, with rhythm and rhyme. One teacher will work with these forms of expression for a year, and another will have worked with them with the same children before, and still other teachers will work with them with the same children in the years ahead. An English teacher who has had the tenth graders looking at the visible world and writing similes which the visible world suggests perhaps has occasion to visit the first-grade room. Printed large and tacked to the walls of the room are the "poems" which the first graders have written, and all of these poems compare one thing with another. One of them says: *The reflection of the moon in the water is like a long golden eel.* The English teacher smiles to himself, remembering that one of his girls has just written: *The reflection of the moon in the water is like my broken, wavering thoughts.* In short, the teacher of the six year olds and the teacher of the fifteen year olds have both been working with the same elements of creative writing, and it is a natural assumption that there will also be many points at which they will both be working with the same elements of creative dramatics.

In *Playmaking with Children*, Winifred Ward cites a delightful situation which illustrates our point. The teacher reads the first graders a poem which goes as follows:

Hand in hand they dance in a row,
Hither and thither, to and fro,
Flip, flap, flop, and away they go,
Fluttering creatures as white as snow.

When the children have guessed, with the teacher's help, that these fluttering things are clothes on a line, they take hands, and, while one of them is the wind and blows on the others, they "try to feel limp and floppy" and to act like creatures fluttering in the wind. When this fun comes to an end, they sit and talk with the teacher. Each child has thought of himself as some particular article of wash. One has been a pair of stockings, another a torn sheet, another a party dress, another a pair of jeans. Under the teacher's questioning, they begin to think of some of the things they might say if they were, indeed, such articles. "I wish someone would mend me," the sheet might say. "I'm going to be starched and ironed and go to a party!" the party dress might say. So again they play at being clothes on a line, but this time without the poem. Instead they go merrily about the business of improvising the dialogue of their own play. Thus, in a single sitting, the little children have moved from one of the two essential media of creative dramatics to the other and, combining these two, have made up their own play. More mature children can do no more—they can only express more mature things through these same media.

The two main media of dramatic art are human speech and the movements of the human body. Speech and movement have their sources in thought and emotion and spring from our impulse to express what we think and feel. This is perhaps why children and even adults find dramatics so releasing, because the difference between living and dramatizing lies only in the fact that the situation in which we move and speak is in one case real and in the other imaginary. Growing up in a complex society imposes many restraints on our impulses. But in imaginary situations we can do and say many things we cannot do and say in reality.

Dramatic expression made by the movement of the human body is called *pantomime*. Under different circumstances, it will also be called such things as *action, movement, blocking, stage business, exit, enter*, etc. But if one keeps in mind at all times the central content of the word "pantomime," the creative aspects of these other terms will not be lost sight of. In work with children, pantomime is perhaps more important, certainly more underlying, than speech. This is so, not because in a play the pantomime is more important than what is said or how it is said, but because, as we grow older, our minds and souls tend to become chained to words and we lose, in large measure, our animal capacity for thinking and communicating with our bodies.

The "I" of Stanislavski's *An Actor Prepares* goes home in the evening so tired from the strenuous demands of the acting class that he can't think and, in this state of mindless fatigue, soaks up important lessons for an actor in the movements and relaxations of his cat. The purpose of pantomime is to put us in touch with our bodies, to make us know through the creative act of memory how it feels to lean against the wind, how we raise our knees in deep snow, how we pull our clothes from our sticky flesh in muggy weather, how it feels in the muscles of arms and fingers to turn a doorknob or brush our teeth, how it feels to lift a weight, to thread a needle, to be a piston and a piston rod, to be a billiard ball, to fly, to subside and rekindle as a flame, to sway in ocean currents like the fronds of a sponge. The purpose of pantomime is to unfold within the imagination the kinaesthetic experiences which the soul has stored up, both those which are memories of our own muscular or tactile experience or those that were empathic in the first place—the muscle tensions, for example, with which one responds in seeing an erect old man of ninety, or a person biting his tongue in anger, or concealing derision, or holding back tears. The purpose of pantomime is to reactivate such memories in new muscular experience and reintegrate them in new creative forms.

For the younger child, says George F. Willison in *Let's Make a Play*, "the body is still a primary and flexible medium of expression." It is for this reason that a program of dramatic activity involving body movement should begin with very young children so that their natural use of the body for expression will continue to be a natural thing in later years. Over and beyond the spontaneous make-believe of the "play period," there will often be "instruction" of a kind, a program of rhythmics which helps the child to learn coordination and control. The teacher will strike different rhythms on hand-drum or wood block or piano, and the children will walk, skip, prance or gallop to these rhythms, learning to distinguish between rhythms and to change from one kind of body movement to another as the rhythm changes. Sometimes the children themselves will sit and beat out, clapping or striking the floor with their hands, the rhythm which the teacher is giving them. At a later stage, they may form little rhythm bands, using hand-drums, wood blocks and triangles; and part of the group may move about to rhythms supplied by the others. At another point—or even in another organization which, for example, may take a dim view of such disciplined work as this with kindergartners—their rhythmic activity will take on a dramatized content as they move about being the things suggested by the music which the teacher plays for them. Or again, poems with strong rhythmic content may carry the work in rhythms in the direction of dramatization:

Jack be *nim*ble, Jack be *quick*.
Jack jump OVER the candle*stick*.

The child who acts out this poem is dramatizing, because he is *being* Jack. The dramatic content is slight, however, for Jack's central characteristic is that he jumps over the candlestick in a manner that relates his movements to the rhythm of the poem. In Miss Ward's example of the wash on the line, the poem itself also establishes a strong rhythm to work to, but the act of *being something* takes on a much stronger imaginative content, so that the transition from rhythmic exercise to creative expression in pantomime is now complete.

As children move from the primary grades into the lower elementary grades, the instructional program aimed at body co-ordination and control tends to become disassociated from the classroom program of the group and to be continued, if at all, in special dance and physical education programs. If, at this point and beyond, any openly instructional work is to go on with children in the use of the body for creative expression, it will take the form of dramatic exercises. A visitor dropping in on a sixth-grade classroom, for instance, may see the students, with the teacher among them, sitting in a semi-circle or U, while, at the teacher's desk, a boy is very intently making circular motions, a foot or so above the desk top, with a loosely clenched fist, movements which, for some reason, seem to be meeting with a considerable degree of physical resistance. After a time, the boy stops, and a dialogue something like this takes place:

DAVE: He was stirring paint.

ALICE: No, he wasn't—he was stirring soup!

TEACHER: What did you see, Dave, that made you think Tom was stirring paint and not soup?

DAVE: It was too thick for soup.

TEACHER: Alice, did you notice that Tom took something out with the paddle or ladle at one point and dropped it on the floor?

ALICE: It was a fly or something that had gotten into the soup.

MARCIA: How could it be a fly? You don't just spill a whole ladle of soup on the floor to get rid of a fly!

ALICE: You don't just spill paint on the floor, either!

MARC: None of that's important! When you stir soup, you stir with kind of a slanted oval movement. When you stir paint you sort of get right up over it and stir straight down. That's what Tom did.

TEACHER: Well, Tom, what about it?

TOM: Yes, I was stirring paint. It was old paint and there was a piece of scum that I couldn't mix in. I didn't drop in on the floor, though. I dropped it in another paint can I was using for waste.

ALICE: You stir paint on the floor, not on a table!

TOM: I was stirring it on a work bench!

TEACHER: Well, some of you saw that Tom was stirring something thick—*viscous* is the word for it. He made me see that, and he made others see it. But perhaps some of you weren't really seeing or feeling what he was doing.

What the visitor has looked in on is not a guessing game, but a dramatics exercise. But like a guessing game it poses a "problem"—a problem in this case with a double focus. For the doer it poses the question: *Do I really feel what the imaginary act I am performing demands?* For the watcher it poses the question: *Do I really see and feel what the doer is doing?*

With children a great part of the pantomime exercises should involve just such precise consideration of what is involved in an act of physical doing. A group can sit with its eyes closed and stroke or handle a variety of imaginary objects—the marble top of a table, the back of an Airedale, a billiard ball, an orange, an egg. Or they can "do" any of the things that they commonly do or see done: sew a hem, use a screwdriver, peel a banana, eat grapes. Or with nothing more to work with than a cleared space in the classroom floor, they can lift heavy or awkward objects, pull a rowboat over sand, fly a kite, engage in a ropeless tug-of-war, play hopscotch, toss an invisible ball in the air and catch it, be pitcher, catcher and batter without ball, bat or glove, wash, iron, chop, split, saw, hammer, whittle, eat, pull taffy, spin a top, play imaginary jacks, push their way through an atmosphere thicker than the one we live in, walk in heat, cold, snow, wind, rain, through deep snow, on hard pavements, in tall grass, through tangled forest growth, sway or swim like sponge, shark, octopus or skindiver in an underwater world or reach up and pull down a cluster of stars.

Other exercises will take the player from the act of *doing* to the act of *being*, to the expression, not of what it is like to do something, but of what it is like to be something other than oneself—an old woman, a sailor, a dog, a horse, a waterfall, a melting ice cream cone. Some exercises will call on the player to explore the kinaesthetic feel of emotion and nuance. Still other exercises will help the player explore the possibility for expression of separate parts of the body—the back, the hands, the feet and legs. A curtain can be dropped within a foot or so of the floor, so that the watchers see only the player's ankles and feet, or a puppet stage can be used so that they see only the expressions of his hands. Or an imaginary window ledge is established in such a way that the player, looking out of the window, does not face the watchers and they see him only from behind, and yet he is able to convey who he is, what he sees from the window and what he feels. He is being, perhaps, a boy his own age. An airplane enters, crosses and passes beyond his field of vision, flying high so that its passage takes a little time. As it passes from sight, the boy's head yearns after it and his ankles cross in a voluptuous gesture, the Irish airman's "lonely impulse of delight." Or some exercises will establish, not what one is doing now, but what one is about to do or what one has just done. For example, the exercise calls for the player to enter the acting area and to establish who he is, where he has come from and what he has just experienced. A thirteen-year-old girl steps into the acting area and it is soon apparent that she has just entered her house from her front porch, where, beyond any shadow of doubt, she has just experienced her first kiss.

However, any effort to define these dramatics excercises briefly is bound to be distorting and to conceal the precise problems which the exercises will pose. It is true, for example, that the adult should proceed, in work with children, from the physical doing to the act of being, and from there to exercises which involve emotion or nuance. But what about an exercise which calls for a player to be a carpenter, or for two players to be riveters? Essentially in such an exercise the players would define what they *are* by what they *do*. On the other hand, suppose the doing exercise involves daydreaming, or looking in a mirror, or waiting for a bus. These doings are very passive and noncommital except as they express personality and a situation to which that personality has some kind of emotional response.

Or suppose the exercise calls on the player to open a package. With what do we concern ourselves? The adult can define the exercise in such a way that the player is limited to establishing the size and weight of the package, how it is wrapped and tied and how one goes about untying and unwrapping it. But this same exercise has almost unlimited possibilities for probing personality, situation and feeling. Is it a child opening the package? Is it her birthday? Does she express excitement—or deeper anticipation? And when the package is opened, does her birthday gift thrill her? Or does it overwhelm her and make her quiet and deep? Or does the gift hurt and anger her because, though it is expensive, it shows no recognition of what she is? Or is it a woman opening the package? Who is she and what does the gift mean to her—that is, what are the deepest currents of her life, past and present, that make their confluence at this moment?

The exercises can become very engrossing—so engrossing, in fact, as to present certain dangers. If an adult is going to make use of these exercises with children he must make sure that they are not used—in terms of the amount of time available—at the expense of other more meaningful possibilities; that their use as vehicles for developing certain forms of acting insight does not diminish them as valid vehicles for the child's creative expression of the moment; and that the developmental sequence the adult establishes in the use of these exercises is not too "programmed." When the exercises are used well, the children's experience with them will be both valuable and pleasurable, and their pleasure will be much deeper than simple fun. For in the moment when the mind captures the physical image and the muscles respond and reproduce that image with a degree of precision, one experiences that intestinal stirring which is associated with acute aesthetic pleasure.

There are, however, limitations in the use of exercises with children, and more of their work with pantomime should arise from other things, perhaps, than from the exercises—from the dramatization of short tales and poems, for example. Many tales of the kind traditionally read to or by younger children have a strong pantomimic content. As one example, there is the story of the argument between the sun and the wind as to which is stronger, the denouement of the story completely pantomime: wind blows more fiercely—man hugs his coat more tightly; sun shines more ardently—man removes his useless outer garment. "The Man and the Satyr" is a story that proceeds entirely along pantomimic lines until the man who is lost in the forest comes at last to the house of the satyr. Many, but not all, of Aesop's fables set up a pantomimic situation—for example, "The Fox and the Grapes." "The Fox and the Crane" is another, especially if one thinks of the tall receptacle which the crane uses to frustrate the fox as being purely imaginary. The American Indian folk story, "The Healing Waters," is pure pantomime, and for children to attempt to use dialogue would probably trammel its beauty. On a high school level, young people often find that they can interpret stream-of-consciousness material through pantomime.

For children of all ages, however, the richest source of material for pantomime is poetry and song. In the beginning there is *Mother Goose*. And after *Mother Goose*, there is the body of poetry written for children.

Last night I saw upon the stair
The little man who wasn't there.

He wasn't there again today.
Oh, how I wish he'd go away!

At what age can a child bodily express the sense of formless fear which this poem conveys, or the wry and more underlying wonder—the paradox of the what-is and the what-is-not? At a relatively early age, one must assume, for the child can capture in action what the adult verbalizes. But if such a challenge is too great, for example, for a nine or ten year old, there is narrative poetry—the border ballads, or *Robin Hood and His Merry Men*. There is also funny poetry—Edward Lear's stories, for instance, or the incident Ogden Nash describes of the elephone who tried to use a telephant. By the time children are eleven, the poems they read and dramatize can be drawn more from the main currents of the poetic tradition than from folk and children's sources. At a couple of points in a given school year, for example, one class of eleven year olds dramatized the following songs and poems: a folk song, "The Golden Vanity," James Weldon Johnson's "The Creation" (in shadow puppetry), Edna St. Vincent Millay's "The Harp Weaver" and "The Buck in the Snow," Whitman's "Come Up from the Fields, Father" and "The Runaway Slave" and Langston Hughes's "The Merry-go-round."

Since such dramatizations are complete works of art, and since the child who dramatizes them has something to say, there is no reason why programs of poems which a group of children have been working on should not see the light of day. For the pantomime of children is often so beautiful that it ought to be shared, if only through a less adequate vehicle of description.

Of many lovely pantomimes, this writer remembers five in particular. Interestingly enough—though they have not deliberately been culled to make a point—they are from different kinds of dramatizations, and together they reflect the creative importance of pantomime in all aspects of dramatic activity.

The first, in essence no more than a Doing Something exercise of a purely physical kind, was given an amusing twist for public purposes. A high school boy fully clothed, and remaining fully clothed throughout his pantomime, entered onto an empty stage. Pantomimically he first established a few familiar objects—a chair, a towel rack, a mirror. Then, article by article of clothing, he stripped himself naked and stepped into a shower stall, where he turned on both hot and cold water, getting the water too cold at first and then too hot. He adjusted the water temperature, soaped himself thoroughly, cut down on the hot water a little and rinsed himself, then stepped out of the shower and dried himself thoroughly with a towel from the towel rack, and got back into his clothes, article by article. The writer by this time was completely smitten with the *almost* impeccable precision of the pantomime, but very much on edge because of the one glaring lapse in its impeccability—the boy had left the water running in the shower! But now in his shirt, but not yet in his jacket, the boy noticed that he had left the water running, rolled up his shirt sleeve, reached gingerly into the shower, shut off the water, wiped his arm, rolled his shirt sleeve back down, buttoned it, put on his jacket and made his exit. Immediately thereafter a girl came out onstage and held up a two-word placard: SAVE WATER.

The beauty of this pantomime lay in its physical precision; its greatness lay in the fact that the boy had the good judgment to do nothing more, to avoid the temptation to characterize and farcicalize. The reactions to water too hot or too cold, reactions which were neither underplayed nor overplayed, were the only "human interest"—except for a pervasive aura, a sense of virile pleasure in everyday life.

Of an opposite kind—that is, a piece of very moving pantomime—was that performed by a boy, blond, fair-skinned, very graceful, stripped to the waist, miming the fugitive in Whitman's "The Runaway Slave." He darted in, furtive and terrified, and crept about before hiding in a wood pile created for him by the words of the poem. Found by the poet and brought into the house, the terror still lurked in his head and shoulders and eyes, but gave way to a deep trust as the poet washed the galls of his hands and feet. In this instance, there was little or no conscious artistry—only an eleven-year-old boy throwing himself, body and soul, into his part. Whence, then, the totality of the image? The boy's natural grace and intelligence are part of the answer, but only part. There is also a strong assumption that this child of a wealthy family was making a subjective expression, was finding the symbols for his own fears and chains, for his thrust toward inner freedom and his growing trust in an adult world that had begun to wash the galls of his hurt and sensitive spirit.

Another beautiful pantomime was done by a girl about the same age. A camp director had been meeting with a group of youngsters, most of them twelve and thirteen, who wanted to read poetry together and learn something about it. Among the poems he had introduced which they particularly loved was Ezra Pound's translation of Li Tai-po's "The River Merchant's Wife." When the group decided to dramatize some of the poetry, the camp director wasn't sure it could be done, especially for children of this age. One twelve-year-old girl—a deep creature—had other ideas. She thought it could be dramatized —and dramatized it.

The poem takes the form of a letter written by a sixteen-year-old girl to her husband, whose business affairs have kept them apart for many months. They had grown up together as neighbors—"two small people without dislike or suspicion." When the girl was fourteen they were married, not through any wish of theirs, one supposes, but through the wishes of their parents: their love for each other has come about as the result of their marriage. "At fifteen," the girl writes, "I stopped scowling. I wanted my dust to be mingled with yours forever and forever."

In her performance the child wore a long white costume tied with a sash, and her hair was done up in a tight bun on top of her head. She sat, writing-brush in hand, on a box covered with fabric. In her pantomime, she left this box only twice—both times briefly and absently, as one who is deep inside oneself does something without knowing that he does it. Otherwise she used only the upper part of her body for her pantomime, but used it all—her lovely head, her long neck, her graceful arms and hands, her lithe torso. In a sense her movements were very bold and in another sense they were of extraordinary fineness. At one point, she would convey the wisp of an amusing memory seen as though through tears, at other points the crushing weight, or lifting exaltation, of love remembered in the depths of separation sorrow.

Young as she was, she was a conscious artist. The camp director reports that in regard to the wife's wanting her dust to be mingled with her husband's forever and forever, the player asked him, "Shall I make my body small?"—a dancer's term. She had studied only a couple of years in creative dance class, but had shown great talent. The skill in the use of the body, however, cannot accomplish much creatively unless the image in the mind tells the body what to do. And in the subtlest responses of the muscles of the body to the mind, the mind will not be conscious at all of what the body is doing, but only of its own image. In this instance, it was only the girl's involvement in what she was being that could account, say, for the dilation of the pupils of her eyes in her moments of yearning exaltation.

Another of these memorable pieces of pantomime was done by an older girl playing the part of Polly Garter in her junior-class production of Dylan Thomas's *Under Milk Wood*. At one point the narrator turns aside from the dubious behavior of people and takes up the behavior of one of the more dubious species of barnyard animals. How was the verbal image to be given a visual counterpart? Through a contrapuntal human figure. So Polly Garter, her mop laid down, her scrub bucket by her side, sat on the steps of the stage in the face of the audience, and there—doing nothing that one can put one's finger on—marvelously exuded the disreputable Polly's delicious inner responses to the spring weather, while the narrator lyricized the correspondingly delicious vernal ardors of pigs.

Finally, there was a very stirring pantomime done by an eighth-grade boy in an original play his group had developed through improvisation. It was during the years of World War II, and the group was studying about Japan, on the assumption that an enemy nation is not necessarily an enemy people. About that time a Japanese artist, who had taken asylum in the United States, published a thin volume of woodcuts which dealt with an underground democratic movement in Japan of which he had been a part. The children built their play around this underground movement, weaving into the story many of the things that they had learned about Japanese life and culture.

One scene took place in prison. It demanded a lot of pantomime—in fact, it had been developed rather fully through pantomime before any improvisation was undertaken. For example, there was a stone wall, very thick and high but purely imaginary, which separated the male prisoners from the women prisoners, and the men and women communicated with each other—when the guards didn't catch them—by standing on tiptoe and talking through an imaginary grating above their heads in the wall. In the prison was an old revolutionary, who had been there many years. His spirit was broken, and for the most part he lay supine and had nothing to say. The revolutionary zeal of a new young prisoner, who looked upon the old man as his leader, as the father of the movement, seemed to stir him not at all. Among the other characters was a vendor of fortune cookies who, as the play went along, one came to understand was a contact man for the underground, carrying secret messages and propaganda as fortunes in the cookies. At one point in the prison scene, the young revolutionary had just made an urgent effort to reach the old man and to restore his faith and hope, but had turned away in despair, feeling it was no use. At this moment, the street cry of the vendor was heard outside.

The young man turned to listen. Slowly the old man lifted himself to a sitting position, managed to rise on prison-weak legs, shuffled in his old man's gait to a beam of light and stood looking up at this light—the light from a high window through which had come the voice from the world outside. In a sense, the pantomimic elements were simple ones. But to convey the old man's resurrection, his rediscovery of life and purpose, would seem to call for more depth of vision than one who has not worked with twelve- and thirteen-year-old boys might expect them to have.

Children should not only do pantomime. They should see good pantomime done. This is one of the reasons why good work done by one group of children should be shared with other groups of children. They should see Marcel Marceau and old Charlie Chaplin pictures. They ought, above all, though it is not likely they will have the opportunity, to see Chinese theater.

There used to be a Chinese theater under the bridge on East Broadway in New York, where Chinese classical poetic drama was played to a full house every night in the week. The plays were long, and eighth-grade groups would go to see them with a firm commitment to their parents that they would leave the theater and start home by 10:30—a commitment which could never be met, for at 10:30 the children would be unable to tear themselves away, even when they couldn't follow the story, which was most often the case.

Occasionally, however, the story of a play would be intelligible despite the barrier of language. In one play, the father of a young man and woman dies—drops dead, in fact, as they are together at table—whereafter he disposes of himself by walking offstage, doing so with no obtrusion because he has ceased to be a part of the pantomimic rhythm which goes on continuously and which totally separates the actors from anyone else, such as a stagehand bringing on a chair. Anyway, his death impoverishes the two children. The daughter, much against the brother's wishes, becomes the concubine of a wealthy man, and the brother becomes a beggar. After several years he arrives by chance at his sister's house and the two have a tender reunion. The sister expresses her joy by an act of sisterly love—she washes out his beggar's shirt. The plays were always staged with gorgeous Chinese costumes and beautiful silk hangings and even many authentic properties. But sometimes, apparently, they had to make do with whatever they could buy in the clothing and hardware stores of Mott Street. For the boy's shirt was a gray denim workshirt. And the sister—richly arrayed in Chinese dress, for she was the wife of a wealthy man—fetched, to wash the shirt in, a white enamel washbasin. There was no water in the basin, no suds, and the shirt never entered the basin, never, in fact, left the girl's hands. Yet it was a moment of infinite tenderness. Huge tears were running down the brother's cheeks as he knelt before his sister, and the audience was weeping too. For with this pantomime of washing and wringing out her brother's shirt, the actress did her scarf dance, and the shirt wound and unwound itself in convolutions, sinuous and lovely, in her amazing hands. Imaginary waters gushed from it, a fountain playing a counterpoint to the sister's flutelike singing and the young man's joyous tears.

But though the Chinese theater is gone—at least in New York—Brecht knew Chinese theater and learned from it, and occasionally in college towns or off Broadway young people can see his epic use of pantomime, as in the crossing of the bridge in *The Caucasian Chalk Circle*, or the crossing of a "river of swirling waters" in *The Rule and the Exception*.

6

○○○○○○○○○

Improvisation

LITTLE CHILDREN in their make-believe, even when they are playing alone, adlib their thoughts and feelings with almost unlimited freedom and conviction. Words and tones of voice are as much a part of our inherent capacity for make-believe as are movements. In fact, as we have already indicated, the reason for attaching so much importance to pantomime is that, as we grow older, language tends to replace muscular attitude as a means of expression, and so the use of the body needs to be retained or restored. But it is words which carry the communicable meaning in most dramatizations. Of the five examples of effective panto-mime previously described, only the shower bath, which was something of a *tour de force*, could have been completely clear without words—"The Runaway Slave" would have been par-tially clear. One would have understood that this was a fugitive of some kind, frightened and hurt, and that a kind and loving person had found him, cared for his hurts and won him over from mistrust and fear to assurance and faith, but one would not have understood the historical circumstances. As to the others, we would have sensed something of the importance of the movement of the old man in prison, would have understood that something was revealed to him; we would have felt the impish beauty of the girl exuding her feelings on the steps of the stage, and the profounder beauty of the girl writing a letter with a brush. But without the words which supplied the context for us, we would have felt these things through a haze of ambiguity in which the meaning and the emotion would have wandered loosely on the air.

If children need to be offered experience in order to keep alive their inherent knowledge of how to do things and be things with their bodies, so too they need to be offered a wealth of ex-perience in order to keep alive their inherent feeling for what the person or thing they are being would say under certain cir-cumstances and *how* he would say it. This kind of experience cannot be supplied by dramatic scripts. When children act out in pantomime a song, poem or story while someone else reads it, even though the words are not their own, the dramatization is their own, because they have searched out their own pan-tomimic vision. At a later stage in their development—when they are fifteen or sixteen years old, for example—they can learn how to take the words Shaw, O'Casey, Shakespeare or Euripides has given them and make these words their own, and this *is* a creative process, which will be discussed in Chapter Eleven. When younger children, however, work from a script, the words tend to remain the author's words, and their way of saying the words is liable to become their coach's way. If, under such circumstances, the resulting play has impact and is well performed, it will still not represent the creative vision of the children, but of their coach, who has known how to get them to say things as he or she has wanted them said. They will have held their mirror, not up to nature, but up to the mirror that their coach has held up to nature.

If children are to keep alive their capacity to find language and to use that language to express character and attitude and feeling, they will need a lot of experience with improvisation. Here, too, as with pantomime, exercises can be useful (within limits) with youngsters, say, more than ten or eleven years old —or in game form even with children eight or nine.

Many pantomime exercises can move very naturally into simple improvisations. Lovers walking in the park will not remain forever silent, nor an old man and woman by the fire. Riveters can sit down and have lunch together. A child opening her birthday package will naturally enough talk to herself, or to Mommy or Daddy if they are there. Or if it is a grown woman opening the package, perhaps her husband comes in meanwhile. This is all the adult gives them: *You are a married woman; you are opening a package. You are her husband; while she is opening the package, you come in.* No time to talk about it beforehand, though each may take time to think about his own character without talking with the other. For if they talk together, they will make up a skit, and what they do will not be an exercise. So she decides what she is, and he decides what he is, and he comes in while she is opening the package and, through interaction on each other, they unfold, not only for the watchers, but, more importantly, for themselves, the situation, the drama, comic or regrettable, of their lives. So with teenagers. Eleven year olds might choose to play campers who enter a clearing, and while they pitch a tent and make their fire and cook and eat their supper, they chide each other for clumsiness, reveal their fear of the forest and the night coming on, play on each other's fears, seek adult solace in the person of the boy who, in the course of things, has evolved into the counselor or scout master.

Some adults using these exercises make a transition from pantomime by means of an intermediate stage in which speech itself can be mimed though no words can be used. Thus boys who are being sailors in a storm at sea can shout back and forth in silence to each other and to their unseen shipmates in the tops. In a mass exercise with eighth graders, in which each child was to be an animal and the animals were to make such approaches to each other as suited their animalities, one bright boy was a bear —or so the teacher insisted when the exercise was over, though the boy swore up and down he was homo sapiens. "You were a bear, distinctly a bear!" said the teacher. "After all, everyone else was human, but attaching to himself the attributes of some animal. You attached to yourself the attributes of a bear. On this basis it is my firm decision that you were a bear!" The next time, the boy left no room for doubt that the animal he was being was man, for he stood and delivered himself of a fiery, if silent, political harangue.

The purpose of withholding words, even in the acting out of situations which by their very nature call for words, is so that, with the beginnings of speech, the need to extend the visible communication to its fullest limits is not lost sight of. Sometimes as an intermediate step gibberish is used instead of speech —sounds, expressive inflections, etc.—but not words.

This writer, however, has been responsible only once for an exercise using anything like gibberish, and he cannot take much credit for the exercise, since it came about quite beyond his conscious intent. He was trying dramatics exercises with a very difficult group—that is, though the girls were earnest, cooperative and sober, the boys were difficult and obstreperous. He set the girls to doing something or other by themselves, perhaps working out a skit, and turned his attention to the boys who were apparently alarmed by the subjective implications of dramatics and were resisting it to the point of using every technique of disruption short of open defiance. The writer knew that their resistance would change into its opposite if he could reach them. Somehow—and rather suddenly—out of the rather strenuous give-and-take between him and the boys, he found himself being an ape school teacher trying to handle a class of young apes. Lower jaw protruded, arms swinging in ape fashion, he chased this way and that, trying to lay his ape hands on one or another, no matter which one. In the same ape gait and arm swing, they fled, dodged, approached, scampered. The auditorium in which this exercise was taking place was loud with the highly expressive squealings of apes. Whatever the sober and seemly girls had been doing came to an end, and they watched in stunned amazement, not at all amused. It was a good exercise—that is, morally and tactically good—as good in the long run for the sober girls as for the boys. For the group began almost immediately to pull itself together and do good things.

The things which some young people, especially uninhibited teenagers, will do with improvisation exercises are usually good fun and are sometimes brilliant to the point of being exhilarating. One group of high school seniors was given the following exercise: *Here is a room—any room which any one of you takes it to be. Each of you is to think of who you are, and when you know who you are you are to enter the room.* The first to enter the room was a young man who sat down and began to wait. The second was a psychiatrist, followed closely by a rather inebriated gentleman, whom the psychiatrist tried to deal with as a patient. But the inebriate would have none of it—he was in no fit condition to be psychoanalyzed. Next a hatrack positioned itself. Then a girl approached the young man who was waiting and insisted that he was in her bathroom; he insisted that it wasn't a bathroom and that he was waiting for an interview and wouldn't leave. A she-creature appeared and crawled about the floor on all fours. Two men entered, hung their pantomimic coats on the extended arms of the coat rack and began to discuss a deal. The inebriate thought it would be fun to push over the hatrack. The businessmen got it back on its legs and dusted off their coats. The she-creature continued to prowl; a number of people asked about her, but no one knew who or what she was. The psychiatrist was getting nowhere with the inebriate, who by now had developed compulsions for pushing over the hatrack. The altercation between the young man and the girl was becoming heated. The boy continued to insist on his right to wait for his interview, the girl on her right to use her own bathroom. At length the girl turned toward the watchers and called, "Mother! Mother!" Touched by her appeal, one of the watchers entered the scene as the mother. "What's the trouble, dear?" she asked. "This man won't get out of my bathroom!" "Oh," said the mother, turning on the boy the radiant voice and smile of a first-class receptionist, "you're the young man who is waiting for an interview!" The inebriate continued to push over the hatrack. The she-creature continued to prowl. The psychiatrist took notes on all this, sucked his thumb with infantile abandon and began to cry.

Under the hilarity and release of such an improvisation, there are, of course, serious undercurrents. In a general way, there is the troubled search of adolescents for meaningful communication, and in specific roles there may be elements of psycho-drama and self-exposure. Such releasing experiences are good from time to time, and a self-confident teacher need not be afraid of their happening. However, a depth of knowledge and an expertness that go far beyond self-confidence are needed if an adult is to make programmatic use of such antics to help young people take themselves apart and put themselves together again.

In terms of dramatic art, much is accomplished by such an exercise, but, again, the expertness needed to carry young people through such dynamic chaos to the creative order of art lies beyond the range of most classroom teachers or others who work with children's dramatics, not as professionals in the field of theater, but as educators. And on the whole, the use of improvisation exercises with children, except very casually, is not particularly necessary or desirable. The merit of improvisation exercises is that they shake up a person's wits and liberate his ingenuity. Also, since interactions are spontaneous, as they are in actual situations, such exercises tend to generate energy. One grows loud, angry, sarcastic; one wheedles, one exerts oneself, one "pops off," so to speak, as one does in real life. But these virtues are also limitations. One works cleverly, even brilliantly, but off the top of one's head. In this writer's eyes, improvisation exercises, when used with children, lack the deeper level of aesthetic integrity which frequently arises in pantomime exercises even of a very simple and rudimentary kind. For improvisations which have this kind of integrity, one must turn to material which has, in itself, aesthetic, literary and human merit.

For this purpose, poetry is of little use, unless, as in the case of the poem about the clothes on the line, one takes the poem as a starting point and develops an improvised expansion, as thirteen or fourteen year olds might do, for example, with Hardy's "The Man He Killed" or Robinson's "Richard Corey." But there are many excellent stories which children can dramatize. Those that are most suitable for eight and nine year olds frequently have an excellent base in pantomimic action and do not make too many demands for the improvisation of dialogue. Thus, in "The Man and the Satyr," the man gropes his way pantomimically through the cold forest night until he comes to the satyr's house. There the satyr welcomes him and he has someone to talk with—but the story provides a clear line along which the essentials of the dialogue must develop: The man blows on his hands; the satyr asks him why he is blowing on his hands; the man says his hands are cold. The satyr offers the man some soup; the man lifts the soup bowl to his mouth and blows on the soup. The satyr asks him if the soup is cold. No, the man says, it is too hot. Thereupon the satyr screams at him in wild alarm: "You get out of my house! You get out of my house! I won't have anyone in my house who blows hot and cold with the same breath!''

In the story of the quarrel of the sun and the wind, it is the beginning which calls for dialogue and offers a little more challenge for improvisation, for the argument is heated, but the story gives the children little to work on until it comes time to set the conditions of the test. In the story of the humpbacked cobbler and the elves, the challenge both for pantomime and for dialogue improvisation is subtler and more extensive. But all of these and many more lie within the capability of eight and nine year olds. The Polish story of "The Three Wishes" can be done by nine year olds, too. Here the pantomimic element is very amusing—the sausages dangling from the blundering fisherman's nose and the hopeless efforts to get them loose without using up the third wish. Ten year olds can do such Jewish folk stories as the one about the Chelm goat, or the charming and witty story—witty in a very ten-year-old way—about the miller's clever daughter. It is a long story but an excellent one for a group that wants to develop a play to put on for other children. The lord of an estate is very much smitten with the daughter of the miller, who is one of his humble tenants—so smitten, in fact, that he decides to marry her. He is, however, somewhat wary of her braininess, so before they are married he makes her promise never to meddle in his affairs. In one instance, in a dispute between two of his tenants, he hands down a judgment which represents a real injustice to one of them. The wife conceives a maneuver for getting the judgment reversed and, working cleverly behind the scenes, manages to get her husband confronted with his blunder. He is not an unjust man, and so reverses the judgment, but he recognizes his wife's brains behind the affair and, more in sorrow than anger, tells her to pack and return to her father. He also tells her she may take with her some one thing—whatever is most precious to her. She asks that they have one more dinner together, a request that he willingly grants. At this dinner, she so plies him with food and wine that he falls into a deep sleep. Thereupon, she has the servants bundle him into her carriage, and so carries him off to her father's house. With one group of improvisers, the story ended the next morning with the following exchange:

> THE LORD (*Waking up—very puzzled*): Where am I? What *is* this place?
>
> THE CLEVER WIFE (*Quietly and very sure of herself*): This is my father's house. Don't you remember? You told me I could bring one thing with me—the most precious thing I could find. I looked all over! But— (*She goes to the lord and slips her arm around his shoulder.*) —the only real precious thing I could find was you!
>
> THE LORD (*With characteristic decisiveness, but he knows when he is licked*): All right. Let's go home!

We are not being condescending. It is really a stunning last line—completely in keeping with the character the boy had established for the lord and very much in keeping with the saucy spirit of the story. "All right. Let's go home!" Who but a ten-year-old boy could manage a happy ending with such economy?

What is the process by which children work out the improvisation of a story and what is the adult's role in this process? Again the parable of the clothesline contains the answer. Under the adult's leadership, the children talk together about what they are going to act out; they act it out; then they talk again. If what they have just acted out was complete in itself and they are not going to go further with it, this talk may be little more than a pleasant postmortem:

> "Sally waved her arms too much. If you're the sun, you can do a lot with your fingers."
>
> "Wasn't Robert funny—the way he hung onto his coat?"
>
> "Yes, but I don't think he should have been so funny. I think it's a serious story."

But if the dramatization is to be done again, then these are serious evaluative points and a new discussion ensues about what can be done to make the dramatization better. Then there is another acting out and another discussion, and so on, until everyone is satisfied with what has been done—or reasonably satisfied, as the case may be. The adult's role is to ask questions, to invite comments from the children, occasionally to make suggestions, to watch the acting out closely and perceptively, to point out his observations and invite observations from the children, to help the children reason things through and to help them open their imaginations and their insights.

The process is well illustrated in the development of a short piece of dialogue from a long eighth-grade play about China. One of the scenes was to portray the life of a family who lived on the soil. The group decided in the first discussion of this scene to set up the pantomime and let the dialogue come as it might. The scene began, then, with a father and son working their field.

The father hoes patiently, stopping now and then in an unperturbed manner to wipe his brow on his sleeve. The son hoes with a more compulsive exertion, wiping his brow with greater frequency and with a degree of irritation, and pulling his wet shirt from his flesh. The teacher and the watchers—that is, the part of the group not involved in the scene—like what they see. The characterizations are emerging. Soon the dialogue begins, spontaneously, no plans for it having been made.

> THE SON (*Leaning on his hoe, pulling at his shirt, mopping his brow and scanning the sky*): The crops will be burned up if we don't get some rain!
>
> THE FATHER (*Serenely, continuing to hoe*): There will be rain.
>
> THE SON (*As though bursting with pent-up indignation*): Yes—and it will rain so hard that we can't get the crops to market through the mud!
>
> THE FATHER (*Concerned, looking up quickly*): What's the matter with you, son?

The watchers are nodding. This is good—it will stay as it is. Out of their own temperaments, the boys are defining father and son—the father a man of the soil, whose serenity and optimism, however unrealistic, are a necessity for survival; the son an adolescent, tense, charged with anxiety and urgency. Now the man's wife—the boy's mother—enters. The father rebukes her mildly for her tardiness.

THE WOMAN: I couldn't leave the baby. She has a germ.

The watchers hoot with derisive laughter. A Chinese peasant woman saying, "The baby has a *germ!*" The acting-out phase passes explosively into the discussion phase. The adult asks: "Is it altogether unthinkable that a Chinese peasant woman in the twentieth century could mention germs?" Provoked by this question, new possibilities are explored, and in its final development the dialogue continues:

THE FATHER: Why are you late? There is a lot to be done.
THE WOMAN (*Soberly*): The little one is sick. I couldn't leave her with the old lady. The old lady believes in spirits, she doesn't believe in germs.
THE SON (*Exploding, throwing down his hoe*): The old lady is a fool! I myself have seen germs through a microscope!
THE FATHER (*With far more sternness than he usually shows*): You must not speak disrespectfully of the old one!

And so the girl's original blunder has been utilized to open up more searching possibilities. It has now established the family in time—in changing times, in changing customs, in changing familial relationships. Also, light has been shed on the reasons for the boy's low threshold of angry impatience—a hint of frustrated aspirations, of opportunities that have ceased to exist.

Improvisation sometimes takes a long time and requires a great deal of working through. In a seventh-grade dramatization of *Tom Sawyer*, the boys playing Tom and Huck ran into serious difficulties in their first encounter—they reversed roles. The boy who played Huck was a freer boy, his imagination took fire more easily and words came more readily, and so Huck became master—ideas and proposals poured from him, and poor Tom accepted and went along. They were not incorrectly cast—quite the contrary, it was merely that the boy who played Tom could not unlock his imaginative resources quickly and easily. But as improvisation followed discussion and discussion followed improvisation, Tom grew in force and mastery. Now it was he who had the ideas, while Huck began to search deeper for his own nature and to find it—the realist living in the wonder and freshness of the real, an outcast thoroughly convinced of his wrongness but liking himself with the simple self-liking that was part of his liking others, filled with awe by the imaginative power of his friend, entering into his friend's make-believe world, but trailing clouds of reality, unaware that these clouds were glorious. It was a slow process, in which revelation would often come through pantomimic "posture"—that is, by "feeling" masterful and dominant Tom could find the dominant thing to say, and by "feeling" compliant and deferential Huck could find the compliant and deferential thing to say.

Perhaps the most difficult improvisation for a child, and the most beautiful in its final resolution, was the creation of the character Mottel (pronounced *Muttel*) in a school production of *Mottel, the Cantor's Son*. The book is not strictly a novel—rather a series of episodes centering around a family in the ghettoes of Russia in the early nineteen hundreds. The family is always trying to better itself, and these efforts are all comically and pathetically frustrated until their final effort is crowned with success through their emigration to America. The aesthetic unification is achieved by having Mottel tell the story, so that the reader sees everything through the mischievous, but sweet and terribly penetrating eyes of a twelve-year-old boy. The group selected a number of their favorite episodes—the wedding, the ink-making, the vituperation between Jews and Ukrainians in the railroad carriage and, for dramatic suspense, the comically secretive crossing

of the frontier. Because of the particular genius of Sholom Aleichem, each role offered a creative challenge, for the characters
are all more or less blundering, indulging in great flights of pure
reason on the basis of ridiculously erroneous premises, sharp of
tongue with each other—and these human inadequacies are
blended in an undercurrent of decency, tenderness and love.

For most of the group the challenge was not inventing
things to say, for the author had given them dialogue or active
situations in which words came easily. The creative challenge
was to capture the undercurrent. At least such was the challenge
which most of the youngsters faced, but not Mottel. His challenge was total. For in telling the story through Mottel's eyes,
the author had not involved Mottel in any action or situation,
had not put a word of discourse in his mouth. He was, so far as
the episodes went, only an observer, magnificently characterized, but completely on an inward plane. And yet Mottel's inwardness, the flavor of Mottel's mind and spirit, *was* the story,
and no dramatization was conceivable unless Mottel's inwardness
could be externalized outwardly and unless, on the basis of such a
reversal, Mottel were to become the central character.

While the others worked out the various scenes, using,
where they could, lines the author had put in their mouths and
improvising the rest, Mottel hung around the edges, "mugging,"
experimenting with various possibilities of Mottel-like pantomimic behavior, obtruding himself in annoying and mischievous
ways and occasionally butting in verbally. The things he did and
said in the early stages were usually out of place, rashly experimental and inept, and they were irritating to the others, who
were trying to find their way into their own parts. Once in a
while, however, he would inject something which would get a
reaction from his mother or his brother or his sister-in-law or
some other dramatis persona, not as another child annoyed at a
troublesome classmate, but as the mother or the brother or the
sister-in-law annoyed at a troublesome Mottel. Little by little,
the intrusions as Mottel became more and more, and the intru-

sions as a boy struggling with a part became less and less, and
they began to shape one scene and another until ultimately Mottel emerged as the central humanity, the person through whose
lively inwardness the inner meaning of the play was revealed.
The process took two or three months. In the end, lovers of
Sholom Aleichem who saw the play said that it was not David
So-and-so whom they had just seen, but Mottel in the flesh.

7

Communication and Values

BACK OF ANY DRAMATIZATION lies extensive experience. Dramatic exercises, for example, assume extensive experience on the part of a child. A child cannot very well have trouble with an imaginary zipper if he has had no contact with a real zipper, nor be a sea captain if he has not known a sea captain or read sea stories, or a carpenter if he has not handled, or seen someone handle, a hammer and saw. But the limitation of dramatic exercises is that they fragment experience. They lack that dynamic interplay of relationships—that gestalt, so to speak—through which a good

[78]

story or poem or an important real event unifies and illuminates experience.

Consider, for instance, *Winnie the Pooh* and its collection of stuffed animals with their warm-hearted and incompetent humanity. "Poor Eeyore," says a child who has just read about Eeyore's birthday and Piglet's gift of a wet scrap of burst balloon and Pooh's gift of an empty jar from which Pooh himself has absent-mindedly eaten the honey. "Poor Eeyore," says the child again, and finds the paradox she is looking for. "Poor Eeyore! Eeyore is so funny!" Now if she is to play, not just a donkey, but this particular donkey named Eeyore, she will have something on her child's level to convey—the beginnings of that ironic wisdom in which one sees the human condition as both touching and absurd. She will, perhaps, as she grows up, refresh her vision with the laughter-through-tears of Sholom Aleichem and Sean O'Casey—and Chekhov, and the more disquieting catharsis of Lear's trial of the three stools and Hamlet's disposition of the carcass of Polonius. Yeats was right—"Hamlet and Lear are gay!"

The subject matter of children's dramatizations should be what children have genuinely experienced, whether the experience is real or vicarious. And the communication is the meaning and the value which they find in their experience. Since dramatization is most often a collective activity, the subject matter will most frequently be a common experience. Sometimes the subject matter will be some real experience the children have had together which they found important. Sometimes the subject matter will be developed from a variety of common experiences, such as going places and seeing things, reading textbooks and stories, etc., around a unit of study—as when a third grade makes up a play about Eskimos, or a seventh-grade class conceives a play about the Underground Railroad. Occasionally, though rarely, the content of their dramatization may be developed through the pooling of their diverse experiences, as when eight year olds make up a play about a family, or eighteen year olds thrash out a dramatic vehicle for expressing what they think about life. But, for the most part, the subject matter of children's dramatizations will be some reading experience which they have shared together.

It is in this connection that it is necessary to make a distinction between venial and mortal sins against children. This book has been at some pains to define a creative process in regard to children's dramatics. However, the violation of canons of creativity is a venial sin. It is a venial sin to impose on children a dramatization which is written or adapted, coached and directed, from the adult side of the tracks. It is only a venial sin because such dramatics are probably better for children than no dramatics at all. Thus the small-town Sunday-school teacher who, knowing next to nothing about dramatics and not being a very imaginative or intuitive person, but rather stiff and earnest, has had his Sunday-school class dramatize a Bible story from some script he has sent away for, and whose motivation may itself be impure—that is, he is having them put on a play, not because it occurs to him that it is a good way for children to learn Bible stories, but because it is what the congregation expects—such a person will still probably do more good than harm. Apart from unsupervised make-believe, the writer's first experience of losing himself completely in a role, of becoming the thing he was being—of hearing, not the voices of his everyday playmates, but the voices of angels—was as a shepherd in a routine Nativity play in a small-town church. It was a case, one might say, of the commonplaceness of the treatment being compensated for by the greatness of the matter. For the *mortal* sin is to permit and encourage children to dramatize cheap, tawdry and worthless material—to imitate, for example, except with satirical intent, the debasements of television.

It is the responsibility of the adult working with children to bring them poems and stories to dramatize. And since the communication which they will make is the meaning and value which they find in their experience, the reading which the adult brings to the children must be meaningful and valuable. The adult violates his own integrity, abnegates his educational role and, what is worse, belittles the children if he brings them material—on the supposition that children might like such things —which he himself does not find meaningful and valuable. The poems and stories which children dramatize should represent a meeting point of the things children prize and of the things the adult prizes and wants children to learn to prize.

The resources are very extensive. Responsible and imaginative writers, working with responsible and imaginative editors and publishers, are today producing excellent books for children of all ages. These are books which may or may not become classics, like *Mother Goose, A Child's Garden of Verses* and *Alice in Wonderland*—or like *Winnie the Pooh, Mary Poppins* and *Madeline*, which have become classics in our own time. But they are good things, with sound values and warm human contact. Inevitably, in the flood of publications, there will also be a lot of dross. This is an area where the inexperienced adult will need to enlist the help of a good children's librarian.

But over and beyond the body of literature written for children, there is an extensive world of lore, adult in its origins, still full of adult wisdom, but bold and simple, a lore which originates from a time when man himself was more innocent and which for this reason is common ground for child and adult. The fairy tales of Central Europe and some lore of Asiatic origin, such as *Aladdin* and *Cinderella*, have been the property of children for a long time. But there are sources of less well known but equally engaging material. There is a considerable body of Chinese folk and fairy tales. Many of these tales are full of magic, of fantasy, of wishes fulfilled through supernatural agency, of simple goodness vindicated against selfishness and greed, as in the more familiar European fairy tales; but they are more humanistic and less charged with an overcast of darkly evil forces. Some are the product of a later period and express more directly the concern for the poor and outcast which runs through Chinese literature—the story of the blind boy and his dog Fan, for example. The animal fables of Aesop are part of the accepted lore of children, too. But there is also a store of African animal tales. These do not have the same clarity of purpose which Aesop's fables have, but say things which are ironic and perverse, which both child and adult can enjoy but not fully understand. And there are Slavic and Italian folk tales which, like Aesop, point up clear lessons in terms of human greed and folly, but through human beings instead of animals, and not without perversity, for the Booby, like Aladdin, may blunder into success. Jewish folk tales are very attractive to boys and girls of ten or older, for they are very bright and witty, but have a warm humanity under their comicality and irony. There is a very beautiful group of American Indian literature, which expresses man's relationship with wind and water, with grain, forest and beast. There are the Greek myths, with gods and men visiting together, and Old Testament stories in which men wrestle with angels, pluck honey from the bowels of a lion and leave the gleanings of the field to the Moabite widow. In the folk literature of many people, there are tales of how things have come about—stories of the Creation itself, not only the Bible story and the Greek story, but a Tahitian story, for example, which searches the origins of man and life and death in a similar way. There is also a body of American folk lore, very raw in comparison with more ancient lores, but because it is rowdy and funny it is fun for boys from nine to thirteen to dramatize.

For pre-adolescents, too, there is world literature which belongs to them and to adults jointly. There are some of O'Casey's plays and Sholom Aleichem's stories. There are *The Yearling* and *The Adventures of Huckleberry Finn*, stories in which a pre-adolescent boy has to face up to life's demands, as Jody must face up to the stern demands which an adult recognition of reality imposes on him, and as Huck must face up to the demands of his deepest feelings, even though he believes that a Providence in the aspect of the adult moral order will make him fry for it. In poetry there are the old English folk ballads and *The Rime of the Ancient Mariner;* the humorous poetry of Edward Lear and Ogden Nash; the poems of Edna St. Vincent Millay, Robert Frost, Langston Hughes, Walt Whitman, William Blake; translations of poetry from other tongues—*The Iliad* and *The Odyssey,* short poems from Sappho and from the Greek anthology and, above all and in fairly large doses, Chinese poetry, which boys and girls from eleven to thirteen find particularly beautiful because of the deeper level of meaning and feeling concealed beneath the simple narrative and imagery.

This is a sketchy sampling of the sources on which the adult leader can draw, an abbreviated listing of specific works which, in the experience of this writer and many of his colleagues over many years and in many places, have provided the kind of reading experience which cements a group of boys and girls together in a common bond of feeling and out of which dramatizations develop. In the simplest terms, we are saying that a group of children cannot dramatize a story or cluster of poems unless they have read the story or the poems or have had them read to them. But we are saying much more than that. We are saying that children will dramatize one story better if they have read six together, and will dramatize six poems better if they have read twenty together, for the story or the poems will then represent their own choice, and the dramatization will be their expression of what they have most prized.

It is very regrettable if the time assigned by an organization for work with children's dramatics is so skimpy as not to make extensive reading together an integral part of the program. The poorest situation is one in which the adult begins by saying, "Here is a story we are going to dramatize. Listen, and I'll read it to you." It is a little better if the adult can say, "Here is a story I am going to read to you so that you can see whether you want to dramatize it"—for there is at least the implication that if the children don't want to dramatize it, the leader will fetch another. Better still if the adult is in a position to say, "I've brought in a number of stories that we can read together, and maybe we'll find one that we want to dramatize."

But best of all is a situation in which dramatization will arise more or less in the natural course of events among children with whom the adult spends a lot of time—a classroom teacher, a camp counselor or, under certain favorable circumstances, a parent. A dramatization on the same program of "The Sissy of Hardscrabble County Rock Quarry" and "The Healing Waters" grew out of a sixth-grade unit in folk literature. A program of dramatized poetry, including Li Tai-po's "The River Merchant's Wife," Laurence Dunbar's "The Caged Bird," Robert Frost's "The Runaway," Blake's "The Tyger" and Langston Hughes's "The Negro Speaks of Rivers," was done in camp by twelve and thirteen year olds who had come together originally to read and enjoy poetry, and even to learn something about writing it. The performance by sixth-grade boys of Howard Fast's "The Price of Liberty" (with the inclusion of material from Smollett's *Adventures of Roderick Random*) came about as the result of a weekly period in which the boys and the teacher read sea stories together. The girls of the same class had a corresponding period in which they read poetry with the teacher, the boys taking science while the girls had their reading period, and vice versa. Out of the girls' poetry period came a performance with shadow puppets of James Weldon Johnson's "The Creation." A group of fourteen-year-old boys in camp played hard all day and liked to get their sleep at night; to avoid the temptation of keeping each other awake with horseplay, they had their counselor read to them at night when they went to bed. From this bedtime reading developed their very spirited performance of Washington Irving's *The Devil and Tom Walker*.

The dedication of an amphitheater in another camp raises, in this connection, some interesting theoretical questions. The amphitheater had been built by the teenagers, boys and girls thirteen and fourteen years old, and for the ceremony they decided on an all-Greek program. They themselves would do dramatized readings of Greek poetry: Anacreon in costume, laurel wreath and all, reading one of his own poems; Edwin Arlington Robinson's translation of Sappho's "This dust was Timas," with an interpretation somewhere between pantomime and creative dance of the mourning maidens shearing their hair; a Housman translation of one of the choruses from *Oedipus Colonus,* read by the chorus leader in costume, with a background pantomime of Antigone caring for the blind, self-exiled king. The teenagers told the younger children to prepare a program of Greek myths, and they obliged.

Now, in this situation, there seems to be a large factor of artificiality: that is, because there is a dedication of an amphitheater, there has got to be a Greek program, like it or not. In all too many instances the public appearance of children comes about through just such circumstances—somebody wants to dedicate something, so the children are asked to perform. But what may be artificial and forced in one climate may be a perfectly natural growth in another. Such was the case in the dedication of the amphitheater. The teenagers had been reading poetry together anyway, and it was merely a matter of taking a look at some Greek translations and finding some things they liked. As for the imposition of teenage intentions on the younger campers, there are climatic factors at work in this case, too. First, the younger campers adored the teenagers and would gladly do anything they wanted; second, one of their counselors had been doing a lot of reading with them, with the idea of doing some dramatics, so that the Greek myths, which they loved, represented the introduction of additional material.

In their best forms, then, children's dramatizations come about most naturally, and have the most meaning for children, in situations where adults, working together, have created an atmosphere, a climate, a soil, rich in human experiences, in communal reading and in a general spirit of "doing" which has come about through a variety of constructive and creative activities.

In children's communities in which one sector of the community feels close to other sectors and the adults, too, compose sectors of the community—whether staff members, who are an intimate part of it, or parents, who, though peripheral, love and support it—the distinction which is often made between "formal" and "informal" dramatics breaks down, and it becomes a most natural and not infrequent occurrence for one sector to communicate with another through dramatizations. In such an atmosphere, the PTA sector of the community, for example, will impress children of ten or eleven as neither threatening nor overimposing. Thus, when a PTA meeting took place one time at a point when sixth graders had been dramatizing some poems— Whitman, Langston Hughes, Countee Cullen, among others—in connection with their study of slavery, the abolitionist movement and contemporary problems of segregation and discrimination—the children felt no constraint about saying to the PTA some of the things they felt strongly about, and of saying these things through dramatizations they had been working on in the natural course of their studies. They did, however, indulge themselves in one piece of "formalization"—that is, they made a carousel out of wrapping paper painted in stripes and attached to a framework of sticks. Inside this carousel, some of the children went round and round in up-and-down movements, being simultaneously the merry-go-round horses and their riders. As they rode, a little girl—it makes no difference whether the actual child was white or Negro—approached the merry-go-round man and asked, with a marvelous blend of simplicity, diffidence, insolence and hurt:

Where is the Jim Crow section
On this merry-go-round,
Mister, cause I want to ride?
Down South where I come from
White and colored
Can't sit side by side.

Down South on the train
There's a Jim Crow car.
On the bus we're put in the back—
But there ain't no back
To a merry-go-round!
Where's the horse
For a kid that's black?

In schools where this climate prevails, dramatizations will frequently flow, not from a single piece of reading which the children have shared, but from a whole unit of study—from a number of things they have read together, from things which individuals have read and have reported on to the group, from trips to places connected with the unit of study. The make-believe which goes on with second graders in the fire engine or tugboat which they have built is one example of this kind. Of a more directed kind are some of the plays cited verbatim by George F. Willison in *Let's Make a Play*. These are plays which children improvised with teacher guidance and whose dialogue the teachers had the good sense to copy down for preservation. A group which had been studying about Eskimos one winter conceived the idea of building a full-sized igloo of snow, and this idea eventually materialized as a little play about the life of Eskimos. During World War II, camp children frequently developed their own short plays from newspaper accounts and correspondents' reports from the various fronts—especially stories about the guerrilla resistance movements in China, France and the Ukraine. Chapter Ten will develop in greater detail the process by which an eighth-grade class developed a stirring and beautiful play about China as the culmination of a full year's study.

In the proper atmosphere, a dramatization may sometimes erupt in an exciting way from some important experience a group has shared. One high school class had a touching experience during a group trip in Pennsylvania where they were interested in learning all they could about the religious sects of the

Pennsylvania Dutch. At one point they stopped by the church, or meeting house, of one of these sects. The church was locked, but while the others peered through the windows, one boy made his way into the church through the cellar and opened the doors from the inside. An old caretaker appeared and scolded the youngsters roundly for their intrusion. However, their contrition, their general seemliness, and their purpose in intruding disarmed him and he took them home to his wife, who knew much more about the origins, beliefs and practices of the sect than he did. While her husband looked after the church and grounds, the care of the sacred objects seemed to be in her hands. She was impressed by the group's interest and respect, and before they left she gave them a collection of church relics to take back to their school. For, as she said, it was better for these things to be among strangers who cared than among the young people of the community itself, who cared little or not at all. The young people were deeply stirred, and on returning to school they conveyed their emotions to the student body through a dramatization of the incident.

In another instance, a group camped out in Jenny Jump State Forest in New Jersey. These youngsters were folk-lorists and the name of the place intrigued them. Not having the time or opportunity to research the origin of the name, they made up a story to explain it—a story consistent with numerous American folk tales about Indian maidens who jump from mountain ledges for unrequited love. They dramatized their story with a combination of improvised dialogue, interpretive pantomime and creative dance, adapting to their purposes a folk song about a girl named Jenny, for which they wrote new words.

During World War II, an eighth-grade group "adopted" a United States merchant vessel—that is, they got the names of the crew from the National Maritime Union and each child wrote a personal letter to at least one of the men. Shortly after this, there was a rumor that the ship had been sunk by enemy airplanes. A month or so later, however, a batch of letters arrived at the school, postmarked from Casablanca at a later date than the rumored date of the sinking. The letters were very touching. Most were awkwardly expressed and badly spelled, but the seamen were genuinely, and not at all condescendingly, grateful that a group of unknown school children cared enough to write them. Two or three letters were in the same hand, presumably dictated by sailors who couldn't write English. One of these was a Swedish seaman, who said his letter was the first he had received from anyone in over twenty years at sea.

The group felt impelled to communicate their experience to the rest of the school and set about making up a play. After an hour or so of discussion, they got to work. Most of the girls went off to work on scenery and properties with two or three remaining with the teacher to write a few pieces of background narration. The boys went unsupervised to the stage to begin the actual improvisation of the two or three scenes that had been agreed upon. By the time the teacher got to the auditorium, the boys had the play all worked out. It was lively, vigorous and moving. Among the boys was a "bad" boy—that is, a very squirmy, uncontrolled little fellow. "How did you manage to hold Bobby down?" asked the teacher, and was told, "We held him down *literally*. We sat on him!" The motivation, of course, was great, and the play went on for the school assembly the day after the letters were received.

In the situations described so far, the subject matter for the dramatization was drawn from things which a group had experienced in common. But there is another area which can be utilized, though with greater difficulty—that is, diverse and individual experiences. Life itself, often beyond adult intention or prevention, provides children with many of their deepest subjective experiences—their successes and failures, their frustrations and self-reconciliations, their fears and ascendencies. It is challenging but very difficult for an adult to sit down with a group of young people and thrash out with them the ideas and feelings, the methods through which they can develop a story or a series of expressionistic scenes and give dramatic expression to the antithesis and synthesis which, pooled, represent the group's statement about some important aspect of life. Younger children will work fairly easily, adlibbing saucily, for example, on the subject of families. But it is really with teenagers that this approach to subject matter usually has its greatest value.

Improvisation of such subject matter is very difficult. Most frequently a play will be developed by a process of collective creative writing and then be put into production, with rewriting along the way. Some of these plays are very beautiful and some are not written well enough. But in either case, the teenagers have thrashed their way to their own statement.

Sometimes the teenagers hit out hard at the adult world. One group of high school seniors wrote two plays as companion pieces—one naturalistic, one expressionistic. The expressionistic play was imaginatively preposterous and exciting, at some points very powerful. In it, a youngster named José is suspected of what—in the nightmarish society in which he lives—is the most heinous of all offenses—that is, being in love. He goes through a series of grotesque, absurd and terrifying humiliations—arrests, grillings and ultimately a monstrous trial—at the hands of nightmarish inquisitors—policewomen and judges—who want to crush everything he is. The naturalistic play took more deadly aim. A father, magnetic and idealistic, in the end uses his magnetism—the image in his daughter's heart of a father who has always been right and whom she has always loved—to undermine the very ideals of human relationship which he himself had inculcated. The plot and point were tightly tied together, but unfortunately the dialogue was tight, too, and sounded like something which had been put together by a committee—as, in fact, it had.

Ought a responsible adult leader to be a party to such teenage efforts to lash out at the adult world? The answer rests in some measure with what the adult himself thinks of the adult world. Far more important, however, is the question of whether what teenagers have to say is a valid expression. If we think that the answer to this question is no, then by what standards do we assume that what eight year olds express and what twelve year olds express *is* a valid expression? Is it because they are more likely to express what we want them to express? If we follow this line of thinking, we fall into the trap of the father in the play. The values we teach return to smite us. "All the time I was a little boy, you told me I ought to think for myself. Now when I express any thoughts of my own you get sore!" And so it seems best to assume that what teenagers have to say is a valid expression, even though what they have to say may sometimes seem to us mistaken or wrong-headed. One likes to think, in fact, that an increasing number of imaginative adults will lead creative activities with teenagers, especially in those places where they suffer the sharpest aches and indignities, so that such youngsters can have vehicles for all the aching and indignant things they have to say.

8

oooooooooo
Shadows and Pictures

WE SPOKE, in Chapter Four, of the way an inexperienced adult, beginning with such forms of dramatic fun as guessing games and costume parties, could gather experience with the dramatic expression of children, and could then begin, perhaps, to lead more directed dramatic activities. However, in order to develop certain pervasive concepts, such as pantomime and improvisation, and in order to define certain philosophical positions, it was necessary to deal with dramatizations of a kind which come about when children work with adults who are rather highly experienced. Now we can return to forms which can be used by adults who have little or no experience with dramatics, but who have a little experience with other techniques and crafts, or who may be what is called "handy." Among these forms are shadowgraph, silhouettes, moving pictures and shadow puppets. They are all interesting—even fascinating—in themselves and are capable of being exploited in creative ways.

In both shadowgraph and silhouettes, the action is represented by the actors' bodies, but under conditions which are not nearly as demanding as direct pantomime. For example, a girl is acting the part of St. Joan as she is tied to the stake. In a direct dramatization, every muscle of the child's face and throat, of her back and hands and legs, must be activated by her inward concept of St. Joan in that fearful and exalted moment. In silhouette or shadowgraph, however, it is sufficient that some kind of broad stance be worked out which will create a strong impression. This is more true of shadowgraph than of silhouettes.

Shadowgraph is a technique which has considerable charm and enchantment. It is a bold form, not capable of projecting much subtlety, but it has considerable impact for symbolic or generalized statement. A piece of white cotton or unbleached muslin, as big as the stage allows, can be hung from a batten or stretched on a wire or line. Behind this shadowgraph screen, a light is set, with enough room between the light and the screen for the actors to move about, not only sideways, but back and forth. The light can be a theatrical flood, a household flood, a Coleman lamp or an electric lantern. It is usually set low—on the stage, the floor or the ground—and is aimed just high enough so that the screen is flooded with light without the light itself shining in the eyes of the audience. The actors move behind the screen, between the screen and the light, and their shadows are cast on the screen. In this way they perform whatever actions are called for and tell their story by shadows.

With the screen intervening between the actors and the watchers, there may be more problem of voice projection than in direct dramatization. Hence it is often desirable to have the story read by a reader who can sit with a reading light in front of the screen. Or, for certain material, there can be two casts—one making the shadows, the other speaking the lines. Or the children can be encouraged to speak somewhat louder than they otherwise would need to.

It is an easy technique, and the person unfamiliar with it can experiment with screen and light and the movement of the shadows and the projection of voices until satisfactory results are obtained. There can also be experimentation with the color of the light through the use of theatrical gelatines—blue, red, amber, whatever fits the mood of the play. If a Linobach projector is used behind the shadow screen—and we will describe this instrument very shortly—then a whole scene can be projected in variegated color against which the shadows will move.

Shadowgraph is not a great medium. It is a form which is not capable of handling pantomime of any subtlety or material in which interaction between person and person, or between dialogue and action, is at all close. On the other hand, it is an effective medium for the dramatization of folk songs and simple folk stories, and can even be an impressive, if not sensitive, vehicle for dramatizations of some poetry. It can lend itself, for example, to poems in which the emotional content is itself theatrical—such as Poe's "The Raven," or even "Annabelle Lee," or to poems which are in themselves more sensitive but in which the action is bold, such as Frost's "The Runaway" or Whitman's "The Runaway Slave." Shadowgraph could, for example, exploit the metaphorical leaps of Blake's "London" more forcefully, perhaps, than could direct pantomime:

> How the chimney sweepers cry
> Every blackening church appals,·
> And the hapless soldier's sigh
> Runs in blood down palace walls.

The use of colored light, of monumental figures and shadowed cut-outs, could do a startling job of translating such lines into theatrical images. And this, of course, is the limitation of shadowgraph, that whatever is done *is* theatrical and lacks the creative authenticity which the child must find if his medium is to be, not his shadow, but himself.

Shadowgraph, nevertheless, has several distinct areas of usefulness. It is a good starting point for an inexperienced adult and for inexperienced children. The magic of light and shadow tends to liberate the children, and their concealment from the watchers relieves them of self-consciousness and tension. For the adult who is not yet ready to get below the surface, the tackling of concrete problems is an easier initiation than working with direct creative expression. It is easier to help a child cast an impressive shadow than to help him really *be something.*

Shadowgraph is also an exciting vehicle for dramatizing stories in which there are great differences in the sizes of things to be represented. Since one's shadow gets smaller as one moves towards the screen and away from the light and gets larger—vast, in fact—as one moves away from the screen and closer to the light, it is possible, for instance, to play *Jack and the Beanstalk,* with a life-sized Jack and an outsized giant, or to have life-sized pantomimists or dancers moving in relation to some vast looming figure. Shadowgraph is also an effective form to use as an adjunct to direct dramatizations. Thus, in a play treated more or less naturalistically, night scenes or mood scenes might be done in shadowgraph. Or the pattern of the naturalistic story might be broken at certain points by using shadowgraph to give a symbolic or universal interpretation.

A sixth-grade class used shadowgraph in this way to conclude a Christmas dramatization of Washington's crossing of the Delaware—but with their tongues in their cheeks. The first scene was set on the Pennsylvania side of the Delaware and dealt with the preparations for the crossing—the hostility of the generals to the mad plan, etc. The second scene took place in Trenton, where a couple of young Hessian mercenaries, excluded from the elegant Christmas party given by Tories for the officers, dream nostalgically of the Christmas tree of their German childhoods. (Some historians say that the Christmas tree was introduced into America by Hessian soldiers on that very night.) Anyway, the action returned to the winter darkness on the west bank—the soldiers loading powder kegs into the boats and making other final preparations for the crossing. Then the curtain closed and opened again on a shadowgraph tableau—a boat with boatmen and their poles, a figure seated in the stern, a large figure standing in the bow. The audience broke into applause at this evocation of a famous work of art. But the true intent began to dawn on the audience a moment later when they heard General Washington speak and realized that the shadow in the stern of the boat was his and the shadow standing in the bow was that of the rather stocky girl who played the corpulent General Knox.

> GENERAL WASHINGTON (*Matter-of-factly*): What do you think, Knox? Could we swim the river if we had to?
> GENERAL KNOX (*Very positively*): Oh, no, General—not in all this ice!
> GENERAL WASHINGTON (*With some asperity*): Then sit down and balance the boat!

In silhouette as in shadowgraph, the light is located behind the screen, but the actors perform in *front* of the illuminated screen and are thus silhouetted against it. The effect is similar to shadow movements, except that the figures always remain life-sized and no distortions of size are possible. Also, the movements are much more precise because they are unblurred. It has the same limitation as shadowgraph in that the figures appear two-dimensional, and its disadvantage, as against shadowgraph, is its incapability for distortion—for example, for having a huge hand engulf the moving shadow figures. On the other hand, because silhouettes are "truer," they are a better vehicle for more skilled or creative pantomime or dance.

It is possible in the same performance to get the advantages of both shadowgraph and silhouette by combining them. Immense effects—gigantic figures, monstrous hands or heads, colossal spread legs, etc., or scenery such as trees, skyscrapers or a looming gibbet—can be cast as shadows from behind the screen while the performers mime or dance in silhouette in front of it. So while these techniques can be used by inexperienced people they are capable of considerable refinement and suppleness as one gains confidence in their use.

Very effective use of combined shadow and silhouette effects was made in the concluding scene of a seventh-grade play about the Underground Railroad. The play itself was naturalistic, with a firm and vigorous plot about the escape of two runaway slaves with the help of a family of Quakers. However, the final scene of the play took the message of the play from the specific to the universal. A large group moved as silhouettes in front of the screen, interpreting in bold pantomime the history of the Negro to a reading of Langston Hughes's "The Negro Speaks of Rivers." As the poem concluded, a woodwind began to play, softly at first, "The Battle Hymn of the Republic" and a looming shadow figure of Abraham Lincoln moved against the screen and was seen to sign a document, while, to a reading of the Emancipation Proclamation, the silhouetted figures mimed —or, one might say, danced—the jubilation of the slaves in their freedom.

The Linobach projector is capable of enriching the effects of shadowgraph and silhouettes, and even of combining them, in some measure, with direct dramatic action. It is a big boxlike device containing a powerful bulb. The top and bottom edges of the open end are grooved so that a pane of glass can be slid into the grooves. On this glass slide, a design can be made with transparencies—that is, pieces of colored gelatine, cut out and assembled in the desired design, representational or abstract. If the pieces of gelatine are fixed to the glass with strips of adhesive tape, the resulting projection will have wide black outlines between its elements like a stained-glass window, for the Linobach projector will flood the screen (or back wall, or muslin "cyc") with a whole scene in jewel-like color.

When the Linobach projector is placed behind the screen,

or cyc, the figures then move either behind the screen as shadows or in front of it as silhouettes. But this projector is frequently placed right on the stage, where it can be concealed by some property, such as a large rock or stone. The light of the projector is usually powerful enough to permit some dim direct lighting on the stage, though much direct light will, of course, wash the projected colors out. Thus, when the Linobach is set in the middle of the stage and floods the back wall with a design in color, the actors who move in *front* of the projector will either be silhouettes or dimly lit figures. On the other hand, a figure who moves between the projector and the back wall will, of course, be illuminated by the projector—the colors and design of the slide will play across him in distorted form. He will be splashed with color, and his shadow, enormous or life-sized, will be cast on the back wall, depending on whether he stands near the projector or back from it. Obviously, no actor will pass between the projector and the cyc unless it is a planned effect to have him splashed with color and cast in shadow. The effect is bizarre—and full of possibilities.

This effect was used by high school juniors in Lorca's *Blood Wedding* night scene in the dry arroyo. The woodsmen, the two lovers and the pursuing husband were silhouettes, with a little dim direct lighting, against a very abstract pattern of blues, yellows and blacks, cast on the cyc by the Linobach projector. The old woman—the symbolic figure of death—was also for the most part silhouetted, though at one or two points she was splashed with projected colors of eerie gloom. The moon, however, moved in bold and dancelike ways between the projector and the cyc, so that the eerie-colored light played over him and seemed to emanate from him. Meanwhile, his movements were re-echoed as a shadow and this shadow, because he wore a cape, was vulturelike and vast.

A similar device was used by other teenagers in mounting one of their anti-establishment plays. They set up an opaque projector on the floor of the auditorium, the standard kind of opaque projector which is used for viewing postcards or pages of books. In the play, a fatuous old general is presenting to the audience and the world a philosophical justification for the destruction of a native village, when suddenly a scene in full color of a field strewn with the half-naked dead appears on the cyc behind him. He himself is splashed—stained, so to speak—with the color, and his shadow is cast across the field of carnage.

In the context of dramatic effects achieved through projection of light, something should be said about shadow puppets. Puppetry represents a specialized form of dramatics. In the creative and emotional life of children, it has its own important values and meanings, very different at many points from those of direct dramatization. It is a field that lies outside of this writer's competence, and therefore outside the scope of this book. However, since shadow puppets are very fascinating and colorful, since they are less often seen and written about than other kinds of puppets and since this writer has had some experience with them, it might be helpful to tell how they can be made and manipulated.

The shadow puppets made and used by children in this country are an adaptation and simplification of Oriental shadow puppets, of which the Javanese are perhaps the best known. Shadow puppetry, like shadowgraph, uses a screen with a light behind it. The puppet is cut from oaktag or heavier cardboard, depending on size, and sticks are attached to the cut-out figure. The simplest way is to attach the stick to the base or feet of the figure, in which case the manipulators sit or squat below the bottom of the lighted screen and hold their puppets up, applying enough pressure to keep them flat against the screen. In the other method, a longer stick is attached to the middle of the puppet—that is, the stick is at right angles to the plane of the figure. In this case, the puppeteers stand behind the light and press their puppets against the screen. This way of doing it makes up-and-down as well as sideways movement possible.

Now if a figure cut from cardboard is pressed against a lighted screen the figure will appear black. And in some uses of shadow puppets, that is what the puppets are—black figures, like the actors in shadowgraph. However, in the really fascinating forms of shadow puppetry, the figures are not black—they are transparencies. That is, after the figure is cut from cardboard, the inside of the figure is then cut out—face, arms, legs, chest, stomach, even hands and feet if the figure is large enough or the craft skills fine enough—so that all that is left is a cardboard outline. If this figure is pressed against a lighted screen, the watchers see a figure in black outline. (When oaktag is used, the outline is not black but a muddy brown, so oaktag is usually painted to make it opaque.) But then, if the holes that were cut out of the figure are filled in with colored cellophanes or gelatines pasted over the outline, and if the figure is then pressed against a lighted screen, the watchers, sitting in a darkened room, will see a figure in bright and luminous color.

Scenery is made in the same way, so that a princess walks past the amber walls of a castle in a pink dress among blue and yellow flowers. The prince comes to her in a red cape and yellow pants. Her father, the king, in a purple robe, spies from behind the black trunk of a tree with spreading green branches. Or a Viking vessel with red and white striped sail tosses on a stormy, dark-blue sea. These figures and pieces of scenery, with their black outlines, appear to the watchers as a stained-glass window in which the characters of the depicted story are able to move.

What moving these figures can do, however, is rather limited. They can enter, move back and forth across the screen and bob a little while speaking their lines. Suppose a puppet is to make an exit from the same side of the stage from which he made his entrance? For the most part, shadow puppets, being two-dimensional, are made in profile—otherwise their movements across the screen would seem to be the movements of someone walking sideways all the time. Thus if a puppet is to make an exit from the same side of the screen from which he made his entrance, he must be flipped about quickly. Puppets manipulated on sticks attached to their feet from below can make this about-face maneuver, but the puppets manipulated on long sticks from behind the light have no choice but to back off. With experience a youngster can learn to manipulate more than one stick in each hand, and then he can begin to make and manipulate more flexible puppets with jointed arms and legs.

The shadow puppet stage can be made in a number of ways. An ordinary hand puppet theater can be adapted by stretching a piece of white muslin or cotton across the proscenium. A sheet of colorless cellophane or gelatine will serve the same purpose. The effects, however, are rather different. The cloth softens the black outline and the colors of the puppets, whereas against a sheet of cellophane the outlines and colors are very sharp and clear. The mood of one is therefore different from the mood of the other, but which is more desirable will depend on what mood is desired—except that the cloth will condone crudities in craftsmanship, the cellophane expose them.

If a puppet theater is not available, or if a larger screen is desirable, a screen can be made by stretching muslin taut across a frame. The frame can be attached to legs, so that it is elevated to the height needed and can stand by itself. The screen can then be draped below and at the sides to conceal the puppeteers and keep light from leaking through. A group of eighth-grade boys used an eight-foot screen to enact a Chinese folk tale which had, as its central figure, a five-foot serpent jointed in four places and manipulated with four sticks. Some sixth-grade girls made themselves a six by four feet screen, together with the needed puppets, to dramatize James Weldon Johnson's "The Creation." First white light flooded the screen—the sun appeared and the moon, the stars, the planets—then blue seas and the green earth, vegetation and the beasts—then man was formed, and woman from his side while he slept. It was a magnificent production.

William Blake's "The Tyger" was also done in a camp by girls the same age by using a regular puppet stage, but the tiger as well as the jungle was a fixed piece of scenery, and the movement was supplied by the shadows of a real pair of hands, which handled, as the tools of the Creation, a hammer and chain.

There are no theoretical reasons, but only practical considerations, why the puppet screen should not be as wide as the whole stage, whatever stage is available. One seventh-grade group managed to combine shadow puppetry on such a scale with direct dramatization. The play was a Christmas play. It was cast in the future, and a mother and several children were sitting in the living room, momently expecting Father's return from Saturn in time for Christmas. They decided to turn on the space-viewer and see whether they could see him coming. The space-viewer covered the whole back of the living room—that is, the cyc, the muslin curtain that closed off the rear of the stage from a room behind. The living room lights were turned off and the space-viewer turned on. Stars, moons and comets, even Saturn with its ring, whirled across the screen, utilizing both its breadth and its height, the puppets manipulated by dowels as much as ten feet long. Santa Claus streamed across the empyrean in his sleigh, followed a moment later by Father in his rocket.

It is a beautiful and colorful medium. Children as young as six and seven can make the puppets. The puppets they cut out may be crude, but they will be characterized by the directness and force which mark the art work of little children. Eight-year-old girls in a summer camp during World War II made up several stories of their own and dramatized them with shadow puppets. In one of these, a ship was struck by a torpedo, broke in two and sank, its black hull in two pieces and its red smokestack disappearing through the blue waves.

The moving picture is another projection vehicle that deserves consideration. An adult who can handle a camera and can edit film might get some delightful and very free and spontaneous dramatizations with younger children who—like the eight year old doing her dramatic exercise of looking for something —can make use of the whole outdoors. But then what? To whom would such films be shown? To adults for their entertainment? To the children and their friends? Would seeing themselves in a movie be a worthwhile experience? This writer's only contact with this medium has been with teenagers and he cannot answer the question. He would assume, however, that for a group as young as ten or eleven to make a movie under adult leadership and show it to their friends would be a valid experience.

Obviously, this medium does not in itself militate against creative dramatic expression. On the other hand, the quality of a "performance" will hinge as much on the technical know-how of the person who shoots and edits as on the dramatic expression of the children—perhaps more. Through skillful shooting and editing, a theatrically effective film could result from "acting" that had little creative integrity; and through awkward shooting and editing a very poor film could result from "acting" that was as fresh and spontaneous as could be. The result, however, doesn't matter very much if the spirit of the whole process is a spirit of fun in doing together. The adult who uses a moving picture camera as a way of involving children in their own creative expression is doing valid dramatics with them, no matter what the results. The camera buff who uses children to satisfy his own professional or ego needs is no better (nor worse) than the dramatics coach who works with children out of the same motivations.

When, however, the young people themselves do the shooting and editing, the quality of the result takes on a greater importance. This writer—who can't take an unblurred still picture with a brownie—has had some contact with this type of situation with young teenagers, who had organized their own moving picture companies and handled everything—script, shooting, acting, editing, sound—without any adult interference whatsoever. At one time there were two such companies among the eighth-, ninth- and tenth-grade boys in the same school, together with one free lancer, though the two companies interpenetrated each other to a large extent, and the free lancer penetrated both companies.

The companies did films of two kinds—art films and satirical parodies. Among the latter was one in which an exorcist pursued Dracula with an instrument of exorcism behind his back, cornered the monster by the wall of the castle, and exorcised him with a Star of David! The monster dwindled and the camera came to light on the empty garments where he had been. One of the art films was called *New York Metamorphosis*. It was done on color film, and the camera roved about the city and created a rushing kaleidoscopic sequence of objects and effects of light, the familiar thrown into the context of the unfamiliar. This writer had *New York Metamorphosis* shown to an eighth-grade class by way of launching a short unit in creative writing.

Although these companies had no official standing in the school, they did from time to time show their films for school assemblies—without charging admission. That is, the companies operated on the basis of all debit and no credit. The boys who operated these film companies had no predisposition against their school work in literature and drew on it for their subjects along with other things. One company did a very beautiful short film called *Orpheus and Eurydice*, which opened with a tough-looking young fellow wearing a cap and sitting on a trash can in front of an apartment house. A girl walked by, very fresh and sweet with long hair down her back. The boy saw her and it was very apparent that he was not the young tough that he appeared, but a boy of acute sensibility. He began to pursue her and she broke into a run. But looking back at him from time to time, she sensed what he was, stopped for him and they walked off hand in hand.

The free lancer, when he was in ninth grade, made a short film of *Oedipus Rex* and showed it to his class, which was study-

ing Greek plays. This writer happened to be in on the filming of
the scene in which Oedipus slays his father, Laius, at the "cross
roads in the covert of glen." The boys had got permission to go
out to the park to film if they could get a teacher to go with
them. The writer happened to be crossing the lobby when they
were casting about for a teacher, and, having a free period, was
pressed into service. There were four boys. One was an assistant
cameraman, one played Laius, one was one of Laius's litter car-
riers and the other was the producer-director, who was also
chief cameraman, as well as the second litter carrier and Oedipus
himself, a role into which he moved very quickly by putting on
a copper mask he had made for this purpose. The crossroads
were a divergence in one of the park paths. Cars went by from
time to time in the background and caused momentary interrup-
tions in the shooting. Most, but not all, of these films were made
to be shown without sound. In the case of *Oedipus*, the free
lancer edited his film in such a way as to synchronize the action
with his own reading of a short synopsis of Sophocles's play as it
appeared in a college trot.

Later, when he was a senior, the same boy worked with
some of his classmates to produce two short films which were
part of the senior dramatics program. On these two films, the
youngsters had some help from teachers, to wit: 1. This writer,
sitting with some twenty or thirty high school students, contributed his voice to those of a roaring crowd waiting to hail its
leader, the free lancer taping these sounds for synchronization
with his film based on a short play of Ionesco's; 2. Another
teacher drove the film makers out to a sea beach at sunrise and,
when they were finished shooting, drove them back to school in
time for classes at 8:30 A.M.

By shooting out of sequence at the beach, the young people
were able to transmute the time from sunrise to daylight into the
time from daylight to sunset, the phase of the day required by
their script. The script was later recorded on tape and the film
was edited to synchronize with the tape—a long and exacting

process. The script itself was one of the most beautiful passages in twentieth-century English literature, where, in Joyce's *A Portrait of the Artist As a Young Man*, Stephen Dedalus sees the girl wading like a long-legged bird at the edge of the beach. In this rapturous moment, the young artist's eyes, which have been turned so long into his own guilt-ridden imagery, turn outward at last in joyous affirmation of the sensory world. Joyce's Stephen walked for a long time with little externalization of his inward exaltation. But the boy in the film was his own Stephen, and, like the eight-year-old girl in the looking-for-something exercise, he ran and ran, until, exhausted at last, he lay writhing in happy anguish in the sand.

9

ooooooooo
Dance and Music

PERHAPS THE MOST EXCITING form of children's dramatics, the form which exploits most fully all the creative potentials, is the more or less completely articulated original play, which the children act out, speaking words which have evolved through the process of improvisation. However, such plays, as we have already begun to see, will sometimes draw for their total communication on supplementary dramatic forms, such as shadowgraph, silhouettes, shadow puppets and, theoretically at least, moving picture sequences. It is for this reason that these matters have been discussed in advance of original plays. And it is for the same reason that it is important to consider, at this time, the use of music and dance as attendants to dramatics.

In many of their aspects, both dance and music—vocal music, at least—are themselves dramatic forms, the one an enlarged or transcendent pantomime, the other an enlarged or transcendent speech. Each, however, differs from dramatics in its disciplines. In regard to children's activities, dramatics is the most spontaneous and least rigorous, music is the least spontaneous and most rigorous and dance lies in between. It must be observed, however, that very young children practice all three arts without help from the adult world, and that in a good program for pre-school and primary-grade children, the three arts often remain wedded in an almost inseparable way, as we have seen in the discussion of pantomime in Chapter Five. But as children grow older, the difference in the skills they need to acquire leads to a high degree of separation of the three arts. Because the demands are different, the gratifications are different, and so each of the arts has its own values—its own philosophy, so to speak. To discuss the philosophy of dance and music is, of course, beyond the scope of this book. What we are concerned with are the areas in which these arts can go hand in hand. We are concerned with the possible enrichments of dance and music through the exploitation of inherent dramatic elements, and with the enrichment of dramatizations through some use of music and dance.

We have already seen that music and dance, of a kind, are integral parts of dramatics work with very young children— that the free and spontaneous make-believe of the play period has a counterpart in a more instructional program of rhythmics, that little children will move about being things suggested by music and will act out songs as well as poems. The acting out of songs and poems remains a valid dramatic expression for children of all ages. In fact, the same song may offer rich possibilities over a wide age range. This writer has seen the ballad *John Henry* performed by teenagers in one camp and by ten year olds in another. The differences in the performances were very great, but they were not differences of better or worse. Quite the contrary, both were fresh and vigorous and delightful: the ten year olds' broad and heroic, the teenagers' subtle, wry, poignant—spiced with sauciness. The differences in interpretation extended even to the steam drill. The ten year olds' steam drill was a contraption of corrugated paper over a frame of sticks, in which a boy sat and operated it. With the teenagers, a group of three boys enacted the steam drill with the rhythmic movements of their backs, arms and legs, in a kind of pantomimic dance.

Where children are in a position to learn dancing of any kind, this dancing will incorporate itself very naturally into their dramatizations. Sometimes, in fact, the dramatization may be little more than a framework for the singing and dancing. An elementary school Christmas assembly may express in this form what the children have been learning about the customs of various peoples. A dramatic framework is set up, characters are created—a family, perhaps, with relatives and guests. Through the activities of this family, the Christmas customs are enacted, culminating in the singing of national Christmas carols or in folk dances or in a rip-roaring square dance from the American frontier. Or one group may enact the Chanukah festival, and another the winter solstice rites of other times and other religions.

But even when no dramatic framework is deemed desirable for a program of singing and dancing, there are often certain dramatic elements in the songs and dances themselves. In many folk songs, the singer is a dramatis persona—he is a story teller and he has an attitude towards his story, or he is a lover making his plaint or he is a gay fellow playing a narrative joke on his listeners. The songs will mean much more to children if, as they sing, each feels himself to be the person whose words and feelings and thoughts the song is expressing. It is a subtle business, and any exaggerated dramatization on the part of the singers will ring untrue. It consists perhaps in nothing more than the singer's inner identification with the person of the song. One beautiful program of ballads sung by sixth graders was particularly characterized by this kind of identification. The youngsters had written their own ballads, both words and music, as the outcome of a study of the folk ballad with their music teacher. In their performance there was nothing one could see or hear that could be called deliberate "acting," but there was a sly entering into a role on the part of the singers which created a sense of infectious pleasure.

The folk dances of many European countries have strong dramatic overtones. This writer recently saw seven year olds, under the leadership of the same teacher who worked with the sixth graders and their ballads, perform the Finnish "Old Man's Dance." All the old men have a game leg, but this game leg has a vigorous thump, and it does not prevent the old men from doing some very spirited dancing. For some of the little children, the response to the music had not become a reflex, and one could almost see them thinking, "When the music does *that,* I've got to do *this* with my leg," so that some of them were always running a few notes behind. But the dramatic element was beyond criticism. Boys and girls alike were a marvelously hearty bunch of lame old men.

Even American square dancing has a degree of inherent drama. It represents a kind of on-going dialogue between man and woman, though this dialogue does not emerge until the dancers have gone beyond mastering the configurations and have mastered style. In New England this dialogue of the sexes is carried out with a blithe grace, further west with a rowdy vigor, in Pennsylvania Dutch country with a sauciness that is almost naughty.

To the extent that the adult who leads a dance or music program with children can help make the children aware of these possibilities, the experience of the children will be enriched. The adult working with dramatics, on the other hand, can enrich the experience of the children by helping them find ways to incorporate dancing and music into the dramatizations.

The pre-dramatic activities discussed in Chapter Four, such as carnivals and fairs, can also be enriched through music and dance. At the annual Pennsylvania Dutch Folk Festival in Kutztown, Pennsylvania, there is square dancing every night, both public dancing and exhibition dancing by skilled groups. A group of children setting up an imaginary fair or carnival could well include square dances or national dances in their program. A seventh-grade class presented a charming variation of this type of program—an East Indian bazaar. Some of the booths were merely carnival games run by young people in East Indian garb. One booth was a rummage sale presided over by no less than a maharajah. More authentic booths sold an attractive, hand-illuminated cook book of East Indian recipes compiled by the children and piping-hot East Indian dishes. From time to time on the stage there was a snake-charming act. The snake charmer would play an East Indian tune on a recorder, and the tune would induce the sinuous hand and arm of a girl to rise and writhe cobralike from a basket. Once every forty minutes or so, the attention of the visitors would be called for by the maharajah or the snake charmer or someone else equally impressive and the girls would perform East Indian dances accompanied by recorders. It was this dance that suggested to perceptive visitors that the youngsters had delved deeper into the study of India, culturally at least, than the level of tourism.

At points in this book, in a variety of contexts, reference is made to many kinds of dramatizations which have involved music or dance in one way or another. Some further examples of the effective use of music can be cited at this point:

> In a camp play about the Underground Railroad, the Negro folk song, "The Drinking Gourd," was used as a theme. (The "drinking gourd" is the Big Dipper, Ursa Major, which, revolving around the North Star, oriented the fugitive slaves on their flight to freedom.) In the same play, a slave woman, standing at

twilight in the door of her cabin, sang "Steal Away to Jesus"; the field slaves understood the meaning of the song and stole away to a secret meeting in the pitch pine grove.

In the play about Washington's crossing of the Delaware, the Hessian soldier boys, cold and excluded from the festivities of their officers, sang a German Christmas song to comfort themselves.

In the sixth-grade play about Valley Forge, the Vermont men, who had been transferred to Valley Forge after their victory at Ticonderoga, introduced the "Bennington Riflemen's Song" to the other troops.

In a Chinese-style comedy, written by an eighth-grade girl and performed by her class, a rhythm orchestra consisting of wood blocks and percussions was placed onstage to establish the beat for the stylized pantomime.

If an original play by children deals with people in a given historical, geographical or ethnological setting, it seems natural that these people will have occasion to sing or dance or both, and it will be natural for the children to include this likelihood in planning their play. Or else the specifics of a given play may be broadened by the more symbolic statement of music and dance. Or, again, the mood of a play may be enhanced if, as the house lights go down before the play, or as an act of the play begins, fitting music is played on recorders or such other instruments as the children play well.

But it is not desirable, for the sake of integrating children's activities, to drag music and dance in by the scruff of the neck. (The story is told of the fifth-grade group undertaking to make a play around their study of American Indians. At the same time, in this school which prided itself on subject-matter integration, their music-dance teacher was teaching them East Indian dances. In a staff meeting the crisis was resolved by a compromise proposal and in the final dramatization a travelling company of East Indians, competing apparently with Shakespeare companies and honky-tonk girls for the patronage of prospec-

tors and homesteaders, stopped off at an Indian village and performed East Indian dances for American Indians!)

There are many situations in which the inclusion of dance
or music is right and natural, and the possibility of their use
should be considered, not only in original plays, but also in
standard plays dramatized from scripts. Some scripts call for
music or dance and their absence may mar an otherwise beautiful performance. This was the case in a performance of Lorca's
Blood Wedding by high school juniors. Lorca, who took his
story from a newspaper item, begins his play with two more or
less realistic scenes which lay the basis for the flight of the young
woman with her lover within hours after her marriage to another man. The scene of the wedding fiesta is the pivot of the
play. It has a naturalistic base, but by employing chanted
epithalamies and Spanish dances, it begins to move the play from
naturalism to lyricism. In the next scene, the narrative action
takes place in semi-darkness amid symbolic figures—three mys-
tic woodsmen, the moon and an allegorical figure of death in the
form of an old woman. In the last scene, narrative disappears altogether in favor of universalized lyric lamentation. In the
absence of dance and music teachers, the teacher working with
the children on the play decided to have the wedding guests re-
cite the epithalamies without musical accompaniment and, instead of having dancing on the stage, to use a phonograph
offstage and let the wedding guests come and go as though to
and from the dancing. Unfortunately, there were among the
wedding guests a surprising number of young people who really
found it difficult to play any dramatic role with conviction. The
result of doing without the singing and the dancing was, therefore, disastrous, and a scene that should have been vibrant and
soaring was tepid and heavy.

If, then, a play calls for certain things, the adult must decide
whether his own leadership is competent to supply these things.
If not, he must look for competence from some other source. If
no source is available, he must make the best judgment he can—

whether to abandon the plans for a particular play or to risk certain modifications. It is an upsetting thing for youngsters who have worked hard to feel that they have not done as good a job as they might.

Sometimes, especially in a group of older children, the source for the needed competence will exist among the children themselves. Among them may be someone who can choreograph and lead dances, another who can compose, adapt and arrange music, and someone else who can play an instrument or sing. Two older boys composed thematic music and adapted other music for a performance of Jean Cocteau's *The Eiffel Tower Wedding Party*. In a presentation of Ionesco's *Rhinoceros*, there were not enough parts for all the girls, and one girl agreed to choreograph a dance of rhinoceroses for the girls without parts. The original idea was that this dance would be given as an interlude between Acts III and IV. However, Act IV begins with Berenger asleep and tossing in the throes of a nightmare. So in the final form of the play the dance was not given as an interlude, but was incorporated into the play itself as Berenger's rhinocerotic dream.

Mention of *Rhinoceros* leads to the matter of sound effects. Those required by this play are very difficult for a non-professional group, including as they do the thundering of rhinoceros hoofs, first one beast, then two, then herds—plus the trumpetings of the beasts. In the production of *Rhinoceros* mentioned above, a couple of very creative boys, technically equipped to handle and edit tape recordings, took care of the sound effects with a combination of know-how, diligence and imagination. The trumpetings were lyrical, as though they expressed the bafflement of souls who had un-eaten the forbidden fruit and found themselves returned, disquietingly, to a state of innocence.

In regard to sound effects, the question always arises as to whether taped or natural sound effects should be used. Taping offers a wider range of possibilities. For example, the sound of a running water faucet, if taped and amplified, can create the noise of a waterfall. But taping presents hazards of timing. It is disconcerting to young performers to have a trumpet fail to call on cue, or, even worse, to have it call too soon. Then, too, the "canned" effect of taped sounds must be evaluated. For some purposes, the canned effect is good. The rhinoceros trumpetings, for example, were made softly with the human mouth, and the bestiality of the resulting effect was achieved, not merely by amplification, but by the modifications of tonality inherent in the "canning" mechanism. On the other hand, the actual rattling of a sheet of metal in a small auditorium will probably produce better thunder than the same sound canned. A knock on a door, a pistol shot, a whistle outside in the darkness—the use of canned sounds for such things will disturb illusion, unless the recording equipment is of unusual fidelity and therefore very expensive. Anyway, the producing of sound effects is an interesting technical and aesthetic area. Young people find it exciting, and experimentation should be encouraged.

Lying between sound effects and music is the achievement of a couple of girls in a dramatization of a passage from *The Tempest:*

Be not afear'd; the isle is full of noises,
Sounds and sweet airs, that give delight and hurt not.
Sometimes a thousand twangling instruments
Will hum about mine ears. . . .

The girls loosened somewhat the strings of two guitars and strummed the loosened strings until they were satisfied that the sounds of their twangling instruments would really enchant the vague soul of a scaly monster, groping his way towards becoming man.

Something needs to be said about operettas and other musical plays. All of the things which militate against satisfactory performance and, more importantly, against creative integrity in the production of a standard play are doubled in an operetta. The child is confronted not only with fixed words as in a play script but with fixed musical notes, so that the latitude for free expression is further reduced. Casting, too, presents special problems. Does the person who can handle the dramatic aspects of a role have the voice for it? Can the person who has the voice handle the acting? And, finally, assuming that the musical level of a group is only moderate, what operettas or musical plays are available at their musical level which are worth the great effort in musical or literary terms?

But these difficulties do not negate the validity of undertaking such productions. For, as with dramatics, it is not successful performance that is the criterion but the value of the process, and a performance which leaves a lot to be desired by way of dramatic vigor and musical finesse may have constituted for the children an important musical experience. Of the performing arts, the disciplines of music are the most rigorous for children and the skills take the longest to acquire. But the disciplines can be mastered, the skills acquired, the difficulties overcome, and one often sees young people handle operettas—Gilbert and Sullivan, for example—with vitality and freshness. The most satisfactory performance this writer has witnessed was Mozart's *Bastien and Bastienne,* performed by thirteen and fourteen year olds in a low-income summer camp. Dramatically, it was altogether fresh and unstilted, and there was such a lovely and compatible relationship between the children and the music it was hard to believe they had not composed it themselves. Perhaps the compatibility can be explained in part by the fact that these gifted, imaginative boys and girls were singing music composed by a gifted, imaginative boy about their own age.

If articulated operettas and musicals are difficult for young people, there are some intermediate forms which are, perhaps, more satisfactory—forms, for example, which use a chorus while the dramatization is carried in pantomime. Earl Robinson's

"The Lonesome Train," an elegy on the death of Abraham Lincoln, is a stirring example for children eleven or twelve years old. Walt Whitman's "I Hear America Singing" has been set to music and the poem is excellent material for dramatization for children eleven to sixteen years old, but how suitable the music is for choral groups of the same age is another question. This writer has seen Bach's *Peasant Oratorio* done by a high school chorus with a degree of dramatization, but whether the singers did the dramatizing or whether it was done in pantomime, he doesn't remember. A group of young people, comprising many of the same children who did the Mozart *Bastien and Bastienne*, composed their own oratorio about the history and meaning of their camp.

But the music children dramatize does not necessarily have to be played or sung by children. It can be supplied by recordings, and there are many excellent recordings for this purpose—Prokofiev's *Peter and the Wolf* and *The Love for Three Oranges*, to name two of many. The dramatization of *Peter and the Wolf* is an excellent experience in creative pantomime for nine and ten year olds. Such dramatizations, interestingly, are often initiated, not by adults leading dramatics, but by adults concerned with the musical education of children. For in order to dramatize the story told through music, the child must listen carefully to the rhythms and melodies and to the tonalities of the different instruments, because these rhythms, melodies, and tonalities express the mobile characteristics of the boy or duck or woodsman or wolf, whichever the child is going to be. Music teachers feel that this kind of listening-in-action is a very worthwhile musical experience. In short, the values of music and dance do not war with the values of creative dramatics, but these activities re-enforce each other. For this reason it is important in children's programs that the adults who work with dance and music and dramatics should explore the possibilities at many points of working fruitfully together.

10

ooooooooo

Original Plays

AN ORIGINAL CHILDREN'S PLAY—that is, a play made up lock, stock and barrel by children—does not necessarily represent a *deeper* creative experience or a *truer* originality than any other kind of dramatization. It represents a more *extensive* creative experience, but whether such an experience is qualitatively worthwhile will depend on many things. An original play which a group of children make up may be execrable for a number of reasons. On one extreme, it may not be original at all. If it is a serious play, it may be a mass of life crises, of police blotters and of hospital waiting and operating rooms. If it is funny, it may be a mass of farcical situations without humanity. It may be, in short, a mass of echoes of the mass communication media, of television in particular.

On the other hand—and this is more a problem of teenagers than of younger children, for whom the world in general is newer and fresher—an original play may be self-defeating precisely because by straining for originality it sacrifices creative integrity. For the relationship between creativity and "originality," in the most usual sense of the word, is that between a circle and a line—they go their own ways, though there are important points at which they come tangent to each other. For example, of the five illustrations of beautiful pantomime in Chapter Five, each sprang from the child's individuality, from his unique way of seeing and feeling things. Yet none of these pantomimes made an "original" or in any way unusual approach to its material. That is, they were not inventive. Even the cleverest of them, the shower bath, was distinguished precisely by the player's sticking to business and eschewing the temptation to "invent." For freshness is not a matter of novelty, but of nuance.

This is not to say that inventiveness is in itself an impediment to creative expression, but rather that it is more or less irrelevant. Thus the boy who played the moon in Lorca's *Blood Wedding* was almost wildly inventive. Never in rehearsal or in the performances did he ever cry or wail his lines in the same way or make the same eerie movements. Yet in what he did there was always a genuine fire—or, in connection with the moon, one might better say a genuine luminescence. On the other extreme was the boy who played Nogood Boyo in *Under Milk Wood*. Whenever, in rehearsals, the narrator would come to him, he would stand inert and appeal to the teacher: "What should I do now?" And the teacher, unhappy not to help him be more inventive but hampered by a cast of twenty-six youngsters with some sixty or more characterizations to express, would shrug and tell him what to do: "Pretend the second step of the stairs to the stage is the bottom of your boat. Lie on the step and look up at the sky." So Nogood Boyo would do what the teacher told him to do but he would infuse whatever he did with a lovely and impudent lyricism, as if to say that only we Nogood Boyos, we reprobate ne'er-do-wells, really know how to taste life's sweetness.

The creative factor in originality has its sources in the emotional content of our psyches. The inventive factor is largely cerebral. It has a wide range and can extend itself over vast areas. If, however, in these extensions it fails to carry the deeper inward forces with it, then whatever it applies itself to will not transcend the rational, the clever, the novel. But so long as it brings the deeper forces with it, all of its extensions will be extensions of the creative process.

What are the areas over which human minds have extended themselves in the final performance of a play? Over the action —the pantomime. Over the dialogue—the words. Over the expressive vocalization of those words. Over the invention of situations. And, finally, over the interweaving of those situations into an entirety which is called story or plot. In the adult world, pantomime and vocalizations are usually the specialized field of actors and directors, and the words, the situations and the plots are the specialized field of playwrights. On the whole, this is probably a good arrangement, although the most successful arrangement of which we have any knowledge came about in the Globe Theater in London in the last years of the sixteenth century and the first years of the seventeenth, when William Shakespeare was an actor and partner of the company, and, as such, presumably had at least one finger in the directoral pie. This playwright-actor-director-proprietor was one of the most original, fresh, imaginative, creative, and inventive human beings of which there is any record. It is interesting to note, in this context, that he confined his inventiveness to the acting, and possibly to the directing, and to the dialogue and the situations, but never bothered to extend it to plots—except possibly for *The Tempest.*

This question of plots is one to which we will return. In the meantime, the question is: What are the areas in dramatics over which it is reasonable to suppose that children can extend their invention and their creativity? Certainly over the pantomime. If the dramatization in pantomime of songs or stories or poems rendered by singers or readers is the most elemental form of original dramatization, it remains, perhaps for that very reason —especially the dramatization of poetry—an experience which is at the same time liberating and challenging. Narrative poetry may, like prose narrative, tell the pantomimist what he is to do, but it will seldom tell him quite so much. The characterizations and meanings, though often deeper, will not be so explicit as in prose, and, on the whole, the pantomimist will be more obliged to translate the poem into his own visual image. Thus Robert Frost's "The Runaway" supplies a number of things for the colt to do—to curl a foot at its breast, to "bolt," to mount a wall, etc.—but the eleven-year-old boy or girl who is *being* the colt must translate the colt's actions into a two-legged equivalent, which, if it is not to look silly, must express very sensitively the child's own recognition of the bafflement and alarm of a young animal, still half wild, confronted for the first time in his short life with falling snow.

Children seem to recognize this distinction intuitively; that to dramatize a poem constitutes originality, that to act out a script does not. In a school which had a tradition that the seniors present an original play as part of their graduation exercises, one senior class presented a program of dramatizations of some of the poetry they had come to love through their high school years. It never occurred to them that in presenting such a program they would be violating the tradition. Yet they would have considered it a violation to present a play, for example, by Ibsen or Shaw.

But the prose story, too, dramatized in pantomime to words read by a reader, though it may direct the action more specifically than a poem, makes similar demands for originality. The

American Indian story "The Healing Waters" prescribes a great deal of the action. The young brave must tend a sick wife, he must wrap her up warm against his absence, he must run over frozen ground, he must build a fire, he must sleep and dream, he must wake to the sound of flowing water, he must dig in frozen ground with a stone, he must fashion a clay vessel, he must fill the vessel from the healing springs, he must run with it, swiftly but carefully, to his village and must put the healing waters to the lips of his dying wife. The very quantity of these physical demands is a challenge to invention, but below the invention is the feeling which these physical actions must interpret—the sorrow, the determined will, the deep despair, the rising hope, the fulfillment, joyous and tender, which make up the *emotional* gauntlet which the young brave must run.

The second stage of playmaking over which the inventiveness of children can extend is the dramatization of a given story through improvisation. The necessity for pantomimic interpretations remains as important as before, but now there is the added challenge of dialogue. Some stories will make greater demands for invention than others in this respect. Thus in a program of folk tales and fables dramatized by eight- and nine-year-old campers, there was on one extreme "The Man and the Satyr," which has been mentioned in another context. Here little dialogue was needed and its sequence was simple and clearly indicated. The final line—the point of the story—was supplied verbatim. Thus it was not a child's gift for finding words which made the satyr's part beautiful, but the pantomimic concept which a little boy had of this creature, half man and half beast —warm, kind and unsuspecting, but wild and furtive of movement like a deer, a characterization which foreshadowed the wild alarm of the ending, in which the creature screams: "You get out of my house! You get out of my house! I won't have anyone in my house who blows hot and cold with the same breath!"

On the other extreme was the longer story about the humpback cobbler and the elves. In this story the pantomime tells most of the story, but there are several places where it doesn't. For example, it was necessary for the children to develop an opening scene by which to establish the relationship between the kind but disfigured cobbler and the townspeople, on one hand, and between the townspeople and the envious tailor, on the other. All they had to go on was an opening sentence, "Once upon a time in a little town there was a kind cobbler," or some such thing, and another sentence about halfway through the story, "Now, in the same town there was an envious tailor." Thus the opening scene of their play, a scene involving some six or seven boys and girls, talking to and interacting on each other as townspeople, was almost entirely their own.

(In a very different sense, another one of the stories done by the same group was very much their own, too—a story about a donkey who, seeing a dog climb in the farmer's lap and be petted, decides to try the same thing. The farmer screams for the hired men, who come running and drive the donkey off, laying into him with staves. The children prevailed on one of their young counselors to play the role of the donkey. However, their zeal for the final action of the story was a little excessive!)

Invention of dialogue is not hard for eight and nine year olds. Their problem is more likely to be losing track of where they intended to go when they started out. Once a group of children in another camp were included in an evening program of dramatizations, about five groups of older children being ready to go on after them. The little ones' story was something about a family—a father, a mother, an uncle, two or three children, etc. They had done it once or twice with their counselor and it had shaped up to run about ten minutes. But, stimulated perhaps by expressions of pleasure from the watchers, they adlibbed away for forty-five minutes, chatting on and on in bursts of petulance, merriment and derision, interacting on each other in an unself-conscious and spontaneous—if directionless

—act of creation. The teenagers watched with great pleasure, perfectly willing to hold their skits over for another time. The tens and elevens, however, grew increasingly annoyed and tried to pressure the counselor into cutting the little ones off.

Making dialogue for the dramatization of a given story involves a good deal of invention. Most story tellers use a lot of dialogue for the children to help themselves to. But there are many other passages—passages of description, of narration, of characterization, passages which tell a person's thoughts—which, in the making of a play, have to be transposed as situation and dialogue. Thus the "script"—the improvised dialogue—which emerges when a group of seventh graders dramatize *Tom Sawyer* may be as little as thirty or forty per cent Mark Twain and sixty or seventy per cent their own.

For boys and girls of eleven or twelve to take a full-length book and make it a full-length juvenile play is a very considerable extension of their inventive powers. They must cut the plot to its essentials, select and reject certain episodes, consolidate two or three episodes into one and plan their play scene by scene, discussing it and acting it out again and again, until the dialogue and the action emerge to their satisfaction. But if their play is to satisfy them, they must take that last long stride beyond invention. For if they have chosen to dramatize *Tom Sawyer* or *Mottel, the Cantor's Son,* they have made this choice because of some qualities in the story, some special spirit, which they prize. In other words, to satisfy themselves, their pantomime must be as good as Mark Twain's or Sholom Aleichem's narrative passages, their characterizations as good as the passages in which the writer defines a character or tells a character's thoughts, the dialogue they supply as good as the dialogue the writer supplies for them. That is, they must capture the spirit of their material within their own lights. Children of eleven or twelve cannot write as well as they can perceive. But by dramatizing, by interacting on each other, by thrashing things out—and then by dramatizing, interacting and thrashing out again, and yet again if necessary—they can find their way to the over-statements or understatements, the clumsiness or the grace, the paradoxes and ironies, the laughter, the nuance and the some-what cockeyed humanity—whatever it was that enchanted them with the story in the first place.

In a way, there is no good reason for children to extend their inventiveness beyond this point, but the fact is that they can and will, and there is no good reason why they should not. This next extension may be a fairly short or a fairly long step. While they are dramatizing a given story, they may incorporate into it an episode or so of their own, or an episode or so from another story, or they may take two or three stories and com-bine them into a new story, more or less their own, as Shake-speare combined Homer and Boccaccio to make *Troilus and Cressida.* The example of the sixth-grade play mentioned in Chapter One, based on Howard Fast's "The Bookman," is an example of this process. Besides many adjustments of the mate-rial to suit their wishes—the inclusion, for example, of Blake's "The Tyger" among the bookman's wares—there was a se-quence the children made up about the troops. Actually, How-ard Fast's stories are noticeably improved by such incorpora-tions. A group of sixth-grade boys dramatized his "The Price of Liberty," the story of a Jewish sea captain named Johnny Ordronaux, master of a swift little privateersman in the War of 1812, who, with his band, captures a huge and lumbering Eng-lish frigate. The boys liked the heroics of the story and also its reverence, for Johnny and his men go to the synagogue to pray before setting out on their adventure and return afterwards to give thanks. The boys also adored a passage from Tobias Smollett's *Roderick Random,* in which they had made the acquaintance of the British commander of a frigate—a ruffled dandy who wears rings *over* his gloves, a snob who faints out of sheer snobbism from the reek of the gunners' tobacco.

How could they *not* put this delicious character into their play? But how could they fuse the flavor and spirit of material so different? In truth, the boys never gave any conscious thought to the second question at all—they simply went ahead and performed the fusion. They brought Howard Fast's somewhat exalted manner down to earth a little—or at least down on deck—and they exalted the Smollett by making the British dandy a brave man who goes over with the first boarding party, as disdainful and arrogant toward danger and death as toward his fellow men.

In another case, to which previous reference has also been made, a seventh-grade group took three different stories about families working with the Underground Railroad, extracted the plot elements and made up a family and story of their own. There was no particular spirit they had to respect, for the stories they adapted came from a book written for younger children, and its merit lay primarily in the fact that it had research behind it and the stories were presumably true. In this case, then, the plot was in some measure their own, the family was largely their own, and the flavor and spirit entirely their own. The story centered around the efforts of a family of Quakers to effect the escape of two runaway slaves with the United States marshal and the slave catchers breathing down their necks. The boy of the family encounters the first of these fugitives running for his life, and directs him to hide in the corn field. The marshal and the slave catchers come on the scene almost immediately. They have caught one of the runaways, having wounded him with gun shot. In violation of his religious ideals, the boy tells them a barefaced lie—that the other fugitive has run into the swamp, in the opposite direction from the corn field. The boy even cons the slave chasers into letting him take a gun and stand guard over their captive while they go after the other one. In this way, he gets both fugitives into his house. While the mother is binding the wounds of the fugitive who has been shot, the marshal and the slave catchers arrive at the door, where the father stalls them with legalities until the fugitives have made their escape through an underground passage under the massive hearthstone. By this time the marshal has produced a search warrant and slipped it under the door. But when the Quaker stalls further, they decide to force their way in. Just as they hurl themselves with all their weight at the door, the Quaker, with a deliberate combination of courtesy and timing, opens it for them so that they sprawl in a heap on the floor. On the hearthstone are a sleeping cat and two innocent children, popping corn. The marshal and the slave catchers search the house but find nothing. The slave catchers try to persuade the marshal to take the boy in and question him, but the marshal will have none of it—it is apparent, in fact, through a sly piece of characterization, that this big, bluff man doing his duty under the Fugitive Slave Law is not giving the slave catchers quite the cooperation they would like to have. When the marshal and the slave catchers leave, the father opens the Bible and reads to himself. There is silence among the members of the Quaker family who have just managed such a magnificent deception. Then the boy speaks, a little timidly:

THE BOY: Father? Didn't thee lie when thee told the marshal that there were no slaves in our house?
THE FATHER (*Stoutly*): No, son, I did not lie. In the eyes of God all men are free.
THE BOY (*Sheepishly*): I lied. I told a whopper!
THE FATHER (*Quietly, but there is, perhaps, just a breath of amusement in his tone—or possibly it is the native grace of a man not easily ruffled*): I think God will find his way to forgive thee, if thou ask.

To say that a children's play of this kind is not altogether original is to quibble. Nevertheless, for the sake of quibblers, we can distinguish another and final extension of inventiveness in the making of plays—the play which children make up from scratch, plot and all. Winifred Ward takes a dim view of this phase of playmaking on the grounds that "children cannot make good plots." This is not, however, a philosophical position, but a generalization of a body of experience. In answer to a question which this writer once posed to a psychiatrist regarding some hypothesis about children's behavior patterns, the psychiatrist answered: "I don't know. You people in group practice see many things which we in clinical practice never see at all." So it is with the adults who have worked with the children whose dramatizations form the illustrative material of this book—they are not specialists in children's dramatics, but teachers, camp people and group workers, for whom children's dramatizations are something that flow out of and back into the way of life of this or that children's community. This may account for certain differences of emphasis between this writer and Miss Ward, specifically the importance attached to dramatics as communication. And it may also account for a different body of experience—specifically in relation to the question of whether children can make up good plots.

We have already seen, in other connections, instances of valid and important short plays which young people have made up—the play about the sailors on the merchant vessel, the one about the gift of the church relics, the folk dramatization of the Jenny Jump legend, etc. There are a number of Christmas assembly plays one could cite—especially a very beautiful one in which, on Christmas Eve, the people go to the top of a hill to watch the "blackout," a Christmas tradition whose origins are buried in the past, in something called a war, which no one knows much about. As the people wait, parachutes begin to descend, dropping Christmas gifts, and snow, too, begins to fall. We have also illustrated where children have developed original situations and incorporated them into plays they were dramatizing from stories—the opening situation of the humpbacked cobbler and the elves, for instance.

What is a plot? It is the interweaving of situations to make a point. If children can make up good situations, why can they not weave a number of situations into a good story? The problem is more precisely, perhaps, that children cannot make up good "tight" plots. But they can and do make up beautiful stories of their own sometimes on the basis of a loose plot—the kind of plot which the adventures of Odysseus and Huck Finn are examples, stories in which a series of situations and experiences develop around one person or a group of persons, the episodes strung together like beads on a string, the string being some more or less impelling motive. More impelling in the case of Odysseus, who wants to get home to Ithaca, and more impelling in the case of Huck, who wants to get Jim to freedom. Less impelling in the case of Dylan Thomas's *Under Milk Wood*, in which the impelling motive is the dawning, waxing and waning of one spring day.

Children eleven or older can compose fine plays with this kind of plot. One group in a camp made up such a play, which they called *The Drinking Gourd*, in which two runaway slaves, husband and wife, go through a series of episodic adventures on their way to freedom. It was not a great play, even in children's terms. But it was an honest play, it had something to communicate and a few moments of beauty—for example, when the husband tells his wife of his intention to run away to freedom. He is unwilling to have her risk her life in the same way but she quotes to him the words Ruth spoke to Naomi: "Whithersoever thou goest. . . ." The weaknesses did not reside in the plot, for such a plot is capable of doing anything that one sees to do with it. The weakness was that, in a camp situation, the youngsters did not have the opportunity to invest the weeks of study they needed to give substance to their vision.

In a lighter vein, a seventh-grade group recently put on a play in which the string for the beads was supplied by a couple of creatures from Venus, observing us earthlings from space ships, and the beads were the experimental situations they set up in order to study the human condition. A female Venerean had a space ship in the form of an unusually lanky stepladder set on the floor of the auditorium in front of the audience. The male Venerean was perched on top of a fire exit which projected into the auditorium. The two communicated with each other by means of toy telephones. The play was far from "finished"—and wisely so, for its light substance, good as it was, would hardly have justified protracted work on it. The boy carried the bulk of the dialogue, adlibbing inventively as he went along, either from an outline he carried in his head or from one he had on paper beside him. Among the experimental observations they set up was one of mankind in a subway. The earthlings enacted the situation on the stage, with tongue-in-cheek comicality, two girls being a turnstile and two others the sliding doors of the subway train. In one of the experiments, the Venereans wanted to see to what extent the human's outer skin determines his character. Conveniently, a young male earthling found himself in a room with various skins—a raccoon coat, a woman's hat, a tuxedo jacket, an athlete's sweatshirt—through which in pantomime he culled up, one after another, various Walter Mittylike ego images, and the Venereans noted soberly that "the outer skin makes the man." For the special spirit of this dramatization was its double-edged satire. The earthlings were satirized in that rather incompetent and vain humanity which we all understand, but the Venereans drew very pompous conclusions—not exactly erroneous, but silly, like the conclusions drawn by behavioral scientists from experiments which end up by telling us things we have known all along. In the end, the Venereans grew very edgy and nervous, suddenly aware that they, in turn, were being spied on by creatures from still further out.

Of plays made up in their entirety by young people, the one which this writer, within his experience, considers the most significant, both in the importance of its communication and in the creative level to which it was carried, is a play about China which eighth graders made up during World War II, a very beautiful and sensitive play, though it failed to exploit its pantomimic possibilities fully enough, the teacher working with it being rather inexperienced with dramatics. The play was a culmination of a full year's study of China. Students individually or in committees had done research and presented reports in many areas—geography and economy, home and family, the arts, the historical background of the Republic under Dr. Sun Yat-sen, the break between the Kuomintang and the Communists. They studied the then current situation, the reunification of the country for struggle against the Japanese invaders. The general respect they had already acquired for the cultures and lives of different peoples, together with their patriotic empathy for one of their own country's allies, created a great depth of interest. The students had read Pearl Buck's *The Good Earth,* and had read together in class quantities of Chinese poetry and a translation of the Chinese classical drama, *The Chalk Circle.* They had made several trips to the Chinese community in New York and had seen a couple of Chinese plays in the old theater under the bridge. Finally, each child had written poems and stories which interpreted their factual studies in terms of human experience.

In the planning discussions, the group had little difficulty deciding what they wanted to say. They wanted to tell about the people who lived on the sampans and about those who tilled the soil; they wanted to tell about the life of the wealthy classes, people who seemed to the children oblivious to the lot of their poorer countrymen, but who had preserved, through the advantages of their wealth, one of the greatest and most beautiful cultures of the world, an art and a poetry which were already old at the time of Renaissance art in Italy, and Elizabethan poetry in England. The children wanted to speak about the position of women, and about changes and adaptations of an old culture in the face of a new. They wanted to tell about the scorched earth and the partisans, and they wanted to express their love for the Chinese people as human beings and as valiant allies. They had to plan a play which would say all these things and still have narrative and dramatic unity. The historical moment supplied the driving motive, which, touched on lightly at first, gathered momentum from scene to scene—that is, the approach of the invaders and the development of the resistance.

In its final form, the play began with a waterfront scene.

Night was falling. An old man was fishing on one end of the quay. At the back of the quay, which was constituted by the stage itself, was a sampan sail and the illuminated window of a little vault-shaped cabin, behind which, extending back into the darkness, was a forest of other sampan sails. A little girl emerged from the cabin and chatted with the old fisherman. Soon her father emerged and, standing with his back to the watchers, cupped his hands and conversed across the water with a neighbor on another sampan. The audience learned that the father and his family were going downriver the next morning and that the trip involved a degree of peril because of the imminence of air raids, but that the need to trade in order to eat could not be ignored. The curtain closed, leaving an expectancy that the adventures of this family would be followed, but they were never seen again, since it was not a given family who made up the persons of the play, but a people.

The next scene took place in the countryside, and we have already read in Chapter Six the dialogue between father, son and mother with which that scene began. Then while they were hoeing their field, a neighbor entered, sullen and agitated. The Japanese were coming nearer with each day, and yet the government had failed to send the promised organizer to help the peasants mobilize for their resistance. A meeting was being called to send strong representations to the government for its neglect.

The third scene was a street in the town. The people learned of a Japanese bombing downriver, in which it would appear the family on the sampan have all been killed. The shopkeepers and the peasants, including the father and son, who had come into town to market their produce, gathered together and inveighed angrily against the government delays. A wealthy mandarin swept magnificently through the village streets, followed by his retinue—followed also by sullen looks and angry murmurs voicing the suspicion that he was collaborating with the Japanese.

The following scene was set in the wealthy man's home. The

audience learned that the daughter of the family was expected home momently—a headstrong girl, who, against her father's wishes, had been away for several years as a student. As evening deepened, a servant girl read poetry. Two agents of the Japanese visited the wealthy man and made him a very profitable offer— the control of certain factories in exchange for his collaboration. He was tempted, but dismissed them, promising to consider their proposals. An old philosopher, part of the rich man's retinue, made a speech about the historic greatness and glory of China. Moved, the rich man decided to put his country ahead of his greed. At this point, the daughter arrived. She was wearing a military uniform and was the organizer the government had sent in response to the appeals of the peasants. Her father was shocked and deeply perturbed by her unwomanly garb and call- ing, but, having just waged and won inside himself a battle of conscience, he accepted the new order of things.

The next-to-last scene consisted of a meeting between the peasants and the young woman organizer. She was having diffi- culty. It was bad enough that the government had sent them a woman—but a natural enemy, the daughter of a landowner! It was almost more than the peasants could stomach. The father and son were there and, at one point, the son, who was perhaps closer to the new realities than the others, jumped up in his hot way and blurted out his point of view:

> THE SON: You asked the government for an organizer and they've
> sent one! Why do you reject her because she's not what
> you expected? Why don't you listen to what she has to say?
> A PEASANT (*Addressing the boy's father with a grin*): I see your
> boy has a tongue in his head.
> THE FATHER (*Proudly*): Yes. My boy has seen germs through a
> microscope!

And with this parental irrelevancy, they got down to busi- ness and listened to the organizer.

The final scene opened with the sound of cannonading and the wavering red flames of not-too-distant fires. The women, children and old people of the village and of the countryside were being evacuated. The woman organizer and the young peasant handed out rifles and other equipment to the able-bodied men, who were remaining behind to execute the scorched-earth program and to wage guerilla warfare.

It was a stirring conclusion, and an auditorium full of high school students came to their feet cheering. Of course, the historical circumstances under which the play was given contributed greatly to the acceptance of the heroics with which it closed. Nevertheless, the ending was honest and aesthetically valid. It was a natural outcome of the unfolding story. More importantly, the emotional force of the heroic stance at the end flowed from the slow, thoughtful and sensitive way in which the characters had been developed in their everyday humanity.

One of the distinguished things about this play was the language—a dialogue which was at once both firm and supple, and which had been developed entirely (except for the old philosopher's speech) through improvisation. The dialogue had been carried to a point of very high finish, and the children knew their play so well, without ever having memorized a word by rote, that when one boy was absent on the day of performance, another stepped into his part and carried it without a taint of adlibbing. The words of the play had, in fact, attained such a limpid and crystalline finality that a number of people, struck by their beauty, asked for copies of the script. But there was no script—the teacher had not bothered to take it down, so that nothing is left of the play except a few snatches which the teacher who worked with it and some who saw it are able to remember.

Perhaps the teacher should have taken it down, if only for the school archives, the word "archives" in this case a euphemism for old filing cabinets and cardboard cartons stored away in a sub-basement closet which was once an elevator shaft. In these archives rest the relics of her sect which the woman in Pennsylvania gave to the strange boys and girls, thinking they would be in the hands of people who cared. And, in a sense, she was not mistaken. But though the young people cared deeply at the moment, their caring was not in particular, but was part of a general caring, a *caritas*, which was an element of their lives. And they graduated and dispersed. As for the school itself, though it is deeply committed to caring, the particular objects of its caring are a flowing stream. So it is with a children's play. The eager work, the delight, the moments of creative inspiration vanish in the spasm of a performance. And the children themselves often comment: "Eight weeks of work, and it's all over in an hour!" Sufficient unto its hour the dramatization thereof. For the performance itself is unimportant, except as it may give momentary pleasure to adults or as it may lend new insights or a sense of standards and creative possibilities to an audience of the players' peers. It is the process which is important because it shapes the players' sensitivities, their human understanding, their creative potential and, hence, the course of their lives.

Creative Approaches to Standard Plays

AT WHAT AGE will children begin to dramatize standard plays? The dramatization of a play from a script is, in essence, the same process as that of most of the other forms of dramatization which have been under discussion, such as the dramatization in pantomime of a poem, the dramatizing of a given story through improvisation, or even the development of an original play from material in a history book. In all four cases, the questions are the same: *Here is some reading matter. What are its meanings? How do we act these meanings out?*

[136]

There are several ways, however, in which the use of a dramatic script introduces obstacles in the way of the child's direct creative expression. First, the words are not the children's own, and it is more difficult for them to make the words of a script theirs than the words of a poem or a story. Second, these words must be memorized, a hurdle which some will take in stride, but over which some will stumble and fall on their faces. Third, as long as the words remain unmemorized, the process of dramatization goes forward script-in-hand, and a script in the hand gets destructively in the way of the pantomime.

Dramatization for little children is a very immediate thing. They hear, understand, capture their image and act out with little delay. Their dramatizations are a form of spontaneous make-believe, and obstacles and delays—a script in the hand or a half-established set of words in the hand—will totally destroy their spontaneity. Increasingly, however, the child is able to hold onto his dramatic impulse and his creative image and work across extended, even protracted, periods of time to bring that image to fulfillment—eight or nine year olds from several days to a couple of weeks, eleven and twelve year olds for as long as a couple of months, the interest being deep enough. The dramatization of *The Hearthstone* by eleven year olds, and *Tom Sawyer* and *Mottel, the Cantor's Son* by twelve year olds, and the original play about China by thirteen year olds are all examples of the way children can sustain, probe, refine and unfold their creative image through six or eight weeks of long, hard work. Doubtlessly, the same children, under comparable leadership, with comparable interest, working with scripts which invited a comparable creative expression, would have given performances, in the end, of comparable insight and gusto. But there are reasons why it was better for them to work as they did. For in developing their own plays, they extended their creative potential and experience over wider areas. They had the experience, not only of being their own actors and their own directors, but of being their own playwrights, or, more properly, their own playmakers, since they wrought their plays in the fires of improvisation. Over a three-year span, how many six or eight week blocks from a child's life can be devoted to putting on plays? Three, perhaps, under the most favorable circumstances—that is, one a year. Then, since there are almost no reasons why they should use this precious time for dramatizing someone else's play, it seems reasonable to conclude that they could best use this time making plays of their own.

One is tempted to say that there are no scripts for children's plays. There is a great wealth of poetry, folk lore, history, prose tales and novels which are part of the literary heritage of children. But there is no comparable body of dramatic literature which is part of their heritage. There are only hand-me-downs. There are scripts available, if one wants to look for them, for many children's favorites—*Cinderella, Rumpelstiltskin, The Emperor's New Clothes, Alice in Wonderland*, etc. But these are not part of the natural reading experiences of children. Children do not read *Alice in Wonderland* as a play, they read it as a story, just as Lewis Carroll wrote it, with whatever his nuances are. Why should they try to express a middleman's nuances (or lack of them) when they can tackle Lewis Carroll's nuances on their own—and have a more dynamic, creative experience at the same time?

Thus if we look on children's dramatics as something that flows from their experiences and as a way in which they seek to probe and interpret their experiences, it follows that the point at which children will begin to do dramatics from scripts is the point at which they read plays as part of their literary experience. The reading of plays, however, represents a new and more mature kind of reading skill. In a novel such as *The Yearling* or *The Good Earth*—or, to carry it all the way, *War and Peace*—the writer uses an amalgam of elements to draw the reader into the vortex of his imagery, to invite the reader's participation and to set the reader's powers of association and inference into operation. But plays are not written to be read—at least not in the same way. They give nothing to the reader but what people say to each other, together with a limited description of person, place and action in the moodless economy of the stage directions. The reader's participation must be conscious; his powers of inference must be alerted in a deliberate way. It is a long time before a person learns to lose himself in a play in the same way that both child and adult lose themselves in a story. Most adults, in fact, never learn to enjoy this kind of reading experience. So it is hardly to be expected that a group of children will rush into production with the first good play they read. And the margin of difference between amateur theatricals and creative dramatics will depend largely on the degree to which the reading of plays has become as natural, meaningful and moving as the reading of novels and stories.

However, none of the obstacles that scripts interpose between the image and the acting is insurmountable, and, in the long run, the child can surmount them all, so that the time comes when—through accumulated literary experience and the personal process of maturation—children can handle adult dramatic literature with creative élan. It is wise to assume that this time does not come much before children are fifteen or sixteen years old. It is also wise to assume that it does not come of its own accord, but that it comes as the result of a variety of literary and dramatic experiences. In a sense, all that has gone before in this book is a discussion of these preparatory experiences, and the performance of dramatic literature is itself only another extension of the processes that have been described. The pantomime exercises and the dramatization in pantomime of poems and stories have established that sense of action which is the muscular interpretation of the word. The exercises in improvisation, the adlibbing for fun and the more careful development, through improvisation, of a story—these have established the sense that a word is an act, an interaction between person and person. But back of the act and the word are the meanings. *Here is a piece of reading matter. What are its meanings? How do we act these meanings out?* The child has no way of acting out, no creative vision to bring to bear, unless he has probed the poem or story or passage from the history book and unfolded its meanings for himself. And so, all along, creative dramatization has gone hand in hand with literary interpretation.

As children reach the age at which they will begin to read plays, some of their other reading can help equip them for this new kind of reading experience, for example those poems which are themselves short pieces of dramatic literature—dramatic dialogues, monologues and soliloquies, in which the poet conceals himself and his intent behind the dramatis personae or persona of the poem and obliges the reader, through a process of inference, to ferret things out. The border ballad, *The Twa Corbies*, is such a poem. In the process of planning to dine on the carcass of a slain knight, the two crows give us certain facts. Besides the two crows, no one knows where the slain knight's body lies except "his hound, his hawk, and his lady fair." All three have abandoned him, the hawk and hound to pursue their natural inclinations for hunting—and the lady to pursue her inclinations, too, for she has gone off with a lover. Now, if the knight has been slain, and if only one human being knows where his body lies, there is an inescapable inference that that human being is his slayer. Thus we are forced to the conclusion that it was the lady fair who did him in. (Fortunately for a thirteen-year-old vision of life and love, there is a companion ballad in which another hawk, hound and lady fair all remain loyally by another slain knight's side.)

Among other poems which demand that the reader draw inferences concerning fact, character, motivation, emotion and, behind these, the philosophical attitude of the poet, are Thomas Hardy's "The Man He Killed," Housman's "Is My Team Plowing?," Amy Lowell's "Patterns," and Browning's "My Last Duchess." All these lend themselves to dramatization, no longer in pantomime, but with the players themselves speaking the lines. The two crows cackle and flap scandalously over the circumstances which have provided their dinner. Hardy's soldier talks reflectively about the man he killed to another fellow in a pub. The dead man questions the living about his team of horses, his football team and his sweetheart, and receives answers, kindly enough intentioned, which will forever keep him from his rest. The girl in her stays and brocades speaks her thoughts as she walks the patterned paths of the garden. The Duke gives the Count's emissary to understand that trashy merchandise is not acceptable.

The Browning poem is very difficult but when thirteen year olds—boys especially—have pieced together the structure of inference and are confronted with an arrogance and possessiveness so total as to consider wife-murder a natural prerogative, they find the poem very exciting and want to dramatize it. Girls prefer the more intuitive, less syllogistic processes required by "Patterns." The difference of attitude, in fact, between boys and girls is of great importance in refining the aesthetic tastes and perceptions of both. The beauty of much of the playmaking previously described resulted from the synthesis of the clash between the taste of girls, which contains the danger of being tolerant of sentimentalities, and the taste of boys, which contains the danger of accepting what is coarse and harsh.

It is at this time that children will begin to read plays. In the school with which this writer has been principally associated, the thirteen year olds—eighth graders—read some one-act Irish plays, such as Synge's *Riders to the Sea* and Lady Gregory's *The Rising of the Moon*, and, for full-length plays, they read Sean O'Casey's *Juno and the Paycock* and *Romeo and Juliet*. In *Juno and the Paycock*, they find again that vain, laughable, poignant and incompetent humanity which, when they were small, delighted them in the stuffed animals of *Winnie the Pooh*, and, when they were eleven or twelve, in the stories of Sholom Aleichem. But now the vision is less amiable and calls for a longer and more searching look at the human condition. One is immensely diverted by Captain Boyle's strutting, but one must see, in the end, that he is a poor, shallow specimen of a man. The laughter turns to ashes, the poignancy to sorrow, the vanity and the incompetence bring life down about one's ears. *Romeo and Juliet,* too, begins to prepare the children for the tragic vision which characterizes the great works of dramatic literature—but gently, for it is a young and romantic play, and does not oblige young people to probe those forces of self-destruction which reside, for example, in the souls of Brutus and Cassius.

In ninth grade, Greek plays are read and in tenth grade *Everyman, Doctor Faustus* and *Julius Caesar.* The plays are read aloud and different parts assigned to different boys and girls from one reading to another, so that a degree of dramatization is inherent in the reading process. The teacher does not press for dramatic expression at this point, however, but for meanings. Later, when a play has been read through, casts may be assigned for different acts, and these casts can then do dramatized readings for each other. Infrequently, it may seem worthwhile to carry these dramatized readings to a point where other classes in the school can see them in an assembly.

Throughout this period, the individual student has been encouraged and, in some measure, required to read plays on his own. In eleventh grade, the group reads three plays together, one after the other, while each student reads and reports to the group on other plays at the rate of about one a week. The readings include the great comic tradition—Jonson, Molière, Aristophanes, Congreve, etc.—but are centered on the later work of Ibsen, Strindberg, Chekhov, Shaw, O'Neill, Arthur Miller, O'Casey, Brecht, Ionesco, Giraudoux, Genêt, Duerrenmatt, etc. By now it can be assumed that the young people are ready to choose a worthwhile play to interpret into dramatic action, and to take on the hard work, responsibility, fun, and exaltation of producing a "real" play for the public—though that public will be the same one they have been doing things for informally all these years.

Under conditions of this kind, where dramatization is the handmaiden of the study of literature, the production of a full-length standard play is a valuable culmination of the prior, more informal experiences. Some of the values of such major effort are not present in the more informal situation, such as extensive teamwork, organizational initiative and discipline, workmanship and aesthetic correlation in a variety of areas, and responsibility to an audience.

However, the choice of play usually offers some nagging limitations. If standard dramatics proceeds on a philosophy which puts the interest of the child above theatrical accomplishment, then everyone in a group should have a part in a play, and a high school class may have as many as thirty or more young people in it. On this basis, a vast body of dramatic literature, some of the best, cannot even be considered. If half of a group of thirty are girls, there will be fifteen girls. But dramatic literature is a man's world. Even in modern plays, at least those with sufficient parts, the parts run about two to one in favor of males. One group would doubtlessly have chosen to do Duerrenmatt's *The Visit* on a simple majority vote, had not the teacher first polled the girls as to whether they wanted the play, knowing that most of them would not be in it. They were not willing to make this personal sacrifice in the name of group art. Another group, confronted with this problem, developed a momentary enthusiasm for doing *The Trojan Women* until a count of the parts showed there were not enough roles for boys. One group chose O'Casey's *The Plow and the Stars* on the assumption that they could interpolate additional parts into the street scenes and the scene in the pub, but found, too late, that such interpolations were a serious intrusion.

At length, however, a group will work through this matter and find itself making the best choice it can among several plays. Of the several, however, one may be a play which the adult thinks they ought not to do, and here a very delicate equilibrium exists between the democratic rights of the group and the authority of the adult. The wise adult will not permit a situation to arise in which a group makes a decision which he feels he must reverse, and so he will presumably establish in advance his right to veto, and will, of course, let the group know where he stands on a play before a vote is taken. There are two reasons why an adult may exercise such veto. One is that a given play is too difficult and will lead the group into a sense of failure. The other is that the play is not worth the effort. On the first grounds, this writer has vetoed Sartre's *The Flies* and Genêt's *The Balcony*, feeling that both contained too many non-dramatic, philosophical elements which could be sustained only by professional dramatic skills. Two teachers who were collaborating vetoed Thornton Wilder's *Our Town* because they couldn't stand it. It is important for young people to realize that they can't expect an adult to work long and hard and to give them inspiration on something he can't stomach. One teacher wrestled with his conscience for several days before going along with a group on the choice of *The Crucible*. The group had their hearts set on it, but the teacher was afraid they couldn't handle the powerful emotions. In this fear they proved him very much mistaken.

Perhaps there are under consideration several plays which have almost enough parts for everybody and which the adult approves of. But the group itself is hopelessly divided. One section is all for play A, another for play B, and a small cluster, but enough to obstruct a majority vote, for play C. Under such circumstances the parliamentary skills of the adult may be sorely taxed, yet he must find ways to help the group make a choice. In one instance, the adult resolved a deadlock by posing three negative questions: 1. Would you rather do play A or no play at all? 2. Would you rather do play B or no play at all? 3. Would you rather do play C or no play at all? The vote on this question led to the rejection of plays A and B and a decision to do play C, which had had only a few ardent supporters, but which, unlike plays A and B, had not roused strong feelings against it.

A choice has now been made, let's say, of Giraudoux's *The*

Madwoman of Chaillot or of Brecht's *The Caucasian Chalk Circle,* either of which will meet the need for roles. But now the group learns they can't get production rights. It is a silly problem, one created, apparently, by theatrical legalists, who feel that a high school production will take customers away from a professional production in the same city, though the exact opposite is really the case. So back to the parliamentary benches—or perhaps someone's mother's friend knows So-and-so and it is possible to get special permission through sources—another reason why the dramatization of a standard play by an unselected group such as a high school class might remain a once-in-a-school-career experience, and any additional experience that young people want must be sought in dramatic clubs or workshops.

Assuming that the choice of play has been made, rights obtained, scripts purchased, etc., the question now arises: How is this material to be handled in a creative way? Demosthenes, when asked what, in order, were the three most important phases of the orator's art, is said to have answered: *Delivery, delivery, delivery.* Demosthenes's position, translated to the theater, may be valid for the professional actor who has to hit his audience hard or go hungry, but in relation to creative dramatization by young people, his doctrine must be completely subverted and stood on its head. For the three overriding considerations in the dramatization by young people of a standard play are *interpretation, interpretation, interpretation,* for our assumption is still that make-believe is the essence of children's acting, and if a young person understands what he is to be, he will be that thing.

Thus little Eric, mentioned earlier, was able to be a rooster, but was confused by mother's being a seal and could not have been a seal himself because he did not have a sufficient understanding of sealness. Thus, too, a girl who played Abigail in a school production of *The Crucible,* equipped as she was with great talent, a talent supported by dramatics classes and a lifetime of association with the theater, did a magnificent job and contributed her full share to hitting the audience hard—but did not do a job comparable in depth to some done by other, less expert youngsters because she did not really grasp *obsessiveness*. She understood emotional fire and how one person imposes on another through emotional force—and that that kind of force was part of Abigail's power. But underneath this kind of force was a deeper and darker power through which Abigail's imagery transmitted itself and operated on the suggestibilities of others. And this power was beyond the girl's imaginative grasp at the time.

Obviously, some of the reaches of insight which a given play demands will lie beyond the full grasp of one youngster or another, and certain plays—Chekhov's, perhaps—will lie beyond the reach of a whole group. But between little Eric and his problem with sealness and Abigail and her problem with obsessiveness lies the range of fact, of person, of mannerism, of emotional gestalt, of interaction of person on person, of author's thematic intent, etc., which are to be interpreted.

This interpretive process will begin with the first reading of the play and will end, perhaps, with the decision as to whether the final curtain should be fast or slow. Rehearsals will be a process of refining, expanding, and deepening interpretations. The method is almost identical with the method by which a younger group will improvise an original play—that is, through the alternating steps of discussing, acting out, discussing again, acting out again, though in rehearsing a standard play the line between one step and another gets lost in the hurly-burly. Always there will be the questions of the who and the why, and of the how which expresses the who and the why—a continual probing until character and situation are understood as well as a youngster can understand them: the kind of person, his background, his forms of speech and movement, his emotions at a given time, his purposes, and how—given what he is and what his purposes are—he would do this particular act or say this particular word. He is an artist, for example. On his easel is a charcoal drawing which he is contemplating with disgust. Does he rip it from the easel in a fury, wad it and toss it across the room? Or does he methodically remove each thumbtack, replace them in the drawing board, fold the drawing in halves, quarters, eighths, sixteenths, and then methodically tear it into bits along the folds? What then? Does he let these bits flutter through his fingers into a wastebasket? Or does he, at this point, burst through the methodical trend of his temperament and toss the bits of paper, like a shower of confetti, into the air?

This is pantomime, of course, and pantomime remains the visual base. It is everything the player is and does, except what he says. A player speaks only part of the time—yet all the time he *is*. One player speaks well—in the pitch and inflection of his voice, he captures the character, the moment, the nuance, the passion. But he accomplishes little dramatically if, as he speaks, the watchers do not see that the players to whom he speaks are startled, irritated, baffled, titillated, crushed or exalted by what he says.

Beyond the questions of individual interpretation, there are the broader interpretive questions which the group must answer, for on the answers to these collective questions, the answers to particular questions will depend. What is the author's thematic, aesthetic and philosophical intent? What, within the latitude the author allows us, is *our* intent? In a dramatization of *Ondine*, a group was divided in regard to its own intent, some wanting to handle the play as a witty commentary on illusion and reality, some preferring to exploit the pathos of its romantic potentialities. Had the first of these positions prevailed, it would have been enough that the court lady with whom the knight was keeping company before he met Ondine should be bitchy. But since the other position prevailed in the end, the girl who played this role had to go deeper, into the emotional hurt beneath the bitchiness.

Rhinoceros is a play which allows considerable latitude of interpretation. The play, to borrow terms from art, is less "non-objective" and more "representational" than Ionesco's shorter plays, and the bold symbols invite philosophical interpretation, though the writer himself has masked his own intent in ambiguities. Broadly speaking, two opposed philosophical interpretations are possible. The process of rhinocerosization can be taken as a reassertion by man of his natural, visceral inheritance. Or it can be taken as an ultimate conformity to social pressure, the final denial of individuality. Either way, Berenger is a misfit —in the first case a pathetic misfit who, ironically, having failed to measure up to the demands of civilized disciplines, clings to his poor tatters of civilized disciplines when everyone else is able to abandon himself to the sweeping currents of the natural; in the other, a heroic misfit, whose individuality, however insecure and troubled, is able to assert its own uniqueness and integrity as the supreme law of being. The problem is that, if one gives the play this second, more serious twist, the play itself becomes a rather shabby vehicle for its own philosophy. However, for the boy who played Berenger, this more serious interpretation had a deep subjective meaning, and for him to have developed the more perverse interpretation would have been a *tour de force* and would not have drawn on his deeper emotional resources. For this reason, the underlying interpretation of the play was his, and the rest of the play had to be harmonized with his interpretation.

The group's interpretation of a play will begin to emerge in the discussions through which the choice of play is made. And their intent will grow clearer and express itself in the process of casting, etc. It is, however, not a fixed thing, but fluid. Thus, in rehearsals, the answer to a particular question of character or motive will often hinge on the group's concept of the author's intent or of their own. However, it will sometimes happen that the answer to a question is startling and will unfold a new aspect of the author's intent, or provoke refinements in their own.

And so the rehearsals proceed, an acting-out process alternating with interpretive decisions of both a particular and a general kind. The adult, standing arms akimbo, perhaps, on the steps of the stage, is the "director," while those in the group not at the moment acting are the co-directors. And while the adult is focusing his attention on a tone of voice or the opening and closing of a hand, one of his numerous co-directors may rush up on the stage in a froth about the blocking. It is an interesting and exciting process, very agreeable, really, if one can stand the hurly-burly of democratic egalitarianism in the production of a work of art.

So far the adult has not raised the question of memorization. A boy with unusual facility, say, or a tightly organized young woman may have already memorized, but the adult does not press the matter for quite a while. For the danger is that the way of speaking the lines will be memorized with the lines themselves. But the words must first be grasped and felt as a response to another person or to a life situation, and as that other person becomes deeper, more vibrant or more forceful, and as the meanings of the life situation unfold, the way of saying the words must remain continuously responsive to every change. For this reason inexpert young people should not memorize prematurely. The scripts are often miserably in the way, but the youngsters come to know their parts well enough so that they no longer glue their eyes to the page. They find they can drop the script or pass it to someone to prompt them and go ahead with a piece of important pantomimic business. Meantime, a kind of memorization by osmosis has been going on and, for some youngsters, all that is needed is to fix the lines and cues with more certainty. Thus, at a point when memorization will not interfere with fluidity, the adult will set a date when lines must be memorized and can start bringing pressure to bear on those who don't meet the deadline, keeping in mind, however, that memorization will be a much greater burden for some than for others, and that—if it is a school group—these young people who are putting in a couple of afternoons and evenings a week on rehearsals are also trying to keep up with their schoolwork. Now though the individual interpretations will still receive attention, the focus begins to shift to the more technical, theatrical things, such as projection, greater energy, expanded movement, tempo and pace, and more finesse in the blocking—though of course, in some measure, these things, too, will have been developing all along. Then, ready or not, the play will go on at its appointed hour.

Through all this, the adult's role has been to coordinate and to question, and through questioning to open up interpretive problems, without deciding them. In this process, a new type of discussion has developed—new as against the forms of discussion which have taken place with younger children in regard to their plays. This new form is the individual conference. In a corner of the lobby or library, in a conference room, or, weather permitting, on a bench outdoors, the adult will sit down with a boy or girl and have a talk. These talks need quiet and privacy. They may be personal. The adult may raise questions about things in the child's own temperament which are standing in the way of creative realization—but only if he feels sure that the child is ready to deal with these matters. Or the talk may be about life and love and human hurt and the way human hurt works, so that the young person can better understand the adult he or she is being in the play. But again the teacher will not talk about certain things, or not in depth, unless the child is already standing on the verge of those adult realizations which the idealism of childhood tends to keep at a distance from the conscious mind. Or the talk may be about a period of history, and the adult will help a child to see how the beliefs and moral imperatives of a given epoch have shaped the psyche of the person he or she is playing.

A talk of this kind was held with a boy who was rehearsing Judge Danforth in *The Crucible*. He had been playing the part very powerfully as a man of raging and sadistic inward fires, which were kept in check by the probity of a great legal mind but which, when the law permitted, rendered him vengeful and terrible. It was a forceful interpretation, but it wasn't right, and the talk did not seem to lead to any modification. But then one night at rehearsal, when he was not involved onstage, he approached the teacher and said: "I've been thinking. I've been doing my part all wrong." "Yes," said the teacher, "you've been an eighteenth-century hanging judge, not a seventeenth-century Puritan fanatic." The boy went away but approached the teacher again a little later and said he felt feverish. The teacher felt his forehead and sent him home. He did not return for two weeks.

Meantime, rehearsals went on with someone filling in during the courtroom scene. In all such dramatizations, there is a point when the whole play seems to die, and the play was at this stage, with the courtroom scene the most dismal, when one evening the boy returned and stepped back into his role. The scene came alive, as one who is in a state of lethargy will come alive in the face of terror. The judge's voice was low, his speech of a terrifying slowness which precipitated a mounting tension. The probity was no longer the probity of a legal mind, but of a mind that assumes its own probity is the probity of God. This was a man who could do no wrong, nor take pleasure in doing good. Only the most rigorous adherence to the subtleties of the law could save the people of Massachusetts from the subtleties of the Fiend. The disciplines of the mind were awesome disciplines, and the fires raging beneath these disciplines were the fires of the terror of the Pit. Sometime while running a high fever and convalescing from it, the boy had found his image.

Despite the magnificent job which this gifted group did with *The Crucible*, this writer has serious doubts as to whether teenagers should do too highly charged, serious, realistic drama —that is, whether in make-believe they ought to release powerful emotions, even if they can. His scruples, perhaps, are silly. But he retains these doubts despite his great faith in the resilience of young people and his disbelief that such release will really prove traumatic. Anyhow, an adult helping young people choose a play must use his own best judgment.

The young people's performance of *The Crucible* would doubtlessly have been received with enthusiasm and excitement in a professional theater by an audience that had paid good money to see it and never suspected that what they were witnessing was not professional theater but children's creative dramatics—supposing, of course, that the voice projections and movements were extended to meet the needs of a larger auditorium and stage. This kind of achievement is, of course, unusual. It is never to be expected, though it may take place. Back of such achievement lies the depth of understanding which the young people have attained in the process of dramatizing and some unusual combination of energy, vitality and talent is able to project to startlingly high levels. Nevertheless, when a less energetic or talented group achieves a comparable understanding of their material—and this is more usual and *is* to be expected—their dramatization will carry conviction and depth and will be moving to those people in the audience who really use their eyes and ears.

12

○○○○○○○○○

Casting As a Democratic Process

CASTING, AS SUCH, does not rear its ugly head in informal dramatics. One child, of course, will play one part and another child another part, but who plays what doesn't matter as long as each child is having a good experience. Three or four children, it is true, may want to be the same thing in a poem or story, but they can all have a chance, for the same poem or story can be done several times. Little children, especially, will have favorite poems and stories that they like to act over and over again. What the adult is concerned with, then, is fairness and opportunity. He will try to see that the more expansive or aggressive child sometimes gives way in his desires to other children. Above all, he will see, behind the waving hands, the eyes of the shy, less self-confident child who wants to play a part but isn't bold enough to say so—who won't admit, even to himself, that there are things in a story or poem that he wants to be and do. In short, the question of who is good in a part, and especially the question of who is better than someone else in a part, is utterly irrelevant in informal dramatizations.

Even in informal dramatizations which may eventually lead to a performance for an audience, the situation remains much the same. Of the previous examples where informal dramatizations of poetry were publicly performed, a very simple casting situation took place. In the reading of a number of poems, two or three children liked a specific poem and wanted to do it, and two or three liked another poem, etc., so that each ended up doing pretty much what he wanted to do. Suppose, however, that one poem involves four people—all four want this poem with perhaps all four wanting the same part in the poem. Of four youngsters who chose to dramatize Frost's "The Runaway," the youngest was a boy of eleven, who had his heart set on doing the reading, and the others agreed that he would do it. A twelve-year-old girl had the gumption to be the frightened colt, a role about which the others, a thirteen-year-old boy and girl, had some compunctions. So the two oldest ended up with the least impressive parts—the two people who watch the colt across the pasture wall—falling into these roles through a combination of generosity and default. In another situation, three girls chose to act out Poe's "Annabelle Lee." They agreed quickly which would be Annabelle, but both of the others wanted to do the reading. So they let Annabelle decide which was the better reader, and the one eliminated played the part of the mourning poet. In some instances, the sub-group working on a poem will call on the adult to decide who should do a part. To this extent, the shadow of casting falls lightly across their efforts.

Even when a body of poetry is chosen with the express

purpose of public performance, casting will tend to come about through a rather painless process of natural selection. In the dedicatory ceremony for the camp amphitheater, the selection of Greek poems and passages came about through the enthusiasm of a given child or sub-group for this poem or that, and casting fell into line accordingly. The same thing happened with a senior class which dramatized a program of poetry as part of its graduation exercises. This was a major effort, and the group was putting its best foot forward as much as in the dramatization of a standard play, and yet there was no formal casting—only the inclination of a certain student to do this or that and a general knowledge on the part of the group as to who could do this or that kind of thing well.

A program of short stories—folk tales, for example—does not offer quite the same latitude for individual inclination, for perhaps only three stories can be dramatized in the same space of time as six or seven poems. Nevertheless, much the same process is at work, even when the impetus for dramatization is the prospect of performance. For example, eight- and nine-year-old campers, with the help of a counselor, may read as many as nine or ten stories together. Some like this story and some that, so that in all four sub-groups evolve around different enthusiasms. Within these sub-groups or casts, decisions can be made as to who will be who, through a combination of volunteering on the part of some children and the acceptance of one or another volunteer by the others, all expedited by a perceptive alertness on the part of the counselor who asks children what they think, and makes suggestions and decisions, all so to speak on the wing, and in such a way that everything gets done in an eager and spontaneous spirit. With older children, the approach cannot be quite so off-hand. Nevertheless, if older children are dramatizing short folk material, the sub-groups will take care of much of the casting in such a way that parts get assigned largely through natural selection, and only one or two will require the deliberate making of decisions.

When children in high school dramatize scenes from classic plays informally, natural inclination will also be the determining process. For from the number of scenes in a play and the number of persons in a scene several casts can be made up to give everyone pretty much the part he wants to play or has been encouraged to try by his classmates or the adult in charge. If certain scenes are more desirable than others, then the same scene can be done by several casts. In this way, three or four boys and two or three girls can all be Dr. Faustus—about as many as will want to be, since there will also be great interest in being Mephistopheles or one of the friars or Gluttony or Lechery. And if, because girls are going to be Dr. Faustus, David decides that he wants to have a whack at the greatest walk-on role in all dramatic literature, the adult need only say, "Look, David, it's one thing for a girl to be Dr. Faustus, and something else again for a boy to be Helen of Troy!" Then if these dramatizations should get performed for an audience, there may be some decision-making as to what scenes are to be performed, but the casting has already taken care of itself. Thus, in a school assembly program of several scenes from *Julius Caesar*, there were three Marc Antonys, two Cascas, two Portias, four Brutuses and Cassiuses, the Brutus and the Cassius in the quarrel scene being girls. The girls were very good, too, but if anyone had given any formal thought to casting, they would have been persuaded to trade roles.

The goal, then, of such informal dramatizations is to give every child a chance to do the things he wants to do, and equally to encourage every child to try many different things. It is only in those situations where the goal of a group is the serious performance of an ambitious play that the question of casting arises in more than a touch-and-go way. In general, there are two situations which call for any special process of casting. One is the dramatization of a standard play. The other is with those longer improvisations by eleven or twelve year olds, such as have come up in several contexts—"The Bookman," *Tom Sawyer, Mottel, the Cantor's Son, The Hearthstone* and the play about China, whose title no one any longer remembers.

When a group assumes from the outset that what they have to say through improvised dramatization will be said to an audience, then it is part of their responsibility to that audience and to themselves to choose the best person for each part. In the early stages, the adult will encourage everyone to try many different parts. This approach is time-consuming, but it is of great importance in making up original material. For example, some quick-witted child, who, for a number of reasons, may not be suited for a given part, may make important contributions to the development of the dialogue for that part in the early stages. Or a girl with gifts that may eventually place her in a major role may, in doing minor parts, be an inspiration to other girls who will eventually play these parts. Or, in a very fluid situation, a shy child, new to the group, perhaps, and unfamiliar with such goings-on, may make important self-discoveries and turn out to be the best person for some difficult role, whereas in a tighter or more formal situation she might not have dared to try such a role, or, trying it, might have been constrained. Or it may be that one boy's creative vision develops more slowly; he fumbles things in the earlier stages, but watches, absorbs, feels his way and eventually emerges with a deeper or more integrated interpretation of a character than others have achieved or than he could have achieved if final casting had been done prematurely.

Also, in the improvised play, many parts fall into line by common consent. Parts which, in the story being dramatized, may seem minor may become much greater because an imaginative child has seen the possibilities. Such, for example, was true of the role of the U.S. marshal in *The Hearthstone*. The fact that the final dramatization is original provides room for developments which can make every part important and desirable.

Most good stories are about one individual and his relationships to other people, or about two people and their relationship to each other. Thus there will be several roles which will seem more desirable than others, and there will be some rivalry for parts. But if the process of playmaking has been sound, there will be fewer rivalries than in the casting for a standard play, and ego hurt will be largely absorbed in the esprit de corps.

At a certain point in improvisations—after the dialogue has begun to emerge and the children have observed each other doing various things—formal casting will begin. The leader may say: "We have seen Jane and Adrienne as Aunt Polly. Do we want to see them again? Or can we decide now?" Or he may say: "We've developed Aunt Polly's role and character pretty well, and we've seen a number of girls play her. Tomorrow between ten and eleven, we'll cast Aunt Polly. Now let's see which of the girls are going to try for it." In other words, if everyone is satisfied that Jane and Adrienne are the only contenders, the approach can be more informal. However, if Liz and Betty have strong feelings that they, too, are in contention, then a formal tryout will have to be established.

Whatever the situation, as long as a part has not been settled by common consent, anyone who wants a part has a right to be seen in it, and final decision should be made by the group after a discussion which takes into account such things as the originality of the interpretation, the depth of insight, force and movement, etc. The adult's role is to help the children achieve the highest possible degree of perceptiveness and objectivity.

A casting process of this kind is very time-consuming, and with high school students doing a full-length standard play it is scarcely feasible. For this reason, the casting may have to be done by an elected committee, and the major roles cast before rehearsing can begin. This casting committee should announce a time and place for tryouts, and indicate the pages in the script to be used in trying out for a given part. The widest encouragement should be given to everyone, and both the adult and the committee should have the patience to give everyone a good chance. It is probably wise for the adult to be a member of the casting committee, and have a vote as well as a voice.

Here is a question, helpful in many ways, but containing some dangers, which the adult may put to the group before casting begins:

"Of course, everyone may try out for any part he or she wants and, failing to get one part, may try out for any others. But will you agree, each of you individually, to try out for any part the casting committee asks you to try out for, and to accept any part the casting committee asks you to take?"

It is a difficult question, for a positive answer may commit a young person to play a role he abominates. The adult should not exert any pressure or influence in regard to this question beyond pointing out the group advantages of such an agreement. If all agree—and often all will agree—the work of the casting committee is then free from the problem of temperament on the part of an individual who is a good prospect for a role he doesn't like. If most agree to this proposition, then the wishes of those who don't agree must be respected without pressure. However, the greater number, who have agreed, can be held to their agreement. If most do not agree, then the casting committee must fill the less desirable roles as best it can. Actually, the value of this question is to pose and explore the matter of group solidarity, not to smoke out lone wolves, whose right to keep step to a different drummer is absolute. The good soldier in a group project is to be praised, but the person who would gladly play *this* role and obstinately refuses to play *that* role may have good reasons. Selfishness and personal ambition are not good reasons, but personal integrity *is* a good reason. If the issue of personal subordination to the best interest of the group has been raised, then the individual who is unwilling to subordinate himself must confront himself and see what reasons he has. That is enough. The adult may, in the way of personal guidance, discuss these reasons privately with a youngster; as:

"I understand, Linda. I don't know that I agree with you that the matter is as important as you make it, but if you feel that for you to play Albertine would be insincere and false, I have to respect your reasons."

Or:

"Well, Lucy, I'm not going to twist your arm. You have a right to refuse any part you don't want. But I think you need to examine your reasons. There is something in yourself and your relationship with your classmates that you have to face up to. That is all I'm going to say now. If later you feel you want to talk more about it, we can sit down together."

Most youngsters, however, will prefer some part to no part at all, and a few who might personally prefer no part to a given part will be good soldiers. In *Rhinoceros*, a very gifted and ambitious girl got stuck in an upper-storey window, stage rear. She said throughout the long first act about four or five short lines and after that act she was never seen again. But there she was in Act I, just her head and shoulders, her arms and hands, in a window. And yet in the delicate equilibrium on which the pace of the first act depended, she had to be in her role every moment. Her face, her shoulders, occasionally her arms and hands, had continually to express and respond. A half-hearted job would have destroyed tensions, and yet a whole-hearted job would have gone unnoticed. Her position was like that of an unobtrusive object in a Renaissance painting, an object overlooked by most observers but without which the composition would fall apart.

The boy who played the Reverend Parris in *The Crucible* is another example. Everything in the boy was revolted by the slimy combination of hypocrisy, self-deception and pathetic inadequacy of the character. The boy was an excellent satirist and could have enjoyed the role had he been free to play its contradictions and absurdities for laughs, as he sometimes did in rehearsal. Perhaps it was through this satirizing of the role that he was able to reconcile himself to the fact that he was not only a good soldier but enough of an artist to find in himself the creative image, tragic and profoundly pathetic, of this poor creature.

Anyway, following the fullest opportunity for tryouts and searching discussion, casting goes forward on the basis of committee voting. Once major parts are determined, rehearsals can begin. People trying out for minor roles can be seen in actual rehearsals, working with the people already chosen for the major roles. In this way, formal tryouts for these secondary roles may not be necessary. Some roles will fall into line without competition, and others, which may still be competitive, the committee can decide by calling short, on-the-spot meetings.

Why should the casting of children's plays be done democratically? Isn't the director the best judge of who should play what? Why, then, doesn't the director do the casting? For the simple reason that there is no director—only an adult helping children make a play as well as they can. He is concerned with seeing that the children have a fulfilling, enriching experience and his only concern with the success of the play is that to do a good job is a good experience for children, and to do a bad job is a bad experience. But if they do a good job because he has taken important experiences out of their hands and kept them in his own, they will have had, good or bad, a limited experience. In the young people's first major play, he may feel he cannot relinquish to them the central coordination of the work, or even the all-important task of being the central ears and eyes. But he relinquishes as much of the directoral role that he can. He invites their participation in every aspect of playmaking, and since casting is a very creative aspect, and since it lies very clearly within the competence of children ten or eleven years and older, they are the ones to do the casting.

When casting is done by the children, what is to prevent them from picking the most popular child for a part instead of the best qualified? In one sense, nothing. In another, everything —their desire to do a good play, their traditions and prior history, the personal integrity of the individuals who comprise the group. Children who have been conditioned by shallow previous experience will behave in a shallow way, but they will grow less shallow as they gather experience and come to understand what is expected of them. In this writer's experience, no group or casting committee has ever made its decisions on the basis of favoritism, and only one committee has ever involved itself in other than the objective question of who has given the best interpretation of a part.

As an example of how little favoritism affects the choice children make in casting there is a story. The writer one morning received a telephone call from the unhappy mother of a sixth-grade girl. The girl was not coming to school that morning. The last part open in a group play was to be decided, and this girl, who felt herself, with some justice, the most disregarded child in the class, was competing for the role with one of the most popular girls. The writer talked to the girl and persuaded her to come to school and try out. In the tryout, this child showed a very imaginative concept for the part—the part of an old woman— but she had an uncertain, mousy projection. The popular girl's interpretation was more ordinary, but she had much more force and vigor. Now, this play was to be performed for an unusual audience—not only of parents, but of educators, educational writers and editors. Under these conditions, the group might have felt more secure with a character whose force and projection they could count on. Apparently, however, they prized imagination and insight above projection, so their regard fell on the disregarded girl and they voted her in.

The boys in the group, incidentally, picked up this casting method and carried it over to the ballfield to arrive at the best choices for positions on the team. If three boys, for instance, were trying out for first base, the others would execute certain plays—grounders, flies, throws from second or third, etc.—and everyone would watch the candidates handle their end of the plays. Then they would get together and vote. Looking on one time, this writer heard the team captain using an expression which the writer realized he himself had used several times during casting: "Hey, Allen, you watch the plays. If you don't watch every player on every play, you don't have any right to vote!"

What happens when the group or casting committee and the adult disagree? If the adult sincerely trusts young people and if he is sincere initially in establishing a democratic casting procedure, then the young people will have their way. In the casting of *The Crucible*, the adults and the casting committee were in disagreement on both leading roles—Proctor and Abigail. One of the two adults felt, at first, that there was an element of social favoritism in the choice of Proctor, though it became apparent after a few rehearsals that the committee knew what it was doing and had made an inspired choice. There could have been no shadow of favoritism in the choice for Abigail, however, since the girl chosen had managed to keep herself disliked by writing brilliant stories and character sketches in which her classmates felt themselves satirized. Whether in this choice they were right and the adults wrong, or vice versa, there is no way to know. It was an excellent choice, though perhaps not the best.

Young people like to put on plays, and they take playmaking seriously. And so they take casting seriously. Despite confusions and contradictions of values they feel in themselves, they have a great deal of integrity and will draw on it in situations where, so to speak, the chips are down. So in casting they tend to avoid parliamentary faction and maneuver and work toward consensus as much as possible. They will sit and talk and continue tryouts until they reach the broadest possible base of agreement.

Sometimes, of course, honest differences of interpretation will arise. The casting of *Ondine* represented a kind of microcosm of all the possible problems, and the casting committee was sharply divided between two interpretations of the play. The balance of forces was such that a sincere romanticism, as against a more scoffing, ironic attitude, emerged as the central approach to the play before casting was over, and the development of the play proceeded along these romantic lines. The casting is, in fact, one of the most important interpretive aspects of playmaking.

What are we looking for? What is our concept of this character? The committee discusses this question, then sees someone try the character. Only part of what the committee thought it was looking for is conveyed by the candidate, but something the committee had not thought of is conveyed. The relation of the character to the meaning of the play has been extended. The committee talks some more; it sees someone else try the part. Here is a new interpretation altogether. A third girl tries. She is closer to what the committee had in mind in the first place—and she moves and speaks better than the others. But the committee's thinking has gone beyond her now. They have seen other things more perceptive and original. Is it possible to achieve a synthesis of the best qualities in all three interpretations? The girls are called in and briefed together. Each is told what the committee felt she had achieved and what she had failed to achieve, on the basis of the committee's expanding vision. Each girl gets the benefit, not only of what the committee says to her, but of what it says to the others. The committee does not say: "This is the way we want it." It says: "This is what we have seen and liked, these are some of the possibilities. Go beyond what you did before. We will see all three of you again." Thus the work of casting has already begun those explorations of character and meaning which constitute the greatest part of the creative process in a dramatization.

In the casting of Mrs. Cogan in a performance of *The Plow and the Stars*, a very sharp difference of opinion developed within the casting committee. One Mrs. Cogan was rough and tough, earthy and vigorous, a Dubliner, Dublin born. The other was a Mrs. Cogan whose passionate commitment to the wrath of the moment arose from a kind of confused and childlike naïveté expressed in a musical brogue whose lyricism had echoes, not of working-class Dublin, but of a girlhood spent in the green countryside. The excellence of both characterizations was conceded by both parties. In a final vote of five to four, however, it was decided that the more lyrical Mrs. Cogan was a better choice in regard to the tone and aesthetic of the play. The decision, in this case, was perhaps the wrong one. The group was inherently sensitive and lyrical, but their final performance needed more vigor, and the rough, tough Mrs. Cogan might have sparked it off. Once a choice is made, however, all consideration of the choices not made becomes purely speculative.

Once the choices are made, the adult will, of course, do everything he can to support and strengthen each person chosen and to prevent the group from second-guessing itself if the chosen person runs into difficulties as the play unfolds. The girl the teacher thought to be the best choice for Ondine was rejected out of hand by the committee in the first tryout. In one of the rehearsals this girl—we will call her Marcia—became very impatient with Bobbi, who was playing Ondine, and began to tell her how the part should be played. Everything she said confirmed the teacher in his original judgment that she had had the most intelligent and penetrating insight into the role. But the teacher cut into her sharply, saying: "Look, Marcia, you didn't get the part. Perhaps some of the casting committee felt you should have got it, but you didn't. If you had, then you could do it your way. But Bobbi can't do it your way—she has to do it her way. Unless you can see ways to help her do it her way, just leave her alone!"

This brings us to the question of type casting. Younger children and less experienced teenagers will find it hard to avoid type casting. If a child's stature, appearance and manner of speaking are naturally consistent with the attributes of the character, it is not easy to look beyond that natural coincidence and see how someone else, who is not the type, is *being* the character in a more expressive and creative way. Pre-adolescents, in particular, cling to naturalism rather tenaciously. If some unnaturalistic piece of staging is a lot of fun, they'll do it anyway, but on the whole the adult has to pry them loose from their naturalistic tendency.

In casting *Tom Sawyer*, one of the smallest boys had already been picked for Tom when the girls tried out for Becky. The best choice for Becky was very obvious—a big girl and, as they say, fully developed. But the group hesitated to choose her, feeling that the disparity of sizes was comical because it was unnatural:

A GIRL: It doesn't seem right for Tom to be so small and Becky so big!

THE ADULT: What do you mean it doesn't seem right?

A BOY: It seems funny—unrealistic.

THE ADULT: How old do you take Tom and Becky to be?

A GIRL: About twelve.

THE ADULT: How old are you as a group?

A BOY (Grinning): About twelve!

THE ADULT: Well?

Convinced now that the casting of a big Becky and a little Tom did not violate canons of naturalism, they were able to see that the hilarity of a little Tom chasing a big Becky about the schoolroom for a kiss was touching and beautiful precisely because it was natural and true.

The case of *Ondine*, however, was the opposite of this concern about naturalism. Marcia was rejected out of hand because she *was* the type. She looked like an ondine, particularly the kind of ondine a poor knight-errant would meet once and fall in love with forever. And this coincidence blinded most of the committee to the fact that behind the coincidence was a beautiful piece of acting—witty, imaginative, perceptive and supported by fresh gifts of voice and movement. In other words, they did not disregard type, as they should have, but assumed that being the type constituted, on the basis of some higher order of things, an automatic disqualification. It was part of that perversity of adolescence by which some folk idiom, as pliable as an old bedroom slipper, is damned as a cliché. They look down their noses—lovingly, perhaps—at the taste of their teacher, who seems to prefer Robert Herrick to E. E. Cummings. What they fail to understand is that the novelty of E. E. Cummings was already wearing thin for their teacher a quarter of a century before, and that what he hopes they will discover for themselves is that, fresh and lovely as some of Cummings's poems are, the body of Herrick's work is consistently fresher.

Do such mistaken judgments create a terrible situation? Not at all. Though the casting committee for *Ondine* failed to give Marcia the consideration she deserved, their final choice of Bobbi, who had made a very poor showing when they first saw her, was as much a masterpiece of inspired insight as their peremptory rejection of Marcia was perverse. They failed to see in Marcia what the teacher saw. However, they saw in Bobbi a capacity to grow, to transcend apparent limitations and sweep to authority, which the teacher had seriously underestimated. If one is going to work with adolescents, one must be prepared to love them for their perversity, for this is an assertion of their necessity to discover things for themselves. One must even be prepared to nurture the suspicion that it is frequently they who are right and oneself who is wrong. They are tolerant and will deal kindly enough with the errors of an adult. Being themselves strong-minded and argumentative, they will be able to cope with the errors of a strong-minded and argumentative adult. But they will become evasive, indifferent, even devious, when the adult assumes a mantle of infallability.

Nevertheless, there are some mistakes adolescents will make that are more serious, and in regard to such mistakes the adult must let them know, beyond any amiable acceptance of a margin of error, who is adult and who is not. Within the casting committee for *Ondine* there was a faction, well intentioned enough, who tried to take into account such things as who, for emotional or psychological reasons, would be most benefited by getting a given part and who would be most seriously hurt by not getting it. The adult, of course, must have emotional matters in the back of his mind and must handle everything in such a way that all of the children are strengthened and not hurt. Children, too, should be sensitive to each other and to each other's needs and ambitions, and a casting committee can afford to handle its business in a kind and gracious way. But for a committee of children to set itself up as the dispensers of psychological weal for other children is unwholesome in the extreme. One can speculate inside oneself that for Lucy to get the leading role will only aggravate that sense of personal importance which often gets in the way of her personal relationships; and that if Sally were to get the role, her rather shaky self-confidence would be greatly strengthened. And that if Lucy got the part, then adults who know both girls may say among themselves: "It's too bad Sally didn't get the part." But unless the adult's skills in such matters are as specific as the skills of firemen, life guards and surgeons in their matters, he will not assume that casting is an experience in psychotherapy and will not permit adolescents to assume so either. The youngsters doing the casting should be permitted to direct themselves only to one central question: "Who, all in all, is the best person to play this part?" Under some circumstances, they may have to consider the question of a candidate's dependability, especially in connection with long, hard roles. At most, they may weigh, on the basis of their general knowledge of the group, one candidate's tendency to search things out slowly as against the quicker apprehension of another—that is, they may know that what they have seen of Bob's interpretation is close to the limit of what they can expect of him, but that Dave is the kind of person who will inch his way to deeper and deeper insights. These are legitimate speculations. But beyond these things, personal considerations should not enter, whether they are dishonest considerations of personal attachment or well-intentioned speculations of therapeutic benefit. For it is only the faith each child has in the integrity and objectivity of those making the judgments that makes a democratic casting process possible and prevents the producing of a play from becoming an emotional disaster.

What about hurt feelings? Inevitably there will be hurt feelings. Suppose seven girls want the same part. Two or three entertain no real hope and are not too crushed when they are eliminated. But one of these is not immediately eliminated, and her mood of resignation gives way to a heady expectancy. By now there are three girls under consideration. They will be seen two or three more times before the final decision is made. It is a period of tension, and when the decision comes there will be dashed hopes and unhappy tears. But it is a reality situation which must be faced if young people are to put on major plays. The friendly objectivity of the committee will help: "We have had a very difficult time reaching a decision because all three of you are great. Frannie moves in such a beautiful way. Alice's voice is very stirring. But we think Ruthie has seen more aspects of the character and has a clearer understanding of the dramatic situation. So we're going along with Ruthie, though she'll have to work hard on movement and voice." If Frannie and Alice are hurt, there is really only one thing that can help—the loving expectation on the part of the adult and their group mates that they are strong, resilient and objective enough to overcome their hurt feelings and return to action in some other part or in another aspect of the play's production and have a good time.

Hurt feelings do not represent the only emotional problem of casting. One of the most deceptive aspects is frequently the reluctance of a child to admit that he wants to try for the very part he is deeply eager to do, and this is especially true of parts which demand the expression of what is aesthetically beautiful. For example, the wordless part of Helen of Troy in *Doctor Faustus* may go begging for a time, until at last some shy girl volunteers timidly, and one realizes that this quiet, contemplative youngster has had all along an awareness of her own potential for beauty. A camp director, working with a sub-group on the writing of an oratorio about the history of the camp, felt very discouraged when he got the full group together and no one would volunteer to take part in the most beautiful scene of all, the interpretive pantomime. He felt that the oratorio could not be performed under the circumstances. However, when he adjourned the meeting, six or seven girls and boys remained behind, each ready to confess what they had not been able to admit in open meeting, that they ardently wished to do the interpretive pantomime.

In another instance, a high school senior had written a beautiful stream-of-consciousness story which his group decided to dramatize by using a reader and a pantomimist. At first, there was no volunteer for the role of the pantomimist, in which a solo player would have to objectify inward feelings for some fifteen or twenty minutes. At length one boy agreed to demonstrate something of what might be done with the role, though he refused to consider it for himself. There was another boy whom the teacher felt to be the one who should do it—a boy of highly charged inwardness and of graceful and fluid movement, though relatively inexperienced in dramatization. When the first boy finished his "demonstration" and the session was breaking up, the other boy approached the teacher, looking about him to make sure no one overheard, and said he wanted to try the pantomime in the next session. He was, of course, the one to do it, and this experience oriented him on his choice of college and his college courses—that is, on college and courses that would give him a continuing experience in performing arts. Our point is merely that it is often the very thing that children most yearn for in the secrecy of their hearts that fills them with the profoundest diffidence. The adult must be particularly sensitive to this phenomenon, for it is terribly important that a child dare take the responsibility for beauty upon himself.

13

ooooooooo

Expanded Communication—I, Movement

THE CURTAIN OF THE auditorium opens on two boys squatting in
the center of the stage. Near them is something that looks like a
log wigwam. The boys talk and, to the extent that one can hear
them, one realizes that they are Huck and Jim on their raft on
the Mississippi River. One gets some story background and a
feeling of the closeness of this man and this boy; one understands the dangers they are in and that the danger is intensified
whenever they have to pole their boat in to a bank so that Huck
can go into town for some reason. Apparently a town is looming

ahead, for Huck gets up at last—otherwise they have remained squatting close together amidships. He goes to the forward end of the raft and scans the shore. The curtain closes.

The adult who has been working with these boys, and others, on their play has been watching from the wings. During the play's development, he has experienced some stirring moments when the imagination of either boy, or the imaginations of both interacting on each other, have captured some of the beautiful potential of their material. He knows that these boys feel their parts keenly and that they understand the relationship of Huck and Jim in a very perceptive boys' way. As he watches, he sees their insights expressed in the cast of their heads and the expressions of their faces, and hears the insights in the words which they have improvised and the inflections and tones in which they speak the words. They have done a beautifully creative job and the adult knows it. But he realizes with a pang that these beautiful qualities are lost on the audience, who see two boys squatting together without much animation and who have to strain to hear what they are saying. He grows resentful, perhaps, towards the imperceptiveness of the other watchers. Or he shrugs, consoling himself with the truth—but a truth which, in this instance, needs a little fuller interpretation—that it is the process and not the performance that matters. Or, more wisely, he may wonder what more he might have done to help.

For much more might have been done. When the curtain opened Jim might have been squatting, head on knees, brooding or sleeping. After a moment, Huck might have come out of the wigwam, breathing in the morning and scratching a match on the seat of his pants to light his pipe. They might have talked louder, with a much greater variation in their pace. Rather than squat together all the time, they might have lolled and laughed, talking lazily into some subject which led them to animated disagreement. And Huck might have established the edges of the raft for us, forward, starboard and stern, as he walked along that edge following with his eyes some snagged object in the water. Jim might have established the east bank of the Mississippi, pointing out some object on the shore. In a silence, he might have hummed while Huck stood up, stretched and then hollered to break the stillness of the river. They might have poled the raft in to the bank, where Jim would have crept into the log wigwam, while Huck hit the road to town to pick up some things and see what was doing—whistling to show anyone who might see or hear him that he had nothing on his conscience, certainly nothing like slave stealing!

The adult, therefore, might have helped them express themselves more fully. He might have helped them—to be technical about it—with blocking, with the utilization of time and space, with entrances and exits, with focus and pace, and with the audibility, clarity and variability of their speech. In short, he might have helped them expand and thereby better communicate their creative vision.

For, as children make the transition from make-believe to dramatics, they tend to some extent to become hidebound. The eight year old doing "dramatics" bolts off and uses the whole outdoors. But the ten and eleven year olds have developed the sense of an acting area and a consciousness of watchers. The walls of the acting area on three sides and the wall of watchers on the fourth tend to press them together in the center. The adult's role at this point becomes a double one: he will help the children to raise their sense of the acting area to a higher level of consciousness and to establish the line of the watchers' vision as the line on which their desire to communicate is oriented; and he will help them break down the walls of the acting area and restore their birthright of the whole outdoors.

In a sense the space the children have in which to dramatize is, indeed, the whole outdoors, if they want to make it so. A child with a very fine dramatic sense, whose voice and inflection, whose arms, hands and head convey character with great insight and even with finesse, may be quite unaware of the possibilities in using space and may initially be uncomfortable about using it. The adult must help this child.

Assume that there are two children in a scene, such as the scene of Huck and Jim. The children are intent on what they have to say and on their interrelationship. It probably will not occur to them that the lip of the stage, the very back, or the steps, or the extreme sides, or the uprights of the proscenium, or the great space between the tops of their heads and the battens, or even the still greater space in which the watchers are sitting are part of the material they can make use of. Initially these things will probably have to be suggested to children. But they can quickly learn that two people can sometimes express their relationship by going as far away from each other as possible; that fear or hurt or certain other feelings may lead one to go *in*—that is, as far away from the watchers as possible, and to turn one's back on the world; that expectancy or elation may hover over the heads of the audience, so that one places one's toes over the edge of the stage and yearns forward into the vast space of the whole outdoors, of the world; that when one is sitting, a new feeling or a new understanding may impel one to rise, to be tall; that grief or feline relaxation may lead one to crouch on the floor; or that, under some circumstances, a girl leaning and crying against the uprights of the proscenium may communicate more heartbreakingly than the same girl standing and crying in the center of the stage.

Is it a scene between a man and a woman sitting together? Then it is a matter of some interpretive importance whether they sit close together or at some distance from each other, or whether the woman sits on a chair or a log, while the man, sitting on the floor or ground, leans against her knees. Is it within the nature of the sitting man to dig something out of his pants' pocket or to get up for a moment to fetch something? Does a moment's emotion cause him to rise and go lean on a windowsill, looking out of doors? And does the woman, after a moment's silence, go over to him and put her arm about his shoulders?

Platforms can be set up onstage, or there can be a second-storey window accessible by means of a ladder hidden behind the flat, so that one has the chance to utilize not only space that goes way in and out and way left and right, but that goes up and down. These are some of the things children seldom think of of their own accord. But once an adult has put the ideas in their heads, they will breed further ideas with considerable fertility. This manner of looking at space and time—for each extension into space is also an extension into time—will become part of their thinking about dramatization. The acting area expands, and with it their imaginations. They put on space and time for their make-believe, as long ago, in the "play period," they put on hats and dresses. They see more broadly what they are being, for they have created a broader world in which to be.

This creative concept of time and space should animate all approaches to such technical matters as "stage business" and "blocking." Blocking is the control of the arrangement—usually a transshifting arrangement—of people on a stage, and the positioning of the objects these people are to use. But the arrangement is hollow except as it flows from or contributes to meaning. It is an extension and expansion of the pantomime, which conveys meaning through visual image. Thus one of the five examples of beautiful pantomime cited earlier was distinctly "arranged": the inert old revolutionary was placed in a reclining position well to the back of the stage so that he had not only to get up, but to move across the whole depth of the stage in order to stand in a beam of light. The boy's capacity to express the emotional awakening in the old man was given time and space in which to make this expression.

Stage business, too, is an extended interpretation. For Huck to scratch a match on the seat of his pants in order to light his pipe is a natural, Huck-like thing to do—Mark Twain specified the pipe, and where else would he strike the match? On the other hand, John Barrymore's belching in the role of Mercutio in the movie *Romeo and Juliet* was dis-interpretive—a most un-mercurial thing to do. During one long scene in a play high school sophomores made up years ago about Renaissance Italy, two girls continued to brush another girl's hair. (She was the daughter of one of the great mercantile princes.) It was a strik-ing piece of stage business—and also a mountingly seductive ex-pression of the Renaissance appetite for the sensuous. The busi-ness which prepared the exit of Elizabeth Proctor in *The Cru-cible* was distinctly "arranged"—her bonnet and shawl were deliberately placed at opposite ends of the stage so that when the arresting officers came to take her to prison she had to cross and recross the stage before she went out with them. Why? Because the girl who played Elizabeth was a dancer and moved with such beauty and conveyed with such expressiveness the serenity which this woman found in herself in a time of tribulation that it would have been a sin against the audience not to give them the opportunity to take this beauty in.

These matters are of as much importance in original plays as in standard plays. In the original play, however, most of them should be built in. With Huck and Jim, the conveying of the dimensions of the raft, the flow of the river, the changing scenery along the shore, the stage business, for example, of Jim going into the wigwam and coming out with a loaf of bread and a jug of molasses, the pace and tempo of the dialogue, the inter-ruptions, the reflective silences, all these things should be an in-herent and inseparable part of the development of the play. In a standard play, however, the words are already in existence in final form before dramatization begins. The words, the way of saying the words and the action cannot develop simultaneously, but the players—and the adult helping them—have to make their way into the words and unfold what actions and arrange-ments can best form their visual counterpart. Even generous stage directions may not prove very helpful, for they are written with a professional stage in mind, and young people may be working on a stage that is small and cramped. And so the stage directions may have to be deeply modified, or reversed or completely disregarded. As a result, whenever a scene has more than four or five people onstage at one time, in the earliest stages of rehearsal it will be a mass of incoherent groupings. This situation should not develop in an original play, since there is no reason to do an original job of creating confusion, but in a standard play the problem of clutter can take up a lot of the adult's time and attention.

Under such conditions, the adult must play a more or less directoral role—he must be the central pair of eyes, especially in the scenes which are most difficult, when most of the group will be too involved in the clutter to see it. If a scene is not too cluttered he may be able to block by a kind of "side-coaching" while the dramatization itself is in process. He moves about the auditorium and looks at things onstage from many positions. He tells one child to move left a few feet, and another to move forward or back, or a pair to trade places, one being taller than the other. He may find it helpful to think in terms of the superiority, for his purposes, of diagonal lines, triangles and kite-shaped figures, as against smoother figures, such as laterals, perpendiculars and squares. He may squint and perceive the players, not as people, but as constellations of moving objects, and decide what points of the moving constellations will bring certain of the moving objects into focus. Such matters may be part of his personal way of doing things. But at all events he will help the youngsters as much as he can to achieve an arrangement which has lucidity and focus.

When this has been achieved, he may then have some of the youngsters not onstage watch the action carefully with him so as to perfect the aesthetics of the transshifting arrangements. Since lucidity and focus are central elements in an aesthetically pleasing arrangement, any further improvements can usually be made without much difficulty or further serious intrusion on the process of dramatization. The aesthetics, however, or even too precise a lucidity, is not a matter about which to dog the youngsters. High school children will concern themselves very seriously with all of the aesthetic considerations of playmaking. But younger children tend to be expressionists, and for them it is usually enough that the blocking be expressive. The bonus to the audience in terms of visual delight can be left to the scenery, the costumes and the children themselves.

It sometimes happens, in relation to blocking, that a big cast on a small stage will seem to present almost insuperable problems of clutter. Dramatization will have to come to a halt while the scene is blocked out and mobile arrangements experimented with until some final decisions emerge as to who goes precisely where precisely when. Once clutter is relieved and lucidity and focus attained, then the blocking will have to be run through a few times in slow motion until it is firmly fixed in the players' minds.

Of course, the easiest way to block with a large cast onstage is to stretch them all out in a chorus line and have each one step forward to say his lines. As preposterous as this sounds, it is an arrangement the Chinese theater sometimes makes use of. The line of players is in constant motion with hands and fans, while the two who are carrying the dialogue stand in front, making use of a somewhat bolder pantomimic accompaniment to their words. Then, as their dialogue comes to an end, the orchestra, which consists of percussions, a stringed instrument or two and a woodwind, picks up a tune, and the players move about among each other in a fluid pantomimic choreography, fetching up again in line, moving their hands and fans, while the persons involved in the next piece of dialogue emerge into the forward position.

It is a lovely solution, but it will not do for our naturalistic tradition, the only one we can make any consistent use of. For us, the ebb and flow of movement among a group of people on a stage must seem to be a random arrangement, and the move-

ments and regroupings must seem to be dictated by the character and motivations and the inner or chance compulsions of the
people who comprise the group. If two manage to be forward
and in focus, it must seem to have fallen out this way. If one of
these two drops back and someone else comes forward, this must
also seem to lie in the nature of things. Perhaps the one who
moves back or off to the side has been called by someone else.
Still in focus, the first man stands there, his hands clasped behind
him in the self-important stance of a man who does not go to
others but lets others come to him. And the third party, seeing
the great man alone, breaks off a background conversation, and
seizes the opportunity to talk to him. In other words, the solu-
tions to the problems of cluttering must be interpretive solu-
tions. They must clarify the imaginary realities with which the
drama deals and provide scope for the children's expression of
these imagined realities.

The dramatization of *The Crucible* is an exemplification of
some of these matters, as *Ondine* was for some of the problems
of casting. The ultimate performance of the courtroom scene
was tremendously exciting, but in rehearsal the play almost fell
apart on this scene because of the problem of clutter. Almost
everyone who is in the play is onstage at one time. The semi-
final solution to the problem was to run a huge oak table diagon-
ally across the small stage, thereby creating two triangles, front
and rear, the table itself providing a center. Grouped around the
table were characters of secondary importance—the reverends
and others who constituted theological witness to the legal
proceedings. In the forward triangle were Mary Warren, Proctor, Judge Danforth, Judge Hathorne, etc.—the ones most in-
tensely involved in the dramatic tensions. In the rear triangle
were Abigail and the other town girls, watching intently, for the
trial contains the possibility of exposing their wickedness. At
only one point do these girls have much part in the dramatic
action—that is, when they begin screaming hysterically as Abigail calls up the vision of the yellow bird. This action is so

powerful as not to need a forward position of focus—in fact, it is better played in back, for in this way the audience can see the impact of the girls' hysterical behavior on the others. This blocking, then, was very satisfactory—except for one thing.

There is a point when Abigail becomes the pivot and central focus of the scene and comes forward, but there was very little room for her to squeeze out of her triangle into the other triangle, past the corner of the table. And about here sat Judge Hathorne. The boy playing him had established a very effective, very creative image of this judge—a brooding man, sitting on the end of his spine with his legs thrust straight forward. These legs were the last element in the clutter—they were in Abigail's way. As she came forward the first time this blocking was used in rehearsal, there were those legs. With no change in the injured innocence that played over her face, and with scarcely a break in her stride, Abigail gave Judge Hathorne a swift kick in the shins. It was not, in itself, an interpretive solution to the blocking problem, but it put it squarely up to Judge Hathorne thereafter to move his legs interpretively as she came through.

Children also often need help in expanding their feeling for time and space in the matter of exits and entrances. The script says, *Enter Barchester,* so the boy playing Barchester, unless he is helped to find other ways of doing it, will appear onstage and begin to speak his lines. But perhaps Barchester's entrance is of telling importance. Who he is, where he has come from and what he has just experienced may have an important bearing on his own life and on the lives of the people he is about to encounter. So his entrance must be "arranged." Perhaps a side door of the auditorium is chosen, the stage being small and no adequate entrance being possible from the wings. Now the boy playing Barchester must enter the auditorium through this side door, cross some twenty or thirty feet of the auditorium floor in front of the audience, mount the steps of the stage and enter the house or wareroom or whatever it is through an imaginary door in an imaginary wall. And he must extend his image of Barchester into all this time and space. Since it is the child's creative image of Barchester that is to be conveyed, the "arrangement" for the entrance is a means of giving more scope to his creativity.

A teacher more skilled in music than in dramatics was leading a group of high school students in a production of a Gilbert and Sullivan operetta. He was having trouble, he thought, with the dramatics end of it and asked another teacher to come to rehearsal and give him some help. The second teacher saw that the principals—everyone, in fact—had an excellent dramatic sense, once they were onstage—and the chorus, once they started singing, of who they were and what they were expressing. The dramatization was fresh and sweet and needed help in only one thing—the entrances and exits of the chorus. When the chorus was due, it stumbled onstage and groped its way to an organization demanded by the deployment of the voices. A little discussion—"Who are you people and why are you coming here?"—and a little drill to work out the order and timing of the individual comings and goings was all that was needed to transform the chorus into a group of young villagers coming to a wedding feast, greeting each other and the principals, and falling together, in the natural flow of their relationships, in such a way that they could sing together about the delights of strawberry jam.

Exits and entrances need not be timid. There is a burst of angry voices at the back of the auditorium and a group of determined men drag Injun Joe down the aisle and up the steps of the stage to prison. Or a girl in braids pedals a real bicycle down the same aisle and stops at a platform of the Eiffel Tower to ask route directions of Cocteau's old general. Or we hear a voice in the darkness, and a spotlight picks up a creature from Venus, perched, as we have already seen, on top of a fire exit.

Or in the courtroom scene of *The Crucible*, again, an exit is made in very limited space, but in considerable expansion in time. So great was the blocking problem of this scene that it was relatively late in rehearsals before the teacher saw Thomas Putnam walk off the stage at one point without rhyme or reason. "Putnam!" called the teacher. "Where are you going?" "It says, *Exit Putnam*," answered the boy. "Why?" said the teacher. "What was the last thing you were involved in?" So they went back in the script to where Giles Corey had accused Putnam of encouraging the witch trials in order to pick up the property of the condemned at bargain prices. Putnam has been riding high, but Corey's accusation is the bald truth, and he can give no answer, for inwardly he is a weak, frightened man. All he can do is glare for awhile until his pusillanimous soul prompts him to make the fatuous gesture of stomping out of the courtroom a minute or two later when no one is paying him any mind. This the boy was able to express once he related the delayed exit to the exchange in which he had last been involved. He stood and glared and then stomped out—to an unanticipated burst of applause when the play was performed. Thus an initially unmotivated and blundering exit was transformed into a revelation of character much sharper and more devastating, incidentally, than any of the boy's lines or other movements had made possible.

It would seem, then, that if space is used and time taken advantage of in relation to the interpretation of character and situation, such technical approaches will not mechanize or theatricalize the child's creative image, but will enlarge, refine and intensify its expression. Nevertheless, the creative image and the child's hold on it remain all that matters in the long run. And for the adult to ask for the expansion of a child's image beyond the point the child can sustain is to impose the adult's image on the child. For example, in Elizabeth Proctor's exit, to have placed the shawl and bonnet on opposite sides of the room with a child in the part who could not honestly be that woman over that much space and time would have been theatrical and even cruel.

So in the final analysis the image is more important than its extension. The most beautiful entrance this writer has seen in children's dramatizations was very badly arranged. The boy appeared onstage and spoke his lines, and such extension as there was was the only space he had available, that of his own body. A ninth-grade group was dramatizing some scenes from Greek plays informally. They were making use of the stage and they even had some simple stage lighting and Greek-like costumes improvised from sheets. But they had no audience, except for a couple of teachers and two or three office workers who came and went as their time allowed.

They dramatized the messenger scene from Sophocles's *Oedipus Colonus* in front of the curtain, with the daughter-sisters of Oedipus waiting for word of their father, who had gone off alone into a grove sacred to Apollo. Not only had the messenger's entrance not been "arranged," but he was going to have to grope his way onstage through the division in the stage curtain. But suddenly he leapt among us, his voice ringing, his arms extended, radiant and wild with a miracle, for he had just heard the voice of the god, calling the blinded king.

14
ooooooooo

14
ooooooooo
Expanded Communication—II, Speech

IF IN THE PREVIOUS CHAPTER the messenger's voice rang, it was
not because the boy had been taught techniques of voice projection. It rang because a messenger's voice *would* ring from the terror and glory of what he had just heard. It is to this creative aspect of verbal and vocal expression that most of the adult's
attention will be directed in helping young people with a play. If
we assume that pantomime is one-third, then verbal expression is
two-thirds of what a play is all about. With the improvised play,
of course, there are three elements—making up the action, the
[184]

words and the manner in which the words are said. At all events, given the words, the way in which the words are spoken is the principle component of the characterizations, the motivations, the interactions of person on person, the wit, the comicality, the dramatic tensions, etc., which constitute a play. And it is to this more than to any other one thing that the adult will give the closest attention, helping the children, through the questions he asks, to seek out the image of the person and situation and to articulate it in tone, pitch, inflection, modulation, rhythm, phrasing, timing and stress of voice. But these elements cannot very well be broken down for children and expressed as technique. They must be dealt with in their total meaning. How would So-and-so speak under such conditions? Would he shout? Would he whisper? Is he angry? Is he half amused? What are his attitudes toward life? What is in his soul?

Certainly the last must be the question the boy who played Judge Danforth asked himself when he probed the resources of his imagination. He must have worked by himself, getting the feeling of that soul into his chest and throat and going over the words again and again until they corresponded to the image and manifested that soul. There is no other way, and the adult can do no more than ask questions and discuss meanings, trusting, for the most part, that if the child truly sees what the words mean, he will find his way to their expression.

Nevertheless, there are ways the adult can help the child give that expression fuller communication. As great as was the impact of the messenger's sudden, leaping entrance, his account of the assumption of Oedipus was less satisfactory in its entirety. However ringingly his words were charged with excitement and wonder, in his excitement he ran his words together, and his personal speech was marred with a certain nasality. The personal problem of his speech is something that would not, perhaps, have yielded to the kind of help that could be given by an adult not specifically trained in speech. Our personal idiosyncrasies of speech are deep-seated. The Massachusetts man will continue all his life to talk about taking a *barth* in a hotel on *Pack* Street in *Bahston*. The boy from Castine, Maine, will make a very thin distinction between *boat* and *bought,* though he will make a broad distinction between *boy* and *buoy*. The Italian-American youngster from Reading, Pennsylvania, will perhaps never realize that his completely native English smacks of the Pennsylvania Dutch country. The child who has no trouble saying *le, la,* or *lui* in French will cling tenaciously to *hawwy* instead of *holly* and *dowwars* instead of *dollars*. Men of great scope, elected or appointed to offices in which they represent all the people, will continue, despite speech lessons, to represent their sectional origins in the pronunciation of certain words or the inflection of certain idioms.

The adult who is not specifically trained in speech may be able to do little about localisms, less about personal idiosyncrasies, and still less about actual speech defects, but he can and should correct correctable errors. The boy who, playing Hamlet, said to Ophelia, "Get you-all to a nunnery," can leave the *all* out of *you-all*. Clear mispronunciations can also be corrected— at least in rehearsals, though the eight year old who seems to have corrected her pronunciation of "satyr," when confronted with an audience of other campers, may announce the title of the story about to be dramatized as "The Man and the Stair." A fifteen year old whose group has finally bullied him into saying *pref*erable may revert to pref*er*able on the night of performance.

It is interesting that in those areas of speech which are clearly an aspect of dramatization, children will often tend to resent suggestions rather than welcome them. For the most part, suggestions which are aimed at a more expansive body movement are welcomed, even by a child who cannot make the change immediately but must work his way into it. But when a child is asked to speak louder, he often considers the demand a violation of his integrity. "I am saying it this way," he says in effect, "because that's the right way to say it. If I say it louder, it isn't the same thing, it's something different, it isn't what I really feel."

Nevertheless, the adult must insist that the children speak loud enough to be heard. It is not merely a matter of common courtesy to their audience, but a matter of the amplification of expression, very similar to features of broadened movement. And because an adequate loudness is so obviously necessary to communication, the adult does not need to be too tender about it, even when he encounters a degree of irritability. He can sit in the back of the auditorium and yell, "Louder!" as often as he needs. He can call the scene being worked on to a halt, walk up to the edge of the stage and say firmly: "Look, it just isn't loud enough. Come on, now. Put more energy into it." Or he can stand at the back of the auditorium and discuss a minor problem with the young people onstage, doing so in a natural tone of voice, then adding: "Have you been hearing me? Of course you have. Have I sounded as though I were speaking unnaturally? No. So you see, it's perfectly possible to talk loud and sound natural, just as I am doing now. Go ahead and do the same thing!" In this way, the young people will begin to raise the scale of volume of their voices until, on this new scale, their way of saying things will seem to them as natural, as sensitive and appropriate as before. But inevitably, in speaking louder, they will also begin to react on each other in stronger ways. They will feel more force in their parts, and will accomplish an expansion of speech comparable to that of moving across the whole stage instead of just a piece of it.

The problem may be more difficult in the case of the youngster who understands that the character he or she is being is a person who speaks softly, or that at this moment the depth of the person's feeling can only be expressed through a quiet utterance. In the case of the girl who played Mrs. Proctor, for example, it was necessary to work with her alone for a session or two—not because her own voice was too soft, for her voice

could be piercing if she wanted it to be—but because of her feeling for the character. A passage would be selected and she would
speak these lines from the stage while the teacher sat in the back
of the auditorium. She would go over the passage once, then
again, then again, making it a little louder each time, but holding
tight to her feeling of great depths of stillness, until she could
feel these depths and yet be perfectly heard. It is for such reasons, among others, that speech which in interpretive terms
would be called "normal"—that is, speech which is not respond-
ing to any emotional urgency—should be somewhat louder than
the demands of audibility require. This "normal" speech will
establish a fairly loud and energetic "norm," on the basis of
which the energy of more urgent speech will have a more
powerful impact, and things that are said quietly, though heard
clearly and distinctly, will, by contrast, create a sense of deep
hush.

Not all problems are problems of loudness. It is possible to
split the ears of an audience with incoherence. Professional
Shakespearean actors, at least minor actors, often assault our ears
in this way, though we would have no idea what they were talking about unless we knew the play. There are problems of haste,
of running words together, of poor enunciation. Americans tend
to give lip service, but little tongue-and-teeth service, to *d*'s
and *t*'s.

A boy rushes onstage, wildly shouting: "He slying thenna
dish now, his heh manna with bluh!"

"What did you say?" cries the adult, almost as wildly. "He
what?"

The boy stops dramatizing and, with an overmeticulousness
which expresses his annoyance with both the adult and himself,
says: "He'Z lying theRe in the diTCH now—his hair maT-TeD
with blooD!" But in the end he finds that the force which he has
been attaining through sheer rapidity can be translated into
emphasis, and that *ditch, matted* and *blood* have a character of

their own which he had been trampling over in his haste. They spit themselves firmly.

Like the matter of speaking with enough volume, the matter of not running words together is more than just courtesy. Within the words themselves, within the groupings of words as phrases, phrases as sentences, sentences as passages, lies the potential of a passage for expressive communication. Phrasing is the exploration of that potential. It is a complex matter and, like other expressive aspects of speech, should be left for the most part to the child's way of dealing with it under the impulse of his dramatic image, except where haste and impetuosity are causing his communication to be blurred. And yet, in a sense, it is one of the elements of dramatization which have been building up on the basis of experience, especially the reading of poetry. The adult's help in reading poetry is more welcome to a child than his interference with feeling and phrasing when the child is actively dramatizing. A group of children doing choral reading, for example, will find their difficulty with synchronization disappear when they begin to see a poem as a pattern of phrases. The child reading a poem which others are dramatizing in pantomime wants to read the poem well and will look for adult help. The adult can show the child how the poem tends to phrase itself, and how these phrase elements are the basis for the timing and emphasis and counter-rhythm of speech which plays against the meter of the poem. A girl who read Blake's "The Tyger" for a shadow puppet dramatization broke the poem down into its elements and put them back together in a strange but very effective way. Her initial problem was that she followed the rather bold rhythm of the poem monotonously. Instead of correcting this fault, she turned it into a virtue. She slowed the poem down to the point where the strong beat, together with her own resonant and rather beautiful voice, established an independent existence, long and bell-like, for each image-giving word.

A boy who read Eliot's "The Hollow Men" achieved tremendous tension through such slowness, but with a more skillful use of phrasing. His pauses were daringly long and strained attention almost to the breaking point. The pantomimists picked up his tensions, and altogether it was a stunning dramatization. It would have been futile for an adult to have discussed phrasing with this boy before he found the image he wanted, but once he found the image he wanted he also found the phrasing to go with it.

Nevertheless, it may sometimes be valuable for the adult to call a child's attention to the possibilities which an examination of phrasing may unfold for expanded expression in a passage from a play. He may sit down separately with certain children —especially those who have long passages which do not yield readily to spontaneous attack—and help each one explore the possibilities. He may say: "Very good, Nancy, very beautiful. But I want you to do something. When you go home tonight, I want you to go over that passage and break it down. Put long pauses everywhere that a pause can go—prepositional phrases, verb phrases, noun phrases, things like that—you know what they are. Also try putting pauses in some places where they don't normally go. When we feel something strongly, we often break our normal ways. So try it. Read the passage this way several times. Then put it together again and see what happens." This would be a gratuitous and even dangerous piece of advice to a youngster who isn't ready for it, but for a girl or boy with a fine sense of language, it might open the doors onto a new dynamic of expression. This is an area where the adult will do what he sees to do, keeping in mind, however, that meaning without technique is valid, but technique without meaning is worthless.

Related to this matter of phrasing, but more closely related to some of the hidebound attitudes of children touched on in the last chapter, is the assumption the child automatically makes that a passage assigned to a character is of one piece. For example:

BOB (*Ashamed and bitter*): Well, now you know.

ANGIE: Yes. Now I know. And I understand. But I can't help wishing you hadn't told me. By the way, John and Alice Greenough are dropping over this evening.

The girl who is playing Angie reads these lines, stops, comes out of character, and looks with embarrassed appeal to the adult.

THE ADULT: What goes on in this passage, Angie?

THE GIRL: Angie closes the subject. But what have John and Alice Greenough got to do with it? I mean, I'm not stupid —she's changing the subject—but it sounds so silly.

THE ADULT: But does she change the subject in a split second? Allow yourself a little time, a little space.

THE GIRL: Oh!

She runs through the passage again and now it goes like this:

ANGIE: Yes. Now I know. (*She pauses and gestures as though to put her hand on Bob's shoulder.*) And I understand. But I can't help wishing you hadn't told me. (*She goes to the window, center rear, and looks out on the yard.* [At this point someone in the group suggests that children should be heard at play outside.] *She speaks without turning, but not quite mastering her hurt.*) By the way, John and Alice Greenough are dropping over this evening.

So she has made sense of it, because she has seen that Angie's passage is not of a piece, but of two pieces, and with the perception she has developed a broader concept of the realities she is dramatizing. And she has improved the communication of these realities through a more deliberate tempo and pace.

In regard to cues, the child's tendency is to think along the same lines: "When Constance is through saying that, I begin to say this." Or: "When Tom is through saying that, I enter and say my line." The adult can encourage the child to think more along such lines as: "Before Constance is through speaking, I cut in." Or: "After Constance is through speaking, I wait, I think, I rap my knuckles on the arm of the chair. Then I speak." Or: "I come rushing in while Tom is speaking, blurting out what I have to say as I rush in." Or: "When Tom is through speaking, I stay in the wings and permit him to reflect his disquietude in panto-mime, *then* I enter. I study him for a few moments, and only when he looks up and sees me do I begin to speak."

Even high school students with a good dramatic sense are often unimaginative in such matters. Many times in a script, a line of dialogue is cut off in the middle. The youngster who has such a line stops at an "and . . ." or a "but since . . . ," then the next speaker says what the script gives him to say. Big boys and girls feel foolish when this happens, especially when they are the ones who have the unfinished sentence. No one stops a sentence in the middle because someone is *going* to cut in—they stop be-cause someone *has* cut in. What happens in reality and what should happen in a play is that one person's words overlap the words of another. This is something children enjoy when they see the possibilities. They find a quickened pace in this new sense of naturalism. They can then see other places where two or more people can be speaking at once, because this is the way people talk in life and, if it is managed carefully, it won't cause an audience trouble. In a Broadway production of *The Three Sisters*, two of the sisters talked simultaneously for a fairly long time to two groups of guests, though, in the characteristic man-ner of Chekhov's negative tensions, no one was paying them much attention, except the audience, who could hear them both and found them touching and beautiful. But to return to the un-finished sentence, an unfinished sentence must of course be inter-preted. For it may not represent another speaker's cutting in. It may be that the speaker is flustered. It may be that his thought trails off as his emotions rise and silence him. It may be that he thinks better of what he was about to say. Even very perceptive youngsters may not think of these possibilities for themselves—they will need adult help.

It is difficult to leave the question of speech without touching on the use of "dialects." Given the American melting pot—a melting pot from which the rich ore of the nationality group cultures has too often been poured out as though it were slag—children can often "do" all manner of "dialects," but imagine for a moment a group of American children doing Sholom Aleichem's stories with a Jewish accent! The people in the stories are presumably speaking their native tongue among themselves, and we must suppose that they speak their native tongue natively and not with some foreign accent. Therefore, if we transpose their native tongue into English, they must seem to speak English natively—shrewdly, pointedly, with certain idioms of mind which are the idioms of their way of looking at life—but not with a foreign accent!

Fortunately, there is not much good material for children to dramatize which poses this problem. The exception is the Irish plays. These are great plays, and, as we have previously indicated, excellent material for boys and girls as young as thirteen. Certainly *Riders to the Sea* does not have to be done with a brogue. The lilt and music are inherent in the language that Synge has written, and if children can capture this lilt and this music, their native American way of pronouncing English words will be beautiful and right. In O'Casey's plays, however, the brogue is part of the texture, and the play cannot be done if the brogue cannot be done. What is wrong, of course, is that children will accept the various stereotyped "dialects" of various peoples as the real thing. The real thing is not wrong. If children have real opportunity to hear different ways in which different regional or nationality groups speak, if their adult leadership is able to help them to capture what they really hear, and if the material they are working with does not use the speech patterns of a people in ways that are disrespectful or contemptuous, then they will have extended their insights into the musical potentials of speech. The high school juniors who performed *The Plow and the Stars* spent a good deal of time in conversation with women who worked in the school cafeteria. The speech of these women was the native English of people who had been born and brought up in Ireland, and it was sweet on their tongues.

The question of speech patterns strikingly different from those young people normally use is closely related to the question of dramatic style. Our tradition is realistic and naturalistic. The force and beauty of many original plays of younger children or of the performance of standard plays by teenagers reside primarily in the integrity of vision and the dramatic expression of that vision in naturalistic ways. Within a group of children working in a naturalistic tradition, the discrepancies in personal manner and style, and even discrepancies of talent, are often not different in kind from the differences between one person and another, so the differences do not greatly mar their collective achievement. When, however, they attempt to dramatize in a given style—the high style of classical French comedy, for example, or the conventions of Chinese poetic drama—the discrepancies between the skills of one child and another can be aesthetically damaging. In many cases, too, creative integrity will be suffocated in drill and mannerism. A French adult leading children's dramatics with French children might find it easy and natural to work toward the style of Comédie Française and Chinese children whose experience in seeing plays is of a certain kind might move toward that kind of style, but style involves either an existing tradition or else a depth of acquired knowledge on the part of the adult leader, and this specific knowledge most adult leaders of children's dramatics do not have.

A high school senior, directing a play he had written, tried to make use of a style very much like Brecht's adaptation of Chinese style. He and the teacher were in conflict on this matter, the teacher feeling that the boys he had to work with could support what the writer-director wanted to say much more forcefully if they were permitted to handle the material with naturalistic vigor. He did not convince the boy, however, and so the play was performed in as close an approach to the style that the author-director wanted as his cast could achieve. The outcome was hard to evaluate. The actors were painfully awkward in their handling of the stylization, and yet there was no doubt that the stylization, however faltering, was more appropriate for the play, more searing, than naturalism could have been. There is also no doubt that young people should not be discouraged from experimentation.

High school students working with an imaginative French teacher, especially one who knows French life and culture first-hand, often do exciting things with Molière. One cannot say that they achieve the style of Comédie Française, but they will sometimes have seen that company do Molière in one of its visits to America and will have picked up some pointers. Anyway, they achieve a sprightly style—a sharpness of tongue and gesture as authentic as their French. Frenchmen would not mistake them for French, but Americans, without knowing, would not assume they were American youngsters—especially some of the marvelous Dorines! They throw back their hands as if to say, "How can M'sieu be so irrational!" and, maidservants though they are, chew out their wealthy employers for their stupidities with a voluble combination of candor and archness.

A foreign-language play is a good place to experiment with style and technique, for its educational goals are somewhat different from those of other dramatics, the very achievement of a play in a foreign language being something of a *tour de force.* Comedy, too, is an opportunity for stylistic experiment—even broad and "hammy" comedy. For "ham" is a kind of style—an expansion, an overdoing for comic effect. Some youngsters, feeling the relationship between dramatic expression and personal integrity, will resist for a time the demands which some comedies make. This was true at the outset of a high school dramatization of Cocteau's *The Eiffel Tower Wedding Party*—when the youngsters relaxed, however, they had a lot of fun. The play

is a marvelously hammy fantasy—a comic forerunner of the theater of the absurd. But its absurdities are rational absurdities.
That is, they are funny. Every time the photographer who is
taking a picture of the wedding party says, "Watch the little
birdie!" some enormity comes out of the camera—an ostrich in
white tights and tu-tu strutting and blinking her eyes in delicious
overstatement, or a lion down on all fours in a lion suit. Hidden from the tender eyes of the audience by a tablecloth, the lion
makes a meal of pure ham—that is, he eats the fatuous old general, and emerges with the general's boot in his mouth. Later the
general is restored, yielded up by the camera. He walks with
only one boot and seems to have returned from a long journey.
As he rejoins the wedding party he strikes, according to one of
the "phonographs" who narrate all this, a "modest pose"—that
is, a pose of outrageously overstated pomposity. Such stylistic
extensions are not very important, but they are liberating and
give young people a feeling for bold movement and enlarged expression.

For obvious reasons, most of the illustrative material relating to expanded communication, whether of speech or movement, has been drawn from the work of older boys and girls.
They can sustain their creative concept over longer periods of
time, and this concept can stand up under the intense rehearsing
in which the techniques will be worked out. Nevertheless, many
of these matters, in modified form, will find their way into the
help which an adult gives to younger children. He will make
suggestions and ask questions to help the children improve their
play, but he will do so in such an easygoing way that the children won't lose their sense of fun and, with it, their spontaneity.
"I can't see some of you, you're all bunched together," an adult
working with eight or nine year olds might say. "Do people always stand still when they're talking? Don't they sometimes go
on with what they're doing and talk across the room? . . .
Would Jack just walk in? How would he come in? That's right
—he'd tiptoe in. How would Maureen go out? Of course—

Betty's right. She'd toss her head and walk out proudly. . . .
Tommy, I can't hear you. . . . Stop mumbling, Lucy—yell.
Anything—I want to hear you yell. Good. Now talk that loud.
. . . You know, when you did this part the first time, you were
all talking at once. It was better that way. Go ahead—talk all at
once for a ways. I'll tell you when to stop." If such observations
are made by the adult in an easygoing way and with not too great
a frequency, the children will appreciate this kind of help very
much. For in their own way, and within the framework of en-
joying themselves, children of this age want to do a good job. If
the adult's manner is not a nagging one, they won't feel nagged,
but supported. Their spontaneity will not be impaired, their own
approach not interfered with. The adult will not give them
mechanisms in place of their own image, but will help them, in
much the way he helps older children, to do a good job of dramatizing their story or yarn.

15
ooooooooo
Scenery and Lighting

MOUNTING A PLAY is an exciting process for children. It includes a wide assortment of activities, some of them technical, all aesthetically important, many dramatically important, some requiring great ingenuity, others requiring creative vision. Lighting a play, constructing the scenery, acquiring and building major properties and hand properties, improvising and making costumes, applying make-up, etc., are all part of the business of mounting a play.

A good children's play can be performed with no scenery

at all, or with only a few symbolic elements to suggest a scene, or with fully articulated backdrops or flats. In summer situations, nature itself can provide the scenery—woods, a lawn, a body of water, a vista of mountains or tillage. The group can choose the setting most appropriate for its play and mark off the acting area and the audience area. Some camps build outdoor amphitheaters, the seats on a slope, the acting area on level ground at the foot of the slope. Amphitheaters have several distinct advantages: flats can be set up, electric wiring can be installed for night performances, a curtain, even wing curtains, can be rigged and poles planted from which scenery can be suspended. The disadvantage is that the scenic background is fixed, so that the amphitheater loses the exciting possibilities of different settings.

A camp group presenting *The Drinking Gourd* had planned an ingenious staging. They planned to dramatize the scenes at different parts of the camp grounds, using a narrator who would invite the audience to get up and move from place to place. The scene at the slave cabin would have the audience seated about an old well head, facing a brick summer kitchen. This building was to be the slave cabin and the action would take place in front of it and, to some extent, inside, seen through an open window. The meeting with a conductor of the Underground Railroad was to take place at the campfire site in the woods. For the slaves' escape, the audience was to sit on the beach of the pond and watch their flight by water. There was talk of borrowing a neighboring farmer's beagle to act as a bloodhound, but the general opinion was that he was too good-natured for the part. The scene in the barn of the Quaker—in which the slaves, wearing broad-brimmed straw farmer's hats, pitching hay in the presence of the slave catchers—was set, appropriately, in the barn. The final symbolic scene on Freedom Road was to take place on the county road itself with the freed slaves, singing "The Drinking Gourd," sweeping past an audience lined up as if to watch a parade. It was exciting staging and very effective in rehearsal,

the natural terrain inspiring a bold and natural action. If one is
acting out creeping through tall grass and climbing into a boat
by actually doing it, the pantomime is impeccable and yet
dramatically inspiring, for the weariness and the wariness, the
fear and the resoluteness, which are the content of the pantomime, take on the same impeccability.

Unfortunately for this imaginative experiment, it rained on
the night of the performance. Fortunately, however, the group
had rehearsed indoor alternatives, and the play was given in the
barn. For the final scene, though—while the audience watched
from the shelter of the barn eaves—the freed slaves swept down
the road, singing "The Drinking Gourd" in the rain. Outdoors,
children can play perfectly well without scenery, whether the
scene they are enacting is supposed to take place indoors or out.
Indoors, however, children like to have scenery and ought to be
encouraged to experiment widely with it. The simplest, the most
usual, and—up to the point where experience confers a higher
sophistication—the most creative way of setting a scene is with a
large backdrop made of wrapping paper, extending the full
height and length of the stage. Let us assume that the height is
ten feet, the length twenty feet. Two twenty-foot strips are un-
rolled from a roll of five-foot-wide wrapping paper. These two
pieces are stuck together with a twenty-foot length of gummed
tape, four or six inches wide. This ten by twenty foot sheet of
paper is then spread out on the floor or the ground, wherever
there is room for it.

Following a discussion of what a scene should contain, it is
sketched in with charcoal or chalk. Then the drawing is painted
with tempera. The less the adults do, the better it will be. Very
seldom do children get a chance to paint in such a large way, and
anyone acquainted with children's art work—the color, the impact, the two-dimensional force—will understand that this is an
opportunity for magnificence which children will not fail to
take advantage of. The furrowed terrain of China, terrace on
terrace, mounting toward distant summits; a sea coast; a forest; a

garden and flowering trees; the half-timbered interior of an English tavern; a hay loft; a basement room with water pipes and a dirty washstand—any conceivable setting can be expressed in striking shapes and colors.

When the backdrop is finished, it can be hung on a batten and hoisted. It is a good idea to have another batten attached along the bottom of the backdrop to keep it from curling. If there are several scenes, each can be attached to a separate batten, then rolled up and tied with string. If the stage permits, these battens can all be hoisted, one behind another, but if the stage equipment doesn't permit a series of battens, it is possible to rig up a clothesline on pulleys to serve the same purpose. When the play starts, one of the backdrops is already in place. At the end of the scene, the batten holding this backdrop is lowered and the backdrop either cut away and discarded, or, if it is to be used again, rolled and tied, and the batten hoisted back into place. Then the batten on which the backdrop for the next scene is rolled is lowered, the strings cut, the batten hoisted again, and the scene is in place. Ingenious youngsters, with a little practice, learn to make such scenery changes very quickly. Some youngsters know a way of releasing the strings from a rolled-up backdrop without lowering the batten. By this device, the new scene simply flutters into place. This writer has seen this done many times in plays he has helped children produce, but he has never been able to figure out how they do it.

Backdrops of this kind can have windows and doors painted on them, or doors and windows can be cut out. A door, however, would have to be merely a doorlike opening, for a real door cannot be hung on one of these wrapping-paper backdrops. For a real door a substantial flat must be used. The windows cut in these backdrops, however, are functional. Pasted-on strips of paper can give the appearance of panes, so that the audience can see through the backdrop into a garden, for instance. A player can be seen passing by, and he can even stop at the window, either talking or waving to someone inside.

Most of the major furnishings of a room are better come by if they are painted on a backdrop than by real acquisition—a Victorian sofa, for example, a tester bed, an enormous stone or brick fireplace with objects on the mantel, a grandfather clock or a cabinet full of rare old china. In this way, only such large properties as the players will actually use need be bothered with.

Children with their ingenuity and sense of fun can often see ways to make painted things in a backdrop play a tantalizing counterpart against real elements. For example, a boy sucks on a sourball which he has magically abstracted from a candy jar painted onto the scene. The members of a Japanese underground run off actual leaflets on an actual mimeograph machine, and then wash their hands in pantomime at a washstand painted on the backdrop. This kind of interaction of the actual and the imaginary is more exciting—more titillating, certainly—than a consistent naturalism.

Wrapping paper can do many things. A group of eleven year olds once dramatized the folk song "The Golden Vanity." The scenery committee provided a stretch of wrapping-paper ocean waves twenty feet long and about three feet high, mounted on sticks and wooden bases and set on the floor of the auditorium at the foot of the stage. Into this sea the heroic cabin boy jumped, and the watchers could see his head and arms as he swam over to sink the Spanish enemy; from this sea, they saw him pulled, ex- hausted and dying, by his shipmates, and lowered again into this sea, his watery grave. The waves were stylized—curling peaks about to break, and as alike as peas in a pod—the stylization sup- porting a subtle tongue-in-cheek which the children brought to bear, but without parody or travesty, on the sentiment of the song.

Another group made a huge yellow taxicab out of wrap- ping paper, big enough for two people to sit in, one in back and one in front. They cantilevered it on two office chairs on little wheels, and maneuvered it onto the stage, changed a tire and picked up a passenger, the passenger and driver both visible through the cut-out windows. However, the limitation of the stage wings being what they were, this taxicab, which had come on stage frontward, had to back off. A life-sized nag used in the same dramatization suffered the same limitation, as did the life-sized nag and goat in *Mottel, the Cantor's Son.* The Chelm goat used in a camp dramatization transcended this limitation and looked like a goat from either side, though end on he looked like two sheets of wrapping paper stapled to sticks. Obviously such staging is more suitable for broad humor or zany fantasy than for more serious expression, where illusion is important.

What can be done about staging, of course, will depend greatly on the kind of stage available. Many church parish houses and community centers have raised platforms with a back wall and no wings. In the case of a stage with no wings, wing flats can be made, or draperies hung at the sides to conceal players who are waiting to make their entrance. Most public schools have long, high stages with good wings, but they are usually shallow and have back walls, being designed not so much as places for children to put on plays, but as elevations from which children can be talked at by adults. If such stages have battens, backdrops can be used. If not, then the wrapping-paper backdrops can be secured—"secured" is perhaps a hopeful word for it—against the back wall with gummed tape. Under such conditions, quick changes of scene are out of the question and a base scene will have to be used. If the back walls are of unpainted brick, or if they are strongly colored, it is difficult to do anything with them. If, however, they are white or off-white, a good deal can be done through the use of lighting combined with more sophisticated approaches to scenery.

A more sophisticated approach is when a scene is created, not by elaboration, but by suggestion. In its simplest form, a scene consists of lighting plus one or two symbolic elements. For example, in the dramatization of the American Indian folk story "The Healing Waters," the muslin scrim, or cyc, was lighted in such a way as to establish the mood of the story. Beyond this, the stage contained only a wrapping-paper totem pole, which established, by a kind of metonymy, an Indian village. In a blackout, the totem pole was slid offstage and two trees, similarly made from wrapping paper mounted on wooden sticks and wooden bases, were slid on to represent the forest. The change required only a few seconds, the narration continuing during the blackout so that the story suffered no interruption.

In an outdoor amphitheater, eight and nine year olds set up a single, broken Greek column (also made of wrapping paper mounted on sticks) as a setting for the dramatization of Greek myths. For the final scene of a long original play dealing with the evolution of man's thinking from imitative magic to scientific inquiry, eighth graders asked the stage crew to give them "sky blue pink" lighting for the final scene. The stage crew obliged, lighting the cyc with vaporous colors suggestive of dawn. In the middle of the stage the eighth graders set one thing—a crossroads signpost, white, with the lettering in black in various languages, the signs pointing in a variety of directions. It was a striking scene—very symbolic and ethereal.

Except for spanning the entire length of a stage with an unbroken surface, flats can do anything that wrapping paper can do and more. They can create three-dimensional scenery, and provide a hanging for actual doors, etc. A painted backdrop may represent a street in a medieval town. But one or another of the buildings may be extended by flats into the third dimension, characters coming and going through an open door and a woman appearing at a second-storey window. Flats, however, cannot be made quickly. In a children's institution which does a lot of dramatics, a variety of flats of different sizes should be made and stored as permanent stage equipment. Then wrapping paper can be stapled to whatever flats are needed to make up a scene. Where fire regulations prevent the use of paper, the flats can be covered permanently with fire-resistant cloth. When a new play is given, the youngsters need only paint their new scenes over old ones. Scenery made of flats cannot be rolled up and hung on battens but flats can be put on wooden feet, or on hinged braces, and moved quickly in this way.

Cloth can be stretched on both sides of flats so that, by skillful positioning, a change of scene can be made by merely pivoting them around. In the case of *Blood Wedding*, one side of a number of flats was painted white to approximate the plastered interior of a farmhouse. The other side was built up with chicken wire and papier-mâché (mixed with asbestos powder for fire-proofing), the finished rocky surface painted white. By pivoting these flats around and changing the position of one or two of them, the change from the farmhouse interior to the whitewashed interior of a stone cave was made in a matter of seconds.

In their most sophisticated use, flats will be non-representational—that is, they will have aesthetic content through their color and their positioning, without looking like anything in particular. Of two professional productions of *Under Milk Wood*, one was done in the round without any scenery at all and with no costume changes; the other was weighted down and encumbered with its scenery. The approach a high school group made to mounting this play was quite possibly better than either. Each character had some one strong, identifying costume element—a hat, a scarf, an unbuttoned shirt, something which could be slipped into or out of almost instantaneously. The scenery was completely abstract. Tall, narrow flats were placed apparently at random, but actually at carefully studied intervals on the stage. Each flat was painted a single strong color—one a dark blue, one a lighter, purplish blue, another ochre, another a darker earth color. They formed a looming, labyrinthine darkness for the opening of the poem before daybreak, a bright town by daylight, a forest—Milk Wood itself—with the coming of night. These simple non-representational flats were extremely "active." They were active in regard to changes of lighting, and they were active in regard to the movements of the players. Because of these flats, they could emerge from many places, appear suddenly and be gone, ceremoniously or unceremoniously, as the narration darted swiftly from one to another of the people of Llareggub.

In the Walden School, with which this writer has been closely associated, the stage is small, about twenty by fifteen feet in the acting area. The wings stage right are so small as barely to provide room for the wing flats. The wings stage left are more ample. The stage has, however, one feature which has made possible some very exciting stagings: it has no back wall, and the rear of the stage is hung with a scrim of unbleached muslin hung from a batten. The advantages of this are numerous. The muslin cyc is more sensitive to lighting than a solid wall. It can be lighted from behind so that shadowgraph and silhouettes can be used or a scene can be back-lighted; slides and projections of all kinds can be cast on the cyc; and, most important of all, it can be taken down and the green room in back can become part of the acting area.

The green-room floor is on the same level as the auditorium floor, so that the stage forms a kind of island between the two. The green room contains the theatrical switchboard, made by the high school stage crew, along with stacks of flats, A-ladders, bins of floods, spots, gelatines, the Linobach projector, extension cords, assorted properties from plays given years ago, etc. There are two fire exits and a door to the men's room, which is used as the boys' dressing room during performances. On one occasion, a father went to the men's room during an intermission. The scene immediately after the intermission was one of the scenes for which the cyc was taken down and the green room opened up as part of the acting area. No one noticed the father going to the men's room or that he was still there when the next scene started. As a result, his exit from the men's room constituted an unexpected entrance into the scene, a bit part which he played with dignity under the circumstances. Of course, when this green room is opened up and made part of the acting area, no central action can take place there. However, a character can make an entrance in depth from there, or an action can begin there and be brought up onstage for focus.

Two prison scenes have used this staging. Black strips of paper hung from a rear batten provided the prison bars. The prisoners were onstage, but prison guards and other officials made their entrances from the green room. The deep space behind the prison bars intensified the sense of confinement.

In a performance of Arthur Miller's *A Memory of Two Mondays*, the stage was the shipping room and the green room the storage area of an automobile-parts warehouse. As the working men left with order slips and returned with axles or differentials, they would be seen going down the steps and picking up the merchandise and returning with it. In this instance, much of the green room paraphernalia—the A-ladders, the fire extinguishers, the fire buckets, the lighted exit signs, the bins of junk—became part of the *mise en scène*. A large NRA poster and a huge picture of Franklin Delano Roosevelt set the period of the play and at the same time masked out the switchboard and other inappropriate things. The play called for dirty factory-type windows, which two of the more salvageable characters of the play wash on their own time in order to let in some sunlight. In this production, these windows existed as a purely imaginary barrier between the audience and the players. As the actors wiped away with cloths at the imaginary dirt, the lights brightened, and the audience found itself occupying part of the vast space created by the staging of the play.

In *Rhinoceros*, the opening scene is a sidewalk café in a French city. For this the cyc was taken down, but the green room was not exposed. Instead, flats, painted in sharp perspective of an avenue lined with buildings characteristic of a French city, were run back on either side, converging toward each other eight or nine feet into the green room. The two flats were set at such angles to each other as to mask the green room out entirely, yet a player could make an entrance between them. The effect was an exciting *trompe d'oeil*, in which painted depth and actual depth were combined to project a very deep vanishing point. Such a deep vanishing point pulls the eye into it. As a result, a characterizing first entrance, made between the two flats, was in extraordinarily sharp focus. First Jean and, a little later, Berenger, made their first appearances as though from far away, and climbed the steps to the stage as though they were climbing a little rise of ground at the end of an avenue.

A camp to which previous mention has been made had a stage with similar advantages, except that when the back curtain was taken down, the audience looked through the stage into the out of doors beyond. On one occasion the camp goat intruded himself into a play on this account.

The scene was very sad—the burial of a young fighter in the French Resistance movement. The back curtain was open and the youth was being buried in the out of doors. It was raining and the players stood in raincoats at the grave of their comrade. At this moment the goat entered the scene, but somehow or other he seemed touched by what he saw, and stood still and said nothing. It was deeply impressive—the players in wet raincoats, the real rain dripping steadily from the leaves of a great maple tree, the countryside beyond, and the silent goat contributed such a sense of reality to the sorrow of the play as to make it almost overwhelming.

This camp had one season as its nurse an old woman who, to put it tactfully, was eccentric. One evening a teenage group was performing a play of their own about some crisis of social conscience in a lower middle class family. The curtain at the back of the stage was drawn against the out of doors. As the crisis of the play approached, this curtain parted and the nurse appeared, walked across the stage and took a place in the audience. Her completely unrehearsed role was as strangely appropriate as the goat's appearance at the burial, for she seemed for all the world like one of these old women some families keep, who appear unannounced from time to time on their way to

bedroom or kitchen—they are never introduced to visitors, and
no one seems to know just who or what they are.

But of course, neither the children nor the adult working
with them can bank on such felicitous accidents of staging. If an
adult would like to have stunning ideas for staging, he should let
it be known to the children that stunning ideas are in order.
Then the ideas will come from the children, often with more ingenuity than from the adult. On the other hand, the adult
should play a somewhat directoral role in regard to the mechanics of getting one scene off the stage and another on. It is unfair
to young people that their good work in enacting a play should
be cooled off by long stage waits. It is very much worth their
while to think out methods for quick scenery changes and to
rehearse them to achieve maximum efficiency. Young children
tend to develop plays with a number of scenes. But if the acting
time of a scene is seven minutes and the time between scenes is
ten minutes, it is difficult for an audience not to become condescending, or even bored. Except where scene changes coincide
with intermissions, it is usually necessary to make out worksheets,
to assign to this boy or that girl exactly what he or she is to take
off the stage or put on it, and to determine in what order things
go off and on, so that the scene changers don't bump into each
other. A change of scene which, handled haphazardly, could
require as much as ten or twelve minutes can be reduced to two
or three minutes and the change of pace is a lot of fun. (In a
play put on by thirteen year olds, the crew handling the changes
of scene attained such efficiency that in one of the rehearsals the
curtain no sooner closed on one scene than it somewhat ludi-
crously began opening on another. So in order not to distract the
audience by a display of organizational virtuosity, the curtain
puller was instructed to count to five after he got the curtain
closed before he started opening it again.)

A good children's play can be given with no scenery at all,
but unless one is going to disregard pantomime altogether and

present what used to be called a "radio play," some form of illumination is necessary. This writer has worked with lighting of the following kinds: daylight, out of doors and in camp recreation halls; campfires (or flambeaux made of oil-soaked rags on poles); kerosene, gasoline and sportsmen's-type battery lanterns; outdoor floodlights of the kind used on farms (or merely strings of bulbs); ordinary indoor electric lighting; improvised spotlights made from number 10 tin cans attached to poles; similar improvised spots made portable by mounting them on stands and running them on a couple of hundred feet of cable; theatrical lighting from a good switchboard made by a high school stage crew.

The staging plans for *The Drinking Gourd* included several kinds of lighting. The scene in front of the slave cabin was to be lit by a farm flood, attached, as such floods are, to the corner of a building. The meeting with the conductor of the Underground Railroad was to be lit by a campfire, the escape by water by portable spots. The barn scene was to be lit by the more or less permanent arrangement of number 10 tin cans which some of the campers had rigged up. Sholom Aleichem's retelling of the folk tale of the Chelm goat was done twice in the same camp by different age groups in seasons some six or seven years apart —both times by daylight. The program of Greek myths and poetry used to dedicate the amphitheater was illuminated by improvised spots rigged to poles with cross trees, a permanent installation.

These improvised spots are not hard to make. The camp kitchen supplies the number 10 cans, with one end already cut out. After the can is scrubbed good and shiny, a powerful bulb is inserted in the other end—properly insulated, of course. The can is swung on heavy wire or a bracket, so that it can be aimed. It is set up on a rafter or a pole or on cross trees, or, if it is to be portable, on a stand. With a little ingenuity, a frame can be made over the open end of the can so that colored theatrical gelatines can be slid in and out for colored lighting. Or the gelatines can simply be wired around the end of the can, though in this case color cannot be changed quickly.

One camp where exciting dramatizations were done had no electricity. It was for this reason, perhaps, that the camp went by daylight saving time. That is to say, many camps find it better to go on standard time so that there is darkness for certain evening programs, such as campfires, hay rides, dramatics, etc., and in hot weather the bunks have time to cool off before bedtime. Anyway, this was the camp where older boys dramatized *The Devil and Tom Walker,* Washington Irving's adaptation of a New England devil tale. It was presented late in July, after supper, but by daylight, in a recreation hall with open sides. A wire was strung across the hall to separate the acting area from the watchers and blankets were hung to this wire by safety pins to form curtains, which were pulled apart by the players at the start of a scene. Following the performance, the eight and nine year olds asked the big boys' counselor to do dramatics with them, and a week or two later they presented some simple folk tales to the rest of the camp, also after supper and by daylight. Then the older girls asked the counselor to do a play with them. They chose O. Henry's "The Last Leaf," but they reckoned without the inclination of the ecliptic, and by the time their play was ready, it was late into August and darkness fell between the end of supper and the beginning of the evening program. The only light that could be provided was furnished by a couple of old-fashioned kerosene lanterns. For dramatic purposes the light could have been brighter—the watchers had to stare alertly to catch any nuances of facial expression—but it was a lovely soft light, and the whole situation—the shortening days heralding the approach of fall—was very much in key with the autumnal mood of the story.

There is, of course, a close relation between the lighting that is available and the kind of scenery that recommends itself. There is no sense in developing elaborate scenery made up of backdrops or flats if daylight is going to expose painted scenery too candidly or if there is not enough light to give it meaning. *The Devil and Tom Walker* used no painted scenery at all, but established the scene through properties, using real felled tree stumps for the scene in the forest. The girls, for *The Last Leaf*, had one strip of wrapping paper hung up in back and painted to look like a brick wall. On this brick wall a vine without leaves was painted, and to this vine they attached paper leaves by means of pins, so that the leaves could blow off in the storm that took place between scenes, leaving only the one leaf which the watchers had seen the painter paint on the wall—a simple enough arrangement to be visible by the light of the kerosene lanterns.

Such lighting arrangements are at best only adequate. Jury rigged spots made from number 10 cans, if there are three or four of them, can give enough light and aim it in such ways that painted backdrops can be used. But none of these forms of improvised lighting constitutes an expansion of the visual image. It makes it possible to see what is in the acting area, but doesn't make any contribution to what is going on. Such contributions can be supplied only by a theatrical switchboard of the kind that public schools can afford and which are sometimes made as a project by teenagers, under expert adult leadership, for a school or settlement house. Such switchboards can do wonderful things. They can unify the elements of scenery and setting, or they can provide a very sophisticated setting without any scenery at all. They can vary the amount, scope and intensity of light. They can create changes and miracles of color. They can spot a small circle of the acting area, leaving the rest in darkness. They can wander about the auditorium and pick up players and action in strange places. They can dim up slowly and bring a scene slowly into visibility so as to draw the audience into its mood before the action begins. They can end a scene with almost instantaneous swiftness, if that is desired, or dim down slowly on one that needs a lingering conclusion. They can change the time of day, can bring daybreak or nightfall or the gathering or lifting of a storm. They can differentiate outdoors

from indoors and summer from winter. They can express the
burning of a nearby town and can change, by degrees, a not-too-
offbeat room into a surrealistic nightmare. They can express that
tonality of life which we call being "in the pink" or that other
tonality which we call being "blue."

This is all possible through a coordinated organization of
the number, the intensity, the positioning and aiming of the
lights, and of the colored gelatines that are set in frames over
the lights. The lights are rigged to a central switchboard with
switches and plugs and a rheostat or two. For the adult working
with children's dramatics who, like this writer, cannot do any
electrical work beyond putting a new plug on an extension cord,
there is something miraculous in such switchboard lighting, and
he feels acute gratitude for the technological interests which in-
spire many boys and some girls to make such switchboards and
to set up and operate the lighting for a play.

At Walden School, for example, the high school stage crew
will put in three or four long evenings, to the neglect of their
homework, to light an elementary school play. The teacher
working with the smaller children will come in to discuss the
scenes with the stage crew, recounting for them the gist of each
scene and some of the dialogue. When the teenagers feel they
have got the tone and mood of the play, they will get to work
aiming, positioning and coloring the lights which will express the
tone and mood in its various transshiftings. One boy is on the
top rung of a ladder, where he is adjusting the aim of a spotlight
and feeding different colors into it. Another boy is backstage at
the switchboard. A third stands on the stage, and seems to be
running the work. He calls to the boy on the ladder: "Left a little. —A little more. —There!" Then he calls back to the boy at
the switchboard: "Bring up seven! Bring down six! Cut borders!
No! You cut four! Bring back four and cut borders! What an
idiot! This time you cut six!" The boy at the switchboard responds: "Keep your shirt on! There—how's that?" "O.K.," says
the boy giving directions. "Come take a look."

The boy leaves the switchboard and the other comes down

off the ladder. All three look over the lighting. The switchboard boy shakes his head: "Try straw instead of pink in three and nine and a lighter red in seven." The ladder man climbs his ladder again with a new sheaf of gelatines. When he changes the gelatine in one spot, he drops down one or two rungs and, by making jerking movements, "walks" the ladder across the auditorium floor a few feet to the next spot, where he makes another change of gelatine. The three boys look again. The boy on the ladder says: "Bring four down a little and bring up three and two. Bring borders up a little—just a soupçon." The boy who had originally been giving directions goes to the switchboard and makes the changes. "Hey, great!" yells the original switchboard man.

"O.K.," says the boy on the ladder, "let's get it down." All three pull cue sheets from their pockets, check the lighting and jot it down. Then they run through the whole lighting of the play as it is shown on their cue sheets, one boy at the switchboard, the other at the curtain, the third standing in the center of the stage, feeding the cues from the play. The boy on the curtain whispers these cues to the boy on the switchboard through an intercom telephone—an instrument of their own devising. At one point the teacher intervenes: "No—don't start bringing the lights down when you hear the cue. There's a moment of silence, and then the lights come down." They go over it again. "Say when," says the boy onstage. He speaks the cue and starts counting: "One . . . two . . . three . . . four . . . five . . . six . . . seven . . . eight . . ." "When!" calls the teacher. "All right," says the boy to the others, "change your cue sheets. *Cue 17: 'Have a safe journey.' Count eight. Dim slowly to blackout. Narrator spot.* Get it?" "Good," says the teacher—which is about all the adult guidance these boys need in this aspect of their lives.

16

ooooooooo

Properties, Costumes and Make-up

BESIDES THE BASIC SCENE established by backdrops or flats, a
stage setting will usually require a number of major properties
—chairs, tables, a sofa, a log to sit on in the forest, a throne, a
wedding canopy, etc. In most situations with children doing
dramatics there is neither time nor skill enough to make major
properties, nor time enough to acquire the materials even if there
is the time to make them. And since the budget is seldom big
enough to buy them, the only means known to this writer for
acquiring major properties is scrounging. The nursery school

can be raided for cots—or, better still, the nurse has a large cot in her office which she is willing to lend for after-school rehearsals providing it is back in her office during the school day. For café chairs in another scene, six can be borrowed between two homes—and perhaps when we go to fetch a pair of these, they are given to us outright, a precious gift to be stored away when the play is over, for use in other plays. For café tables the school desks will do—they have thin and unobtrusive metal legs, and their tops will be covered with muslin tablecloths dyed in bright colors determined by the aesthetic requirements of the scene. A café awning can be made of wrapping paper and cantilevered from a flat by means of sticks. A huge driftwood log is called for. A girl spends the weekend at the beach, and on Monday morning her father drives her to school and the log emerges from the trunk of the car smelling of brine. A massive table is needed and there is one in the lobby. The rabbi at the temple down the block is most cooperative in providing a wedding canopy. Scholars' robes or religious vestments? The local parish priest is most obliging—and perhaps, too, he will lend a red velvet chair from the sacristy. A set of shelves from the English room comes into service as a bookcase—which can be turned around and painted with tempera to become a fruit-stand for a later scene. A three-dimensional fireplace? Wrapping paper over a framework of sticks. But a moveable hearthstone the slaves have really got to go down under for the play to make sense? A trap door in the stage! But the shop teacher is too busy to make one and the building superintendent has no authorization. This is a matter whose political subtleties evade the children, master scroungers though they are. So the teacher makes an appointment with the principal. It would be shameful to let the children down, he says in ten or twenty different ways. The building superintendent receives his authorization. An old-fashioned kerosene lantern is needed. A boy appears one morning with one that has red glass and is in sound working condition. It looks like the kind one sees on a barricade around a trench in the street. "Where did you get it?" asks the teacher. "I found it," the boy asserts firmly, but no account of where he found it can be pried out of him. "Well," says the teacher, "wherever you found it, put it back. There's money enough in the budget to buy one."

Minor properties and hand properties usually present less problems. Pans, dishes, books, lamps, knitting needles, and yarn are not hard to borrow. Swords, riding crops, magic wands, walking sticks, hoes, and spears are easily fashioned of wood or cardboard or combinations thereof. Even more authentic properties are not usually hard to come by. A pistol shot is called for. The athletic coach probably has a blank pistol he uses for starting races. Some boy collects old swords, another old guns. In fact, the only play in this writer's experience where there was much difficulty in getting minor properties was one which called for a lot of automobile parts. The group solved the problem by using wrapped-up cartons and packages. But it was a poor solution, and a little initiative, time and money spent at an automobile junkyard would have deeply enhanced the play's sense of reality.

As for costumes, they also can be scrounged or they can be rented, improvised or made. Renting costumes is expensive and unimaginative. In the play about China, some of the costumes were loaned by China War Relief. It was a reciprocal arrangement, for China War Relief received all the proceeds from admissions. These costumes were of wondrous beauty, and it was an aesthetic education to see, handle and wear them. They were worn, however, only by the wealthy characters. The peasants wore blue jeans, white T-shirts and those broad straw hats we see in pictures of Chinese laborers—but these hats were made of wrapping paper, painted to look like straw. The mandarin's daughter wore a khaki skirt she made for herself and a borrowed World War I soldier's blouse, whose decrepitude was appropriate to the historical situations with which the play dealt.

Most children's plays will be costumed through just such a

combination of borrowing, improvising and making. Plays which deal with modern life will call for clothing of a more or less usual kind but they must characterize. If Michael does not have any pants or ties which fit his characterization, possibly David does. David's own pants and ties seem everyday enough on David, because he can carry them, but on Michael they seem a little loud or extreme—and that, perhaps, is what we want. Similarly, Judy will be transformed by wearing Alice's mother's skirt and blouse.

When the action of a play takes place in a remote time or a different culture, borrowing may become difficult. In the ebb and flow of little girls' fashions, there will always be certain periods when red winter coats are very popular. In such periods the pickings are rich for costuming boys as British soldiers in plays about the American Revolution. But sometimes the only approach possible is the most creative one—that is, for the children to design, cut and sew their own costumes, though, given limits of time and skill, this approach may have to be combined with some improvisation. Chain mail can be made of cloth, breast plates of cardboard or even thin-gauge aluminum, helmets of cardboard, papier-mâché or even copper. The long dresses and bonnets of colonial women can be made up from a simple basic design, the dresses being dyed different colors, and character and class position being differentiated by collars and cuffs, the simplest of which can be made of light cardboard or heavy white paper. Crêpe paper, of course, will do wonders for costuming, but it may not stand up beyond the dress rehearsal and has a tendency to rustle quite audibly. Colonial men can wear collars and cuffs by which modern jackets can be adapted; pants can be stuffed into long stockings, and cardboard or aluminum buckles attached to loafers. The more costumes the children actually make, the more extensive their creative experience will be.

In this connection a question arises as to the importance of authenticity in costuming and properties. There are two answers to this question, one dramatic, the other educational. In terms of a dramatization, the question is one of aesthetic unity and of illusion—that is, of pleasing an audience, of drawing them into the story and of making them feel that what they are witnessing is real. Thus a rifle with a telescopic sight across the lintel of an eighteenth-century Pennsylvania fireplace would prove distracting, whereas a rifle jury rigged with a wooden stock painted brown and a barrel made of a dowel and painted black would not. Huck Finn and Tom Sawyer in blue jeans instead of nineteenth-century knee britches would not strike an audience at all amiss, but the same audience would be seriously dismayed if Tom were to appear in tartan plaid shorts. In other words, for dramatic purposes, one need only consider two things: Do the costumes and properties create an aesthetic unity which contributes to the mood of the story? And do they represent a reasonable enough facsimile of the time and place we are trying to depict as not to disrupt the illusion?

Educationally, however, there is much to be said for authenticity. When enough time is available, the children should be encouraged to do considerable research on the costumes, household objects, architectural details, landscape, instruments, etc., of the time, place and people in books, historical societies and museums. If a play is the outcome of a study of the people of Polynesia, it is to be presumed that the terrain—whether coral atoll or volcanic island—the houses—whether grass or wood—the garments—whether cloth or bark—the boats—whether catamaran or outrigger—the carved paddles, the ritual masks, and the pots, if any, will have been part of the study, and that, in putting on their play, their interest in the beauty of the artifacts will be one of the things the children will want to communicate. A similar concern for communicating their interest in artifacts may also be an element in the motivation of a play about China, or Italy, or Brazil, or colonial or federal America. Even so, there may be serious limitations as to how much can be done authentically, and a mixture of acceptable facsimile with some striking pieces of authenticity may be all that can be achieved.

A high school class once achieved a most complete approach to authenticity in the costuming and properties for a dramatization of Shaw's *Caesar and Cleopatra*. The crafts teacher, the art teacher and the teacher working with the play took the youngsters several times to the Metropolitan Museum to study Egyptian artifacts and dress. Researches were also undertaken on the garb, armor, weapons, etc., of Roman officers and foot soldiers. Except for the huge sphinx and the deployment of a few flats, not much was done with scenery. But costumes and gear had an almost total authenticity. Costumes, jewelry, daggers, swords and Roman pila were made by the students and were very colorful and beautiful.

Coiffures, however, presented difficulty. By means of a flesh-colored skull cap ringed with white hair, Caesar was made to look bald, but this rig never looked quite right. Charmian was the only one of the Egyptian women who had black hair long enough to be done in those gorgeous multiple Egyptian braids. Cleopatra was blonde and very fair skinned. She came to rehearsal one night with her hair experimentally dyed black—at least she had used a black dye (fortunately a very unstable one) but the effect of this dye on her hair was to make it look like dark greenish mud. Moreover, the girl's beauty lay to a great extent in her coloring, her features being delicate and regular, but not striking, and the green mud, by neutralizing her coloring, made her look rather plain. Fortunately, one of the more erudite boys was able to talk up a case for Cleopatra's Hellenic origins, and it was agreed that a blonde Cleopatra could be an assertion of historical ambiguity—and as a blonde her role was played.

Children's plays can be given without costumes at all—that is, the adult may think that the children are going to do their play without costumes—nothing may have been said about costumes, nothing planned about costumes—but on the afternoon or evening of the performance, the children will appear with all manner of rigs, some borrowed, some improvised, some secretly and laboriously made. A sophomore class presenting some scenes

from *Julius Caesar* at a school assembly agreed that everyone
would wear either dark pants and skirts with white shirts or
blouses, or vice versa. In the quarrel scene, however, both
Brutus and Cassius showed up in sheets wrapped around them
like togas, and the poet who intrudes fatuously on their argument wore a floppy beret and carried a cigarette in a ten-inch
holder.

The use of make-up has an importance similar to the use of
costumes in children's plays, by contributing to the aesthetic
unity of the play and to illusion. It helps establish certain facts
about the characters—age and even subtler things—and whenever young people are doing a more or less finished performance
under lights, all should wear some make-up, even a boy playing
the part of a boy of his own age, features and complexion. For
the absence of cheek coloring, lip coloring, eye shadow, etc.,
tends, under lights, to make the players look washed out, radiant
though they may be under other conditions.

Make-up can be improvised in large measure. For camp dramatics, the older girls and women counselors can supply powder
base, rouge, lipstick, eyebrow pencils and eye shadow. Charcoal
or burnt cork, or even burnt matches, can supply age lines and
cotton from the infirmary will supply full beards for ancient
men. In August, but not earlier, unless it is picked beforehand
and dried for awhile, cornsilk will provide younger men with
moustaches and whiskers. To stick these on, spirit gum is recommended. However, a strip of adhesive tape, folded double and
the two halves glued back to back, will achieve the same end—
one side being stuck to the cotton or cornsilk, the other to the
player's upper lip or chin. Of course, an organization which does
children's dramatics with any consistency should equip itself
with a kit of theatrical make-up, and a staff member should learn
how to apply it. In this connection, incidentally, cornstarch is to
be preferred over paste for whitening children's hair to make
them look gray, because it is more easily applied and washed out.
There may be a problem of allergies to certain make-ups. The

boy who played Jean in *Rhinoceros*—the character who turns into a rhinoceros more or less before the eyes of the audience—was seriously allergic to the green make-up which he was supposed to apply in increasing doses as he thundered back and forth between his bedroom and his bathroom. Despite M. Ionesco's insistence on things in his plays being done the way he wants them done, there is more than one way to skin a cat. The transformation, because it was achieved, not through theatrical device, but through the imaginative power of the boy who played the part, was far more powerful than it might have been if he had had to constantly break his concentration in order to slap on green make-up.

What do these things—scenery, lighting, costumes, make-up—amount to? There are four answers. The first is that they amount to nothing. In respect to the inner core of a child's dramatic creativity, they have no importance whatsoever, and the most beautiful children's dramatizations imaginable, whether the children are six or sixteen, can be done on a back lawn to an audience of a handful of friends, a couple of dogs and two or three parents. The second answer is that these aspects of play-making are valuable activities in themselves—valuable organizational, productive and creative experiences. The third answer is that they mean something to an audience. Whatever the dramatic achievement of the players, good scenery, costumes and make-up will intensify the illusion and draw the audience into those meanings which the players are trying to convey. The fourth answer is more complicated and to some extent contradicts the first. That is, in the final performance of their play, a group of children, set off by their own excitement and by the lights, the scenery, the make-up, the costumes and the first ripple of appreciation from the audience, may transcend itself. It is not that any child will do anything better than he has done in rehearsal. Quite the contrary. In the developmental stages of playmaking, there will be gestures, intonations, energized expressions, moments of insight, beautiful moments which will never quite so authentically recur. Even in regard to tension, to inter-action of one player on another, to pace and freedom, there will be times in the rehearsals whose magic is never quite recaptured. For this—and for more serious educational reasons—the process remains more important than the performance, which is merely the last, most crystallized phase.

Perhaps the word "crystallized" is the key to what we are trying to say. If we think of a crystallized stage as rigid in con-trast to fluid, then the concept escapes us. If, however, we think of crystallization as a qualitative change in which the molecules that compose a substance suddenly coalesce and unify them-selves in a shining way, then what often happens with a chil-dren's play when the curtain goes up on the scenery and on the children in costumes and make-up can be better understood. Though no one thing in the performance transcends that same thing as it was, at its best, in earlier stages, the play as a whole will often transcend itself, and the children will sustain their characterizations, their dramatic actions and their interplay in ways which seem inspired.

17

∘∘∘∘∘∘∘∘∘∘
The Adult Leader's Role

EXPERIMENTAL STUDIES support the experience and intuitive assumption of many teachers and most group workers that a democratic atmosphere is the best one for children to grow in— for example, the extensively documented study of Professor Kurt Lewin back in the thirties. Back of the stockyards in Chicago, groups of boys had established packing-case club houses for themselves in emulation of the Hooverville residences which adults were living in at the time. The University of Chicago was able to establish contact with a number of these boys' clubs and

[224]

to furnish them with adult leaders specifically trained, for purposes of the study, to give the boys either anarchic, autocratic or democratic forms of leadership. In broad terms the conclusions were much what one who had learned to look on children as human beings would expect. First, children will be rudderless and tend to waste their energies wrangling and pushing each other around if they are without adequate leadership. Second, a maximum of efficient operation will result if the adult leader is a boss who makes all the decisions and tells the children what to do. Whatever the adult wishes to accomplish for himself will be better accomplished in that way, but at considerable psychological cost to the children, a cost which the experiment showed to be far more disturbing and inescapable than one would have supposed. Third, children will be happiest together and will learn more extensively when the aim of the leadership is to help them develop their own ideas.

The leader of children's dramatics activity, then, will not be a "director." The "director" of a children's play tends to exploit children for his own ends, as a painter exploits pigment. The play director's creation is a play. But for the person concerned with the growth of children, it is not the play that is the thing, but the child. Creative dramatics, creative activity of any kind, the educational process in general—these are the means by which the adult gives shape to a creature whose principal business it is to shape itself.

In specific reference to children's plays, the question of whether a play will be better or worse if it is more the children's and less the adult's is irrelevant, for it is not the business of a person who works with children to put on plays, but to work with children. However, the question, though irrelevant, is capable of an answer: A play put on by children under the leadership of an adult who works well with children will usually be better than a play put on by children under the leadership of an adult who works well with plays. For the fact is that the creative potential of a group of children, once released, surpasses the creative potential of an adult who is using the children as the vehicle for his own self-expression. In this way, then, a democratic process is better both for the children and for the play.

But the last statement is just as false as it is true. For if this statement is to be true, the democratic process must greatly transcend democratic formalism. Let us look at the application of formal democracy, for example, to casting. Tryouts are held. One child gets a desirable part and another loses it by a vote of fourteen to six. The decision has been democratically arrived at. But the contest was a popularity contest and not an objective test of a child's handling of a dramatic role. The situation is flagrantly unfair in human terms and dishonest in creative terms. But the situation does not stop with casting, for a group that will vote for the more popular child will also vote to accept the ideas of the more popular or more powerful person, even when these ideas are distinctly inferior. Under such conditions, the play which the group produces will not be the product of its collective vision, but of its politics and tensions.

This is not the kind of problem which an inexperienced leader, or even an experienced leader with an inexperienced group, can solve all at once. He must, over a period of time, in order to create a climate of attention and respect for the less popular and less easily liked child, use all his skill, his wisdom, his insights and, when necessary, his authority—plus, above all, his long-range trust in children—to encourage the timid to speak out.

He will seek to get ideas considered on their own merits, but, more importantly, he will seek to get, from the stimulation of these ideas, new and better ideas, until an animated and open atmosphere is created, so that the question of who suggested what is lost sight of in the combat around the ideas themselves. Out of the combat of ideas, of interpretations and evaluations, grows a group working together toward common goals, its energies released toward common goals and not turned against each other. In this way the hurt a child suffers in not being cast for a part, or in having an idea rejected, is not intensified by the feeling that others are unfair to him or her as a person, but only, as President Kennedy said, that "life is unfair"—that is, that one person is really better for a part than another and that one person really does have a better idea than another, a reality to which children must begin to make an adjustment as soon as they go to school. The thing that hurts is to feel that one is less loved, less considered, or given less of a chance.

In case anyone remembers the Kurt Lewin study after thirty years, there is one point in its findings which needs clarification. The study showed that in the democratic group, the children learned more in *breadth* and in the autocratic group, they learned more in *depth*. What these terms meant in context was that a boy in a democratic group would learn something about the use of a hammer and a saw and a chisel and a plane, and that a boy in an autocratic group would learn much more about a saw *or* a hammer *or* a chisel *or* a plane or whatever tool the adult assigned him to. Translated into terms of children's plays, this use of the word "depth" would mean that one child would become a specialist in lighting, another in cutting and sewing costumes, another in designing and painting scenery, another in acting—this use of the term "depth" bearing no relation to the use of the term in such phrases as "depth of imagination" and "depth of insight." These are depths which autocratic leadership will stifle and which democratic formalism will trammel.

For depth of imagination and insight reside in the individual; they are subjective depths. If this kind of depth is to be released, if the individual is to feel free to expose his own subjectivity, to bring out into the open what he most deeply thinks, sees and feels, then the kind of leadership which the adult offers should create an atmosphere far more receptive, tolerant and more basic to sound human relationships than formal democracy. Historically speaking, the tradition for this form of American democracy is not the parliamentary tradition, but the individualism of the transcendentalist tradition, the right, which

Thoreau expresses, of a person to walk to a different drummer. It is characteristic of the parliamentary situation that the group begin with an issue and settle it after discussion by a vote. It is characteristic of the kind of human give-and-take which we are defining that issues arise and are resolved or synthesized as the discussion progresses, and that whatever line of action emerges from the discussion seems to have come about, not as a decision arrived at by debate and vote, but as a natural growth from the soil of the group.

The leader, perhaps, begins as a firm and contributing chairman of a democratically organized body. He proceeds from there, learning to ask the questions that elicit deeper or more imaginative responses, learning to understand the import of what a child says beyond the words the child uses, learning to talk with children and listen to them, learning to trust them and be trusted by them, learning, in short, to evoke from them that atmosphere which springs from children when they are at their best. It is an atmosphere which is at the same time dead earnest and hilarious, animated and self-contained, deeply respectful and totally permissive, in which each child feels free to be himself and to bring his values and insights into the open. And if the subjective freedom of this atmosphere is threatened by the use of personal or raw democratic power on the part of some children, the leader will meet such threats with an unmistakable show of adult authority. For he is, after all, the adult, and must be able to master the paradox of his own position.

In more practical terms, how much, in the production of a children's play, does the adult contribute? If the adult makes too few suggestions and these are inappropriate or not important or not well timed, the children will feel rudderless. On the other hand, if he makes too many suggestions, and they are too firmly made or are timed in such a way as to anticipate discussion, the results will be inhibiting. There is no question but that the best children's plays bear the stamp of the adult who has worked with them. This does not mean that he imposed his own ideas. It means that in the making of the play, he was not just another member of the group, but that there was a polarity, with the adult one pole and the children the other. The adult evoked and the thoughts of the children were evoked. Inevitably, then, a play will reflect much of what the adult leader is able to evoke. One teacher will help the children to see and conceive more boldly, another to see and conceive more sensitively. A strong-minded adult working with strong-minded children begins, perhaps, as a moderator and synthesizer until the discussion reaches a very animated stage. Then, perhaps, he gets in on the discussion, throwing out ideas along with everyone else, assuming that his ideas will be accepted, rejected or synthesized, or that they will stimulate new ideas. If the children really are strong-minded, his assumption is presumably correct. But another adult—another teacher, perhaps, in the same school—feels that this free-wheeling participation of the first teacher goes too far. She scrupulously avoids any imposition of her own ideas but in the eyes of the first teacher her moderating role seems bland and inhibiting—he feels that she keeps too tight a ship. Meantime, some young thing still in her salad days, who feels guilty that the children are often rude and unruly, will get more beautiful things from them than either of the others, because—for reasons that reside in the nature of her own subjectivity—she asks the children better questions.

There is, incidentally, among some teachers and children's leaders, the notion that the democratic process, if used skillfully, is a means by which the leader gets children to do what the leader already has in mind. Such manipulation is a fraud. If the leader has his mind made up, he should tell the children so and tell them they are to do what he says. Children should not be permitted to make decisions which do not lie in their competence, and if a decision does lie in their competence, then the decision should be genuinely theirs. The leader who cons children into believing that they are doing what they want to do when, in fact, they are doing what he wants them to do outwits himself as seriously as he outwits the children. For in his self-conceit, he is depriving himself of that growth, that constant youthfulness which comes from really hearing what children have to say and modifying one's own vision through the vigor and honesty of theirs. The leader need not, of course, feel guilty if once in a while the children decide to do what he hoped they would. The rapport between the leader and the children will sometimes lead to such a coincidence.

The wise leader will, as we have indicated before, make a clear distinction in his own mind, and will convey this distinction to the children as the occasion arises, as to what lies within their competence and what does not. He will presumably maintain veto power over their choice of material, not permitting them to do things so difficult as to guarantee a sense of failure, or things which are tawdry and unworthy. He may exercise veto power over elements in the dialogue which they improvise or write—racial or religious slurs, for example. On the other hand, sentimentality, cliché, corn, schmaltz—these are things the leader would presumably not veto, but would deal with by other means, primarily more searching evaluative discussions.

But again, what we are dealing with is not parliamentary democracy with its competences, votes and veto powers, but with a relationship. And none of these matters are much of a problem where there is mutual trust. The leader's position is rooted in the Socratic idea that when choices are clear, young people will make the right choice. If the leader's skills in evoking—and, where necessary, elucidating—thoughts, feelings and ideas are good, then the choices will be clear, and he can trust young people to "choose the better and eschew the poorer." The youngsters, finding themselves trusted, will reciprocate the trust. It is precisely when this kind of rapport and mutual trust exists, in situations which are most permissive, in situations which make the closest approach to egalitarian dialogue between child and adult, that children are least distressed when an adult whom they trust exerts his authority. It is precisely in such situations that the adult's show of authority—on those rare occasions when he needs to show it—is accepted gracefully, absolutely and without resentment. First, because in most instances such an adult will be right and the children will know it. Second, because if he happens to be wrong, the children will be able to deal with him.

One such teacher, away with a group of high school sophomores on a trip, refused to tell them a promised bedtime story because they had misbehaved. His anger was natural enough, and this the youngsters understood, but the decision not to tell the story was hasty and ill-considered, for this story telling was an element in his relationship with them going back to the time when they were eleven years old. After a time, three boys approached the teacher very respectfully and asked to speak to him privately. "We feel your decision was wrong," one of them said. "The raid on the girls' room shows that our unity is breaking down, and we need the story to pull us together." Since their position was the correct one, the teacher admitted error and told the story. When rapport exists, the adult need have no fear of admitting error and reversing position. Quite the contrary. He should show that accountability which anyone who is set over others owes to the people over whom he is set. Such accountability on the part of an adult is deeply moving to children and cements the ties of respect and love.

Obviously this kind of relationship cannot be developed overnight and will often prove extremely difficult among children who have not had such a relationship with other adults. Fortunately, in some communities this kind of relationship exists as the dominant pattern in the home, between children and their parents and aunts, uncles and grandparents. Much will hinge on whether the adult leader, appearing among a group of children for the first time, establishes his image as that of an uncle or a school teacher or a policeman. A white adult leader was working for the first time with a group of Puerto Rican children in New York City on a shadow puppet dramatization of a poem by a Latin-American poet. The children ranged in age from eight to fifteen, as such groups will in economically deprived areas, and the relationship was one of love at first sight. The children were as warm and at ease with him as with their own fathers. It was a good working atmosphere and a lot was getting done. At one point two older girls who had been particularly warm-hearted and cooperative went out into the hall for some reason, perhaps to go to the ladies' room. Returning, they were talking rather loudly, at which point an old man, also white, burst out of another room and upbraided the girls for their racket. They turned on him with a raucous and shockingly smutty line of abuse. Apparently these children, set down in a new and hostile ethnos, had developed an alternative, non-familial way of dealing with the adult world, and they could relate to adults quickly enough in either way.

This two-pronged relationship of children to the adult world is universal. To a great extent, parents love their children and live with them, however gropingly and sometimes turbulently, on a basis of give-and-take. Society, on the other hand, fears children and establishes all manner of defenses against them. This dichotomy in attitude toward the adult world is particularly marked presently among Puerto Rican children, whose familial atmosphere is particularly warm and pleasure-giving, whereas the other sector of the adult environment—at least on the continental mainland—is particularly hostile. But the dichotomy can be seen in almost any community of the United States. Some homes will be hateful, and the children of these homes may never discover the possibility of a warm relationship with an adult, or they may discover the possibility in a settlement house or a camp, or in the person of a teacher or a librarian or the proprietor of a candy store, or even a policeman—that is, in one or another individual in the very segment of the adult world which seems most hostile. The point is that young people will usually have formed some image of the possibility of relating to adults in happy and fruitful ways. The image may be very tenuous or deeply buried and in situations in which an attitude of mistrust is the habitual way of relating to adults, the trust may be longer in coming. But when it does come, it is all the more gratifying, for it is precisely in such situations that children have the greatest need for a warm and trusting relationship. Thus, if an adult who wants to do creative work is confronted with thwarted or hostile children, he can in all likelihood, through patience, love, understanding and imagination, make important contributions to their lives.

While the kind of rapport we are talking about lays a basis for more or less continuing affirmative behavior on the part of children, it does not guarantee that any individual group will not misbehave from time to time, especially since, in such an atmosphere, they do not fear the adult but tend to assume that he is well disposed and understanding. For this reason, they can let go a little in his presence and don't have to do really bad things behind his back. In this situation there are two dangers for the inexperienced adult. The first is that, because he doesn't want to do anything drastic, he will tend to plead or nag. Far better to settle a disruptive child by swift, if temporary, exclusion, and to settle a whole group by some one, telling stroke—a ringing command, for example, or a sudden adjournment of the activity for that session.

The other problem of an inexperienced leader may be that he thinks he has to control more than is really necessary. A man who visited an experimental school some years ago made, as he was leaving, a comment which he thought brilliantly snide. "The classrooms," he said, "seem more like newspaper offices than classrooms." So be it! In regard to children's dramatics, it is better that the discussions seem like a free-for-all and the rehearsals like a madhouse than that either seem like this gentleman's concept of a classroom. Control of discussion should be aimed only at giving everyone a chance to speak and be heard. To this end, some children must be restrained from monopolizing the discussion, and others will have to be hushed when others are speaking. But this kind of control should not eliminate the possibility of an idea being blurted out out of turn, for otherwise good ideas may be lost. In this animated and far-from-classroomlike give-and-take, the adult will have a roving eye, independent of his attentive ear, which will see a hand raised timidly or tentatively, or even the play of a thought across a face—and he will part the river of voices to let such thoughts get through. He will, of course, rebuke children who deal with the ideas of others in insulting ways, and will act firmly against disruptions, both in the planning sessions and in the rehearsals. But at the same time that he probes for the thoughts of the shyer child and limits the influence of the domineering child, he will not hold the voluble enthusiasts in too tight a control. This, of course, is not specific to dramatics but is the proper approach to any matter in which children are talking through a point of view or a line of action—in fathoming the meaning of a story, for example, or setting up an experimental project in science, or in evaluating issues of past history or of current events.

Generally in early rehearsals, the children not at the moment onstage will watch and listen with great interest to those who are. Later, however, when the scenes are being gone over more painstakingly, the children not onstage will get bored. They may talk loudly among themselves, or bounce balls, or chase each other, or wrestle, or chase each other "with intent to wrestle," as one teacher put it. Sometimes children bring dogs to evening rehearsals. They have to walk the dogs anyway, so they bring them along. How much of such sociability the leader will put up with will depend on his answer to any of these three questions: 1. Is what is going on physically dangerous or emotionally hurtful? 2. Does it distract the children working onstage? 3. Does it distract the adult's attention from the children working onstage? If the answer to any one of the questions is yes, the adult will exert controls. If what is going on is dangerous, he will point out the dangers. If it is emotionally hurtful— for example, one child is being picked on or taunted—he will deliver a sharp rebuke or will stop the rehearsal long enough to talk matters out, depending on whether the hurtful behavior is conscious or innocent. The answer to the third question will vary from adult to adult. This writer is more distractable than he was twenty years ago, but he is delighted to see a new young teacher working magnificently from the auditorium floor in the midst of a lively flurry of sociability and dogs. One adult had such enormous concentration with what was going on onstage that the racket behind him would sometimes build up to an astonishing pitch before he noticed it. At this point, he would turn the palm of his hand back towards the noise makers and shake it at them without taking his eyes off the stage. If they happened to see his gesture, they would quiet down. If not, no matter—he had dealt with the intrusion to the extent that he could be bothered with it.

Misbehavior onstage is another matter. The children onstage will also get bored from working the same thing over and over. First one and then another will start horsing around—but in context! There will be an explosion in which they start hamming things up—overexpressing their lines, experimenting with outrageous inflections, overstating their movements, committing imaginative but inappropriate pieces of stage business, turning the scene, no matter how serious, into hilarious parody. The whole scene takes on a new and preposterous vitality—it comes to life. The adult is jubilant. Now the children know the scene, they have made it theirs, they have mastered it and they can do anything they want with it. The leader has been spared the necessity of using artificial respiration by having the youngsters sing or chant their lines, or whisper or bellow them, of having them waltz or prance through their movements, or go through them in slow motion—good techniques, but artificial, and not as good as this joyous explosion of self-satirizing mischief.

Not all forms of misbehavior, however, are so benign as these. All adult leaders should know that behavior is a manifestation of something in the child, that two similar pieces of behavior on the part of two different children may have opposite causations, and two opposite kinds of behavior may come about in different children for almost the same reasons. Madame Montessori cites the example of two young children, one of whom was totally withdrawn and submissive, the other monstrously demanding and aggressive, both of whom were found to be slowly dying of undernourishment. These same two extremes can be seen in well-fed children who feel themselves unloved. Sometimes a behavior pattern changes into its opposite. The bullying child withdraws, the withdrawn child becomes a bully. In the first instance, the despair has grown deeper perhaps; in the second, a glimmer of hope may be expressing itself in an act of will, however perverse.

Dramatics activity will offer an opportunity for an observant adult to get to know children and understand them. It is enough to our present purpose to describe one phenomenon that sometimes occurs—that is, that "good" and "bad" children sometimes reverse roles in doing dramatics. A youngster who is usually disruptive or uncontrolled in other situations may become marvelously cooperative in a situation in which he can assume a new identity in place of the one that gives him so much trouble. Some very quiet and conforming youngster may become disorderly and deliberately uncooperative, as the task of putting on a new identity forces him to see that he has an identity of his own, but one which has sought its security in seeming not to exist. An extravagant and flamboyant personality may suddenly become pensive and restrained, and a shy child may flower as a creature of extraordinary verve. It is perhaps because dramatizing has this relationship to identity that children find it so exciting. There is probably no other situation in which the inwardness is brought so actively into the open. A painting or a piece of creative writing may express this inwardness, but the act of painting or writing is a private act while acting is a public process.

As we have previously indicated, Winifred Ward, in *Playmaking with Children*, has an excellent chapter on therapy. It is excellent because it deals with the kind of specific therapy which a knowing adult, working with children on dramatics, may undertake. Poor speech habits may be improved. Self-confidence may be so built in this area that the possibility is opened up for the child to build self-confidence in other areas. A child's reading ability may be strengthened in several ways—through a greater interest in stories and their ideas, through greater understanding of books because in acting the child has interpreted the substance of books, and through a more personal and intimate relationship with words. In matters covered by this meaning of therapy, the adult leader has both the opportunity and the responsibility to go as far as he can.

But in regard to the meaning of the word "therapy" as psychotherapy, the adult leader who is not trained in psychotherapeutic processes has only a very broad and general responsibility, and that is to set up as welcoming, as considerate, as human a situation as he can. An emotionally releasing situation, in a sense, but not too releasing in psychological terms. That is, the leader will not knowingly work with psycho-drama. The trained therapist, working with this form, will deliberately try to set up improvisation situations which will impinge sharply on the child's most pressing problems of human relationship and self-identity. But the leader not trained to handle such a whirlwind once it is released will draw his dramatization material from the broader currents of human culture—from history, folk lore, literature or some real experience the children have had together as a group. In this way, the child who tries on a new identity will express through the dramatic metaphor some phase of himself that he would like to be, or is glad he is not, or is amused or excited to be, but not a phase of himself with which he is tormented. It may happen sometimes that a child will choose to play a role whose symbolic relationship to his psyche is highly charged. It may be that such a choice is a wise one or it may not, though a child's wisdom in such matters is to be trusted more often than not. In cases where an adult assumes that a role has subjective symbolism of an important kind to a child, he will help the child probe the role, but not probe himself. He will give the child the same kind of help he gives to all the children, but will leave the symbolism of the role to the secrecy of the child's own inner processes.

It would have been easy, for example, for a camp counselor working with eight and nine year olds on the dramatization of the story of the humpbacked cobbler—a description of which follows—to assume that the role of the cobbler involved a deep degree of subjective symbolism for the boy who played it. But he felt, correctly, that this matter was none of his business. Anyway, the anecdote will throw light both on the importance of the adult's role and, perhaps even more importantly, on its limitations. It illustrates, further, that with the younger child, as with an older child, the capturing of one's creative vision is not always an instantaneous thing, but is something that the child will brood his way into, if necessary, over a period of days or even weeks.

The story of the humpbacked cobbler goes as follows: The cobbler went one day to deliver a pair of shoes in a neighboring village. On his way back through the forest, he was overtaken by darkness and took shelter for the night in a hollow tree. He woke to see elves dancing in the moonlight and, being a sociable person, he came out of the tree and joined them. The elf king was delighted, and as daybreak approached he made the cobbler promise to return and dance with them again. To insure his return, the king put his hand on the cobbler's back and removed the hump, supposing it to be a desirable part of the human anatomy. When the cobbler returned to the village, he was greeted joyously by the villagers, for they liked him very much and were delighted in his good fortune. An envious tailor, however, seeing how richly the cobbler had been rewarded and judging that the removal of the hump was something the cobbler had requested, decided that if he were to join the dance of the elves, the king would give him gold. So, on the night of the next full moon, he went to the forest and hid in the hollow tree, and when the elves appeared he came out and joined their dance. Because of the moonlight and their lack of familiarity with humans, the elves took the tailor to be the same person as their previous dance companion, and when the dance was about to break up the elf king said to the tailor: "You have kept your promise, so here is your hump!" With this, the elf king slapped his hand on the tailor's back, and the tailor had to return a humpback to the village, where, in this particular dramatization, the villagers greeted him with hoots and jeers.

A Negro boy, nine years old and tall for his age, played the cobbler. His characterization was extraordinarily touching, especially in his association with the villagers. One saw an innate friendliness and decency touched with an enduring sorrow because of his disfigurement. However, when the hump was removed, the boy seemed unable to cast off his air of dejection and rejoice in his manly straightness. The counselor discussed the matter with him quietly and not urgently, but with no apparent results. One day on a hike the counselor again took the matter up. "Can't you try something?" he asked. "Can you turn cartwheels, for instance?" The boy thought. "I know now what I'm going to do," he said.

The next time the children worked on their stories it was evident that the boy did know what he was going to do. When the elf king put his hand on the cobbler's back, the hump really vanished. The boy did not turn cartwheels. But he moved! He skipped and darted everywhere, swallowlike—back, forth, around—using every inch of space available to express the joy of his release from the burden of being different.

In suggesting cartwheels, the counselor had suggested a mechanism, hoping, perhaps, that the mechanism would release the insight. But once the boy had worked his way through to his own vision, he had no need of any suggestions. On one hand, it cannot be assumed that a child will make exciting discoveries inside himself if the adult simply lets matters rest and does not help him see that a discovery is needed. On the other hand, the adult cannot possibly make such a discovery for the child—the child must do this for himself.

18
ooooooooo
Children and Audience

AS CHILDREN GROW OLDER, they are able to undertake an increasing responsibility for the quality of their communication to an
audience—for expanding their expression, for greater impact and
for mounting their dramatizations in ways which support a "willing suspension of disbelief" on the part of the watchers. This responsibility is not absolute, however, but relative, their responsibility to their own vision being of far greater importance. The
relationship of young people to an audience is a delicate business.
Of two performances of the same play, one can seem very beau-

tiful to the watchers, the other not. In part, the difference will lie in the eye of the beholder—one audience will see it one way and another audience another way. But the difference in the eye of one audience as against another will communicate itself to the children, so that the actual disparity between one performance and the other will be quite noticeable to anyone who sees both.

The most natural audience for children is a group of other children about their own age. Little children—first and second graders, for instance—are not made self-conscious by the presence of other children the same age, and such an audience is responsive and friendly and loves plays of all kinds. Teenagers, too, make a good audience for little children—at least when the association of the little children with the teenagers is a more or less everyday thing. For teenagers, on one hand, will have a rather sophisticated perception and will not be condescending like adults; and on the other hand, they will yearn back nostalgically to their own childhoods and their response will be loving and not as harsh and critical as that of ten and eleven year olds, who yearn forward. Children of pre-school ages should probably never perform for an audience, though perhaps a small group of other children, or an adult or two, might drop in occasionally while they are acting out a poem or a story or being things to music. Certainly, however, these younger children should sometimes see plays done by older children. For the very little children love plays, too. In the school from which much of our illustrative material is drawn, the pre-school children, when they are let out in the afternoon, wait in the auditorium for the school bus drivers to pick them up. Not infrequently they will appear stridently in the midst of a high school play rehearsal. Some teachers will be with them and will handle their noise to some extent. But the rehearsal itself will soon attract and hold their attention. This writer remembers a rehearsal of *Caesar and Cleopatra* when over a dozen pre-schoolers were sprawled on their bellies on the steps that lead from the auditorium floor to the stage, where for some ten or fifteen minutes, in awed silence, they watched the big boys and girls acting out a story which, one must assume, they, the little ones, did not understand at all.

For high school plays, too, an audience of other high school students is the best. Teenagers are, in fact, a particularly warm audience—even in moving pictures, where their responsiveness will in no way affect the quality of the performance. When Olivier's *Hamlet* was playing in New York, arrangements were made for high school students to be admitted at reduced prices. This writer, seeing the picture one afternoon and pondering the differences between Olivier's interpretation of the play and his own, had his preoccupations rudely interrupted by the far more immediate responses of the teenage audience, who were vociferously shocked by the undercurrent of sensuality in the relationship of mother and son. Another teenage audience, watching *Wuthering Heights*, stomped and hollered with righteous exhilaration when they saw Heathcliff at the far end of a great room, returning, rich and powerful, to give his enemies their come-uppance. Similarly, at a performance for high school students of the Stratford Shakespeare Festival's *King Lear*, the teenagers made the welkin ring when Albany finally took a manly stand against his evil wife and her evil sister.

This acute receptivity is a tremendous support for other teenagers who are putting on a play. The way time works out in a school is such that plays will often be given just before vacation periods, at which points many teachers are winding up units of study and giving exams. As a result, the group giving a play will endure an adult audience the first night and wait exultantly for the second night when their schoolmates will be through with exams and can come to the show. It is not that a teenage audience is less critical, but that, possibly, it is more critically appreciative—it is in the position of the man who bid five dollars for his wife's cake at an auction, even though the cake did not look as impressive as some of the others—for, as he said, he "knew what went into it." The teachers, too, usually know what goes into a play. They will perceive the creative attainment of individual children, will understand the hard work that has kept that attainment alive and has expanded it over the long weeks of rehearsal, and know how slippery the moment of communication of that creative attainment can be. They will understand that the process is more important than the product, that what goes into the cake is more important than the appearance; but they will also understand how disappointing it is for youngsters if what they do is greeted with a lukewarm response. It is, then, within their own community that any group of players can count on finding their natural audience, the people to whom it is most natural that they should communicate.

On the whole, an audience composed in about equal parts of the children's peers and of adults is a good audience, too, for in this situation adults often are able to see with children's eyes. But an audience almost exclusively of adults presents many problems—and in dramatizations by very young children, only the most unusual circumstances can justify the presence of more than two or three adults besides those who are directly associated with the dramatics activity. Younger children should feel no responsibility at all to an audience and should be as little aware of their watchers as possible. On the other hand, adult watchers should feel an acute sense of responsibility to young players. They should feel that watching them doing dramatics is a special privilege, like being in on the birth of a calf or twin lambs, of witnessing a natural phenomenon of a kind which one is seldom in a position to witness. Adults who are so privileged can be most helpful by being totally unobtrusive.

The problems adults create for children—not only in their dramatizations but in many other aspects of their lives—stem from condescension. When adults watch a children's play, they find the children cute—as, indeed, many of them are—but this is irrelevant. The child is usually not trying to be cute, or, if he is, it is because he is struggling to meet adult expectations. The child is trying to be a snowflake, or a star, or a bear, or a humpbacked cobbler, or an elf, or a field slave in the old South, or a

Viking raider, or Robin Hood, or Brutus or Cassius. And none of these—except possibly the bear, depending on characterization—is cute or is considered cute by the child. The child's failure to convince an adult audience that he really *is* the thing he is being has a physiological base. The child isn't big enough, or maturely proportioned enough, or doesn't have a deep enough voice or isn't the right sex. These are all accidental matters and do not affect the child's creative image. But adults are usually much taken with the cuteness of these accidental phenomena and respond to a play which children are seriously presenting by giggles. When these expressions of misappreciation of what they are doing reach the children, they become self-conscious. Some freeze up, some start being cute to beat the band, some become embarrassed and start to cry. A very nasty wedge has been driven between the child and his dramatic image.

Even older children can be upset by this condescending attitude. A sixth-grade play about pre-Civil War life on a southern plantation was received so responsively by an audience of elementary and high school students that a decision was made to give an evening performance for parents. With the first ripple of appreciation from the adult audience, the play died. For the adults had tittered at something which was being said in all earnestness, and this earnestness by an eleven-year-old boy had struck them as cute. The play was not an expansive one, but quiet, sensitive and lyrical. Its creative quality was an essence, a fragrance, so to speak, which, had the audience smelled it, would have grown more pervasive as the evening went along. But after that first titter of adult condescension, the children were thoroughly angry. They dutifully showed the audience the bottle, but kept the stopper in tight.

This kind of detraction has its origins in the difficulties adults manifest in the use of their senses. In regard to dramatics, adults are used to being hammered at by theatrical technique and it doesn't occur to them that they are supposed to summon up their perceptivity and bring it to bear. They are not able to see that a smaller voice or a smaller gesture may express tremendous insight and integrity. They will, in short, be more impressed by a clever show-off of a child, for instance, than by something that rings true—however deep their awareness of things that are expressed in words. For most adults have forgotten how to use their senses except in a limited way. They seldom really taste, touch, hear, see or smell. The senses are merely an aid to cerebration—to decide what is what. "This is a subway entrance and not the entrance to a public lavatory." "This is a subway token and not a dime." Once the identification is made, the act of seeing has fulfilled its function. The opalescent underside of gull wings or the silvery gleam of a fusilage ten miles up in a blue sky are simply not seen. Pantomime, so often a very delicate instrument of expression, is often therefore completely lost on adults.

A problem arising during the school production of *The Hearthstone* should be mentioned in this connection. The play was to be performed as part of an anniversary program, and the final audience was to be entirely adult—parents, educators, educational writers, editors, etc. A preview of the play was given to the school, after which the teacher was not satisfied that the visual deception practiced by the Quaker family on the U.S. marshal and the slave catchers would be evident to the adult audience. When the marshal and the slave catchers finally enter the house of the Quakers, they see on the hearthstone, through which hardly a moment before the fugitives had made their escape into a secret passage, a sleeping cat and two children, who are lying on their bellies popping corn. As a result, it never occurs to the marshal or the slave catchers that this hearthstone might be displaceable and that they ought to have a look at it. Nothing in the dialogue, however, explained how cleverly the marshal and the slave catchers had been put on, so the teacher went about asking one and another who had seen the preview:

"Why didn't it occur to the slave catchers that the hearthstone might be the entrance to a secret passage?"

Every student who was asked the question reacted as though it were a stupid question that didn't need asking, and responded, casually or superciliously: "Because they had the kids and the cat lying on it." The same question was put to every member of the teaching and administrative staff who had seen the play, and every one of these adults except two was baffled by the question.

As a result, the pantomime was broadened. The U.S. marshal—played by a burly eleven year old—strode across the hearthstone, stooped and peered up the chimney, stepping over and straddling the two children and the cat. Then as he walked away, apparently satisfied, he turned again, studied the situation contemplatively for a moment, returned to the hearth quickly and, standing with his back to the audience, "opened" the painted door of the bake-oven and peered inside. In this way, the point was re-enforced so that the adults couldn't miss it.

An important question is raised by this anecdote and that is to what extent the creative work of children should be modified to meet the needs of communication with an audience. The positive aspects of the answer to this question have been dealt with in the chapters dealing with expanded communication. In this case, the marshal's pantomime was an expansion which improved the ending of the play in a number of respects: it clarified the point, it heightened both the suspense and the pleasurable excitement which the audience took in the deception and, most importantly, it gave scope to the marvelous boy who played the marshal for his considerable gifts for characterization. He was able to show that this marshal was a shrewd man, who knew perfectly well that if one suspects there is a secret passage, he will look for it somewhere in the construction of a chimney. So shrewd, in fact, did this man seem to be, and so subtle was the boy's characterization, achieved through this piece of pantomime, that at the same time that he clarified the plot, he developed a delicious interpretive ambiguity in the suspicion he created that this marshal was not deceived at all, that just possibly in leaving the hearthstone and returning to it to take another look, he was playing a mischievous but benign joke on the Quakers, and that he had not the least intention of catching the slaves if he could help it.

Suppose, on the other hand, that instead of conveying the deception visually, it had been decided, as insurance against adult myopia, to have one of the children say, when the slave catchers had gone: "We fooled them, didn't we? By grandma putting the cat on the hearth and by us popping corn, we fixed it so they never thought to look at the hearthstone at all!" This would have demeaned both the children and their audience. Children owe it to their audience and themselves to make what they have to say as clear as they consistently can with the spirit of their expression. They owe nothing more.

Despite some of these problems, it is probably children from eleven to thirteen who can best establish a compatible relationship with an adult audience. In the first place, children are not usually, at this age, particularly cute. In the second place, they are no longer inhibited by being watched, but tend to have a healthy respect for their watchers, whom they like to tease and gull to a certain extent, but whom they are really eager to please. If the adult working with them understands the possibilities, they are able to broaden their creative expression in highly expansive and communicable ways. They are also capable of combining a genuine insight into their material with a great deal of imaginative hocus-pocus. An example of this was the explosive expectoration, in a school play, of the sissy from Hardscrabble County. This man had been expelled from Hardscrabble County rock quarry because of his lack of masculinity, and he subsequently appeared terrifyingly in the bar of a town which lived in fear of the Hardscrabble men. The first thing he did was order a prussic acid cocktail, but the prussic acid cocktail was such a poor, weak thing that he spat it out in disgust, and where his spit landed it burst into flame. (Some of the boys had been at considerable pains to rig up a flash powder for this effect. At the moment the Hardscrabble man spat, the powder was to be set off by the tripping of a switch in the wings. At this time, the senior in charge of the school stage crew was a girl. At the very moment the curtain opened, she tripped over the wire and set the flash powder off, so that the first thing the audience saw was a completely unexplained burst of fire.)

But an example from *Tom Sawyer* is a better one. Such a bold device as poling an imaginary raft down the center aisle and beaching it at the foot of the stage steps draws an adult audience in through a double empathy. In a sense, it panders, tongue-in-cheek, to their sympathetic response to the children themselves. But it does so imaginatively, saying in effect: "Here we are, a bunch of kids you know, having a grand time making believe. Get in on it! Have a good time yourselves!" The early childhood of most adults is buried in mystery, their adolescence in pain and shame. It is with the periods of emergence into the objective that they are most closely in touch, the years between nine and twelve and those of early adulthood, when they began to face the real world with a mixture of responsibility and hopeful illusion. It is for this reason, perhaps, that the communication between pre-adolescents and adults can sometimes be so sweet.

But the relationship between teenagers and an adult audience is often more troubled. As players, they are capable of much greater energy and tension and emotional force than younger boys and girls and, as a result, they can sometimes sweep an audience off its feet. In general, however, it is hardly to be expected that when teenagers do standard plays they will manifest the theatrical skills of professionals. As a result, adult myopia will again be at work, and they will fail to perceive the qualities of lyricism or insight which the youngsters have captured. E.g., a group performing *The Plow and the Stars* was characterized by unusual subtlety and sensitivity of insight. The

boy who played the Covey, for example, was the same boy
who had played Mottel's brother four years before. Both this
brother and the Covey are hard, tight, not very sympathetic
people. Mottel's brother, however, beneath his get-rich-quick
harshness, has wells of familial devotion and loyalty so deep and
ever-present that he himself is not aware of them, but the watchers had felt it every time he rebuked his mother for getting emotional or called his wife a cow—such were the sensitivities of the
boy who played the part. The Covey, on the other hand, is a
Marxist-spouting character through whom O'Casey says, in
effect, that big ideas without humanity in the heart are comparable to boasting, swaggering or drinking, or any of the other
things people do to expose their incapacity to feel the hurt of
others. In short, O'Casey does not give to the Covey any of
those deep sensitivities that Sholom Aleichem gives to Mottel's
brother. But in this case a boy of great sensitivity was in the
part, and when the three cronies witnessed their neighbors' tragedy, the Covey's face was amazing. It was beautiful and frightening. The tragedy of others had reached this shallow man, and
the first promptings of compassion tormented him, so that when
Fluther and old Peter responded by going out to look for a
drink, the Covey joined them, not so much, one felt, to run
away from the tragedy, as to run away from himself.

But facial expressions are a very subtle matter—they don't
hit an adult audience between the eyes unless they are "arranged." In this case, nothing was arranged—the boy had
merely discovered something deeper in the moment of performance—it could not have been planned for.

In teenage performances of standard plays, the line between
a flop and a smash is usually very thin. It may hinge on something as simple as the fact that a boy or girl has trouble remembering a couple of lines. It may hinge on the response of the
audience to something early in the play, a response which either
liberates or tenses the players. For this reason, it used to be the
practice in one school to make sure that the Latin teacher and

the high school principal attended plays on different nights. Each of these men had an explosive, infectious laugh and an effervescent sense of the comical. To hear one of these laughs at the first witty line was most warming to the players, and often one of these men was enough to carry an audience with him. At all events, the problems of performing standard plays are such that it can hardly be expected that teenagers will completely satisfy an adult audience in most instances. The players will seldom achieve the impact which adults have come to expect through their experiences in seeing professional plays. An adult audience comes expecting amateurishness, and will see what it expects to see and will fail to see, behind the weaker projection, the interpretive originality and insight that the group will often have achieved.

In regard to the original plays which teenagers write or improvise, there is a different problem between them and an adult audience, a problem most often of their own making. That is, they will be contentious, experimental, or perverse—often all three at once. This was the case with a beautiful program of dramatized poetry which one senior class presented—a great piece of work but one that was a little rough on their parents. The selection of poetry was on a high level—William Dunbar, Shakespeare, Herrick, John Donne, Byron, James Joyce, T. S. Eliot, William Butler Yeats, Dylan Thomas, some Sophocles in translation, translations of their own of Catullus and Baudelaire, and two or three of their own poems which could stand up in such company. The program was presented without a curtain and for scenery and props there were only a few folding auditorium chairs, a driftwood log left over from several other plays and a huge, paint-smeared A-ladder, which was deployed in various ways—players mounted it, sat on its rungs, leaned against it and circled around it at various times. The youngsters gave a great deal of attention to the aesthetic deployment of this A-ladder and to the aesthetics of lighting. They gave scant attention, however, to the preparedness of their parents for such a program. They refused flatly to brook any interruption in the flow of the poems and the pantomime, and permitted no intermission and only the briefest blackout between the three sections of the program. Similarly, they refused to permit the names of the poems or the poets to be announced. They did provide the audience with a mimeographed list of the poems and the poets, but since the program ran for an hour and a half without the houselights once going up, the audience had to peer at this list in the dark. The attitude of the players seemed to be: "If you don't recognize the poem when you hear it, shame on you!"

Out front, at a grand piano and reading by a music light, sat a narrator. As the houselights first went down, she began: "*Affirmation, Negation, and Synthesis*—a program of dramatized poetry, presented by the senior class." Then, as the stage lights dimmed up on the first poem, she intoned: "Part One—*Affirmation.*" A half hour later there was a brief blackout, and as the stage lights dimmed up again she said: "Part Two—*Negation.*" At the end of another half hour there was another quick blackout, and as the stage lights again dimmed up she said: "Part Three—*Synthesis.*"

In the front row of the audience was an eminent neurosurgeon. He was sitting next to his daughter, who was a member of the class presenting the program. She held an intercom telephone in one hand, a flashlight in the other and she was whispering light cues over the intercom to boys backstage on the switchboard. Her father sat in erect dignity, no slightest cast of his head or back betraying either pleasure or displeasure, until the end of the second blackout as the narrator intoned: "Part Three—*Synthesis,*" when he lost his aplomb and leaned toward his daughter and asked, sotto voce, "What *is* this all *about?*"

This kind of teenage perversity is often expressed in experimentation. Teenagers need to experiment, even to make mistakes. The adult working with them will usually give them the benefit of his thinking to take or to leave. They will often leave it. In one instance, a senior wrote and directed a dramatic fantasy about a bear, a family of geese and a young man and woman who find themselves together at night in a hovel. Through the methods of the theater of the absurd, the play expressed the mixed emotions of expectancy, uncertainty and sorrow which accompany separation from a familiar but thwarting environment. The play was very lyrical, though perhaps a little cloying. Dramatically it was very difficult, and the boy, who was a fine artist and poet, but imperious in his aesthetic sensibilities, insisted that most of such dramatic action as there was take place with the players sitting on the floor of the stage, where they could scarcely be seen. He also insisted on reducing "projection" to a minimum in emotional expression and action too, except for a few eruptive flurries. He seemed to be trying to achieve what only eight year olds usually can—a self-contained play, self-validating in the give-and-take among the players without regard to whether it is seen and heard. It was a daring concept and might have been a great achievement had more than a few of the teenage players been able to attain consciously what eight year olds attain unconsciously—something, incidentally, which Morris Carnovsky attained at certain points in *King Lear*, when the old king maunders on as though he were not in a play at all, a beautiful vision in which "good theater" was risked for true sublimity. Anyway, some of the critics carped at Morris Carnovsky in his greatness, and no one received the boys' play well except a mere handful of teachers and students.

The boy's theoretical position, however, is one that deserves serious thought. He was saying in effect that a work of art has its validity for its creator, that a play is an experience which the players go through together, in which they live out imaginary lives in relation to each other. It follows from this position that no audience is needed for such a play, that if, while the players are living out their imaginary lives together, some people happen to see what they are doing, stop and are drawn by empathy into these imaginary lives, then communication has been achieved. But if the people are not interested and move on, it is no matter, for obviously no communication was possible between the players and them. This position is, of course, the spontaneous and unself-conscious position of children when they are engaging in make-believe or are dramatizing stories as a game among themselves. It is a position which persists and ought to persist in large measure among younger children—for example, the eight year olds adlibbing for forty minutes when they were scheduled to perform for ten. It is a position from which the adult helps children inch away little by little, until a new position develops—one in which the children, at the same time that they are living imaginary lives in relation to each other, are able to see what they are doing with these imaginary lives in relation to the people who are looking on. The boy's position is, in a sense, the heart of creative dramatics: *A dramatization is a relationship among the players.* Its antithesis is "theater": *A play is a relationship between the players and the watchers.* But a dramatization can also be a play—a relationship can simultaneously take place among the players *and* between the players and the watchers. One position, taken alone, denies the creative substance of children's dramatics. The other, taken alone, denies to children a participation in the historical role of drama as a form of social communication of important ideas.

Nevertheless, it would be smug to dismiss the boy's position. Consider for a moment a social order in which people come together in small groups to dramatize—in which, in fact, so many groups of people come together with such frequency for this purpose that no one has any time or interest in being watchers, so that the theater ceases to exist altogether, and drama becomes a social form in which people live imaginary lives in relation to each other. There is nothing deplorable about such a state of affairs—in fact, the idea is rather exciting. On the other hand, the current state of affairs *is* deplorable. Hundreds of millions of people sit passively in theaters and moving picture houses and, more commonly, in front of TV sets and are dramatized at by, on a relative scale, a mere handful of professional actors. Far more desirable would be a situation in which all the members of a community were engaged in creative activity so that the audience at a performance or the visitors at an exhibition would themselves be the performers or the exhibitors at the next.

The plays of teenagers will often be not only experimental in method but contentious in ideas. In one case, the teenage author and the boys performing hoped that their play would offend their audience and make the adults confront the contradiction between the great social issues of the times and the inane preoccupations of their own lives. After the play, the boys were outraged to find their parents chatting pleasurably in the lobby instead of standing silently, filled with shame. But if something offends the parents in connection with these plays, it will be the experimental technique and not the message. The play may say in effect: "Look, Dad, you're quite a philosopher, but your philosophy and your way of life fit each other like a right hand glove on a left hand foot." But the father is proud that his son or daughter is so perceptive.

What young people fail to understand, when they think to shock or anger their parents, is that the current of American intellectual life which makes a villain of the middle class has its source in middle-class self-evaluation. The very fact that the parents have chosen a school in which youngsters are permitted to make corrosive statements about the adult establishment represents the parents' recognition of the paradox of their own established position. Thus, when the children attack what they consider the inanities or the untruths of their parents' lives, they are not violating, but fulfilling, the aspirations which their parents entertain for them. Besides, this teenage attack is not as sharp as that of most of the books which the parents read.

Suppose that in this same school there is a parent named Mrs. King. When she went to school she was poor and was always ashamed to bring her friends home to her underfurnished apartment. But she married an ambitious optometrist, and now she is rich. And in turn, her daughter Alice is ashamed to bring her friends home because she is afraid the apartment is lavish and pretentious. It is a commonplace enough story, but it contains a contradiction. Mrs. King is an active supporter and apologist for Alice's school, which encourages social criticism and that assertion of serious aesthetic taste which attacks her own middle-class follies. On one hand, Mrs. King is the unwitting victim of an economic up-draft, on the other she is an intelligent, independent woman, committed to a philosophy of meanings and values with which the trappings of her life don't have much to do. Thus, when Alice and her classmates attack, in a play, the hypocrisy of middle-class standards, Mrs. King is very pleased, for she agrees with the ideas the young people are expressing.

There is, as a matter of fact, a large element of the paradoxical in the perverse attitude of teenagers toward their parents. When they choose a play to dramatize, or when they write a play of their own, they see themselves as young adults participating in the social, intellectual and aesthetic currents of the times. In this framework, they may look on parents as part of the backward sector of society which has botched things up. But the familial bonds, the ties to Mother and Father, remain very deep, and often strangely sweet. Anyone who looks in on a school lobby some ten minutes or so before curtain time can see that the relationship between teenage players and an audience of parents and relatives is not a tense one. The first time this writer worked with a high school group, the play was scheduled to go on at 8:15 P.M. but had to be held up about twenty minutes until the audience gathered. Meantime, the players had come in at 6:30 to get into costumes and make-up. Once they were in their costumes, it was assumed they would remain backstage out of sight. But within a minute or two after the first of the parents began to arrive, all of the children disappeared and the writer went looking for them. They were in the lobby, in full costume and make-up, shaking hands with their fathers, embracing their mothers, renewing acquaintance with aunts and uncles, kissing sisters just home from college at mid-term. It was a colorful and uninhibited scene. This writer looked on speculatively and decided that this co-mingling of audience and costumed players was one of the more or less irrelevant charms of non-professional dramatics. Except for a one-minute briefing before the curtain goes up, he has never expected to keep a cast waiting out curtain time backstage since.

19
ooooooooo
Image and Reality

THE BUSINESS OF THE previous chapter—the matter of communication with an audience—is of subordinate importance. It is the
process, not the performance, which is of primary importance.
The performance is one step in the process, the last step, but not
the most important step. The most important step is the point at
which one child and another finds his creative image and conveys it with integrity. If this original expression is never expanded and rendered more communicable, a play in which the
children have found the creative image will be a better play in
[258]

the most important respects than a play with more impact but with less vision and integrity. In one of the camps whose dramatics programs have been drawn on for illustration, a professional dramatics coach was achieving marvels of vigor with bold scripts which told stories of heroism and sacrifice. They were very stirring, but they were not good enough. All a player had to do was to throw himself with force into his lines. He was, perhaps, expressing his moral and social convictions, but there was little in the material to penetrate or probe. Meantime some eight-year-old girls, working with a sensitive and quiet young woman counselor, put on a dramatization which was generally not well received. The girls tended to group together and talk softly in the center of the stage, from time to time doing the little bits of pantomime that were called for, such as opening an imaginary cupboard and lifting out imaginary cups and saucers and an imaginary loaf of bread. Their play was weakly communicated. Nevertheless, for perceptive people their play had far more originality and integrity than the plays done in the camp's tradition of "the big bow-wow." The camp director, three or four staff members, one or two younger counselors, and a handful of teen-age boys and girls were aware of the superiority of this play over those they had been used to. Over the next few seasons, by giving young counselors some training, the director was able to establish a more creative tradition of dramatics—one which did not forego all aspects of the earlier tradition, but a new one in which the dramatizations were subtler and richer in human perception, and characterization was achieved, not by throwing the lines, but by the child's finding his way into the character.

The high school production of *Under Milk Wood* is an example of what the adult leader's attitude might be toward failure or success. The teacher was an old hand and knew how to predict a performance on the basis of a dress rehearsal and on the basis of this one he assumed that the performance would drag. He felt that the young people had failed, despite his efforts and theirs, to develop a sense of pace. Instead of anticipating and appearing a moment before the narrator mentioned the character he was playing, each player tended to wait to hear himself mentioned and then appear. The adult felt sure that they would continue to lack pace and he knew that for this kaleidoscopic and plotless dramatic poem, the lack would prove a serious liability in reaching the audience.

He was sorry for the students' sake, because he knew how sweet success tastes to young people who have worked hard on a play. But he himself was completely satisfied. He had seen a poetic work of great beauty whose surface is initially hard to penetrate unfold in the students' minds and imaginations. He had seen them create distinct and imaginative characterizations. He had seen how their capacity for gusty and bawdy humor had taken them to the heart of the poem—and he felt that in the process they had had a most fulfilling experience.

Fortunately, this adult was proved wrong in his assumption that the play would drag. From the outset the group struck a marvelous pace and sustained it through the entire length of the poem-play, which they presented without an intermission. It is good that they did, for by doing so they conveyed that sense of gull cry and cobbled street, of Milk Wood fecundity, of human hurt and absurdity whose discovery and re-expression constituted the dramatic process.

The thesis that it is the process and not the outcome that is of greatest importance has universal validity and is the corrective for two great classical fallacies of educational thought, namely, that the chief goal of education is to provide the child with skills and competences, and, by extension, that the chief goal of education is to prepare the child for life. These positions appear, on the face of it, as truths, for no one in his right mind would deny the importance of a child's acquiring competences, or that one should be better able to deal with life situations because of his schooling. Perhaps, then, they are not so much fallacies as oversimplifications and vulgarizations of a harmful kind.

The error of these positions lies in the concept of time. It is unnatural that a child should learn to read and write and do sums because he may need these competences when he is twenty-one. Rather, he needs to learn to read because there are books he wants to read *now*. He needs to learn about numbers and "sets" because there are questions for which he wants answers *now*. He needs to learn to write because there are things he wants to say *now*. Life itself is a process of greatest complexity; it is a process of which education is, for the child, a very great part. The fifth grader who is adding a column of figures or painting scenery for a play is living his life at the moment and has, in fact, already lived close to a sixth of the years which the actuarial tables predict for him. A high school senior who is conducting an experiment in physics or translating a passage from Camus is living *now* and has already lived a quarter of his allotted span. Education is on-going, like life itself, and the educational process must be, as we have said in another context, "as valid for the child who will die of leukemia six months after graduation as for the child who will live to be ninety." One of the young people to whose work a number of references have been made has lived all of her life in the shadow of death, having been born with a physical condition which did not permit a prediction that she would live to graduate from high school, though she managed to do so. There is perhaps no other child mentioned in this book whose skills are so extensive. And yet not a single skill had, in its acquisition, the smell of futurity about it, but each was acquired because it was needed for things the girl wanted to do or make or say. She has gone about the business of living in a very self-fulfilling way, and school has constituted for her a good life. So it should be for every child.

We can only assume that a child whose heart and mind are open, whose subjectivity finds many gratifications and whose powers of expression are active when he is three years old, and six, and nine, and twelve, and eighteen, is more likely to have an open mind and heart, a more fulfilled subjectivity, a continuing power of expression when he is twenty and fifty and eighty than a child whose subjectivity is thwarted, whose powers of expression are inhibited by the time he is ten or eleven. It is this assumption that gives particular importance to productive, expressive and creative activities, for it sees the child who is being educated not merely in the passive role of learner but in the active role of expresser and doer.

The basic terms of such an educational assumption are subjective and qualitative, not objective and quantitive, and for this reason it would be difficult to test scientifically, except through a complex and extensive use of interview technique. Given, too, the influences which shape human personality, it is hardly possible to say of a given young person—and even less possible of a person of forty or fifty—that it was this and this activity which shaped this and this aspect of his gestalt of meanings and values. For even the very best children's communities suffer real limitations in their role in a child's life. Far beyond the community in which children come together is the community to which they return when the school day or the activity session or the camp season is over—the home, the parents, the sibling situation, the streets, the unsupervised hours, the forces and experiences on which a children's community can come to bear to an extent but which it does not determine. Thus a child may altogether evade the thwarting influence of a poor school or be already so thwarted that he cannot be released by a good one. Or life itself may find ways to reach and fulfill the adult who was a thwarted child or to thwart an adult who was an expansive, expressive child.

For these reasons we cannot follow the careers of any of the boys and girls who were mentioned in this book and say that their careers were given direction because of participation in specific creative activities. Nevertheless, it is interesting—and not altogether without meaning—to see what a few of them have been doing with themselves.

The boy who played the Quaker lad in *The Hearthstone* and who later probed the terrible depths of Judge Danforth in

The Crucible is studying law. By last accounts, the boy who played Proctor was a professional actor. The girl who, in the same play, played Mary Warren with such intensity that she made her hands bleed from her nails decided upon graduating from college to give up her aspiration to be an historian in order to get married. The girl who played Abigail is a reader in a publishing house. The boy who glared and then stomped fatuously out of the courtroom is a mathematician. So, too, is the boy who played Caesar in *Caesar and Cleopatra*. Charmian with her Egyptian braids is a concert pianist. The Quaker who, in *The Hearthstone*, opened the door with such perfect timing for the U.S. marshal is studying medicine. The marshal is a physicist, as is the Greek chorus leader in the dedication of the camp amphitheater. The foppish commander of the British frigate which was taken by Johnny Ordronaux's undermanned privateersman—who was also Mottel, and Fluther, too, in *The Plow and the Stars*—is in moving pictures, but on the producing not the acting end. Johnny Ordronaux himself is a sports writer.

Among these young people, it is perhaps the mathematicians and the physicists who throw the most light on what we are getting at. The boy who played Caesar had, from earliest childhood, loved mathematics beyond other things. Nevertheless, he loved other things, too. In high school he wrote experimental poetry and was one of three students who, over some ten years, were permitted to undertake a difficult comparative study of Chaucer's and Shakespeare's treatments of the story of Troilus and Cressida. He continued the study of literature in college and, as a young man employed as a skindiver by a scientific outfit, spent much of his spare time participating in a local community theater workshop. The U.S. marshal was a Jefferson enthusiast. In high school he was a distinguished student in history, English and Latin; he made several verse translations of Catullus, one of them in terza rima. This writer, who had known both the boy and his family over a number of years and had always assumed that the boy's first interest was social studies, his secondary interest literature, was surprised to find, when the boy was about to enter college, that his first interest had always been science. The Greek chorus leader was generally known for his commitment to mathematics and science, though he wrote prose of lovely and graceful lucidity, whether sly satire or subjective statement of his own relationship with the earth and its hills and waters. He would work over long periods of time on vast pen-and-ink landscapes in which he achieved simultaneously good over-all design and a flawless precision of small detail. In college he found time to be active in the campus civil rights movement.

Why should young people of such obvious gifts for the humanities and the creative arts have chosen fields such as law, medicine, homemaking, mathematics, physics and the civil rights movement as the vehicles for their lives? The answer, of course, is perfectly simple. Each chose the field which had *more* meaning for him, though other things had meaning, too. Each felt that his chosen field was the field through which his particular individuality, on one hand, and his particular humanity, on the other, could best be expressed. In short, it is not the aim of children's dramatics or of any other creative activity to produce actors or other artists, but to enrich the lives of physicists, doctors, lawyers, school teachers, dentists, factory workers, farmers and especially, in these days, parents, giving them a little more sense of what life is all about than they might otherwise have.

Of the players to whom reference has been made, only one has come to the notice of the world—and that under tragic circumstances. This was Andrew Goodman, who, together with James Chaney and Michael Schwerner, was murdered by segregationists in the civil rights struggle in Mississippi. Andy was the mate on Johnny Ordronaux's privateersman. The following year he was Mottel's brother, one of whose get-rich-quick schemes was the making of ink. It was Andy we were talking about when we described the sensitive human insights by which a twelve year old was able to get below the surface of a harsh and superficially rude person and make him as tenderly funny and as loved and—in a deep, essential way—as loving as everyone else. In his sophomore year, Andy was Marc Antony in an informal dramatization of *Julius Caesar*. His gifts were subtle and his Antony was not the flamboyant man who hardly knows where real emotion leaves off and histrionic emotion begins. He was an Antony whose quiet delivery and cunning emphases were as much an incitation to riot as though he had blown up a storm. In junior year, Andy was the Covey in *The Plow and the Stars*. It was his marvelous face which, in the tragic moment, expressed a more disquieting self-revelation than what O'Casey had written seemed to demand. In his senior year he was the author of the stream-of-consciousness story some of his classmates dramatized with readers and a pantomimist. His own role in the senior dramatics program was strangely prophetic. It is best described by one of his classmates in the words she spoke at the dedication of his tombstone:

> "Four years ago I wrote a play in which Andy had the role of a prince who loved life and died to preserve his integrity. Andy gave the part a vitality and impact which my self-conscious attempts at poetic drama did not deserve, and I knew then that this work of his was one of the most beautiful gifts I would ever receive."

It would be a great over-simplification to claim that Andy's participation in creative dramatics shaped the humanity which dictated his decision to go South. But it would be to mistake him altogether not to know that this decision was the direct result of the sensitivities, insights and integrity which characterized both his personal relationships and his creative work. One time when Andy was in sixth grade a lonely boy got himself involved in a wrangle with the other boys and found himself so overwhelmed he ran home and said he would never come to school again. The boys discussed the problem very earnestly, and it was Andy whom they dispatched to the boy's house, feeling that he alone among them could reassure the boy and bring him back—and

Andy did. In college he made his decision to go to Mississippi to work in the Negro voter registration drive. Shortly before he made this decision which cost his life, he talked with his mother about some of the questions which were bothering him. His previous life of creative activity (he had dropped out of college at one point and taken a role in an off-Broadway play) seemed to him detached and he felt a growing need to come face to face with reality. Was his decision a denial of the creative activities that had occupied his boyhood? Or was it an extension of those values which had expressed themselves in creative pursuits? In the absolute way in which young people deal with such questions, it may have seemed to Andy that his decision was a rejection of what he had previously been and of the very tenuous relationship of his boyhood to his maturing concept of reality.

There arises, as they come into adulthood, a disparity in the lives of susceptive young people. While they grow up, they are sheltered from the more severe realities. At the same time, their lives are extraordinarily rich in reflections of realities which they find in literature and history and in the consideration of moral, ethical and social problems and philosophies. It is little wonder that at twenty they find a wide gap between reality and the imagery that has constituted their lives. It is the margin of difference between the person who takes a life and the person who sacrifices his life. Our imagery is the structuring of our vision of reality. Novels, plays, poems, moving pictures, documentaries, editorials and articles, works of art and music, constructs of science and mathematics, our own productive and creative work and that of others—these together with the memory images of our own experiences and the fantasies of our desires—these are the means by which we generalize our realities and see them in relation to the realities of others. On this basis it can be said that what took Andy Goodman to Mississippi when he was twenty was the perceptiveness, the integrity and the humanity which his boyhood had shaped.

These qualities were not, of course, peculiar to Andy

Goodman and the two young men who died with him. These are human qualities which he held in common with others—millions of others, one must assume—with the girl, for instance, who spoke at the dedication of his tombstone and whom we have already met playing Cassius, swathed in a toga and stung by Brutus's barbed tongue. They are qualities which Andy held in common with all the beautiful young pantomimists and improvisers who have threaded their way through this book. It cannot, of course, be claimed that they are qualities which creative activities in general and creative dramatics in particular *plant* in young people. It must rather be assumed that they are more or less universal latencies. They are qualities which are tempered in reality and are of little account if they cannot stand up under the pressures of reality. But in the absence of sufficiently conscious efforts on the part of society to foster them, reality tends more often to thwart these qualities than to evoke them.

What education can and must do—and for this purpose creative activities are its principal tools—is to *hatch* these qualities and bring them out of their latency into consciousness, where they will be available as the means for a more conscious relationship with the real. For many reasons—the probing of important subject matter, the social dynamics of the process, the replica of reality which a dramatization establishes—creative dramatics is a magnificent tool, which education ought to make much more extensive use of than it does.

Sources

ADLER, D. L., and LIPPITT, R., et al. (eds.). *An Experiment with Young People Under Democratic, Autocratic, and Laissez-Faire Atmosphere—Proceedings of the National Conference of Social Work*. New York: Columbia University Press, 1939.

CLARK, KENNETH B. *Dark Ghetto*. New York: Harper & Row, Publishers, Inc., 1965.

SPOLIN, VIOLA. *Improvisation for the Theater: A Handbook of Teaching and Directing Techniques*. Evanston: Northwestern University Press, 1963.

STANISLAVSKI, CONSTANTIN. *An Actor Prepares* (trans. by Elizabeth Hapgood). New York: Theatre Arts Books, 1936.

WARD, WINIFRED. *Playmaking with Children*. New York: Appleton-Century-Crofts, Inc., 1957.

WILLISON, GEORGE F. *Let's Make a Play*. New York: Harper & Brothers, 1940.

ALEICHEM, SHOLOM. *Adventures of Mottel, the Cantor's Son* (trans. by Tamara Kahana). New York: Abelard-Schuman, Ltd., 1953.

———. *Collected Stories of Sholom Aleichem* (2 vols.). New York: Crown Publishers, Inc.

AUSUBEL, NATHAN (ed.). *A Treasury of Jewish Folklore*. New York: Crown Publishers, Inc., 1948.

BETKIN, B. A. (ed.). *A Treasury of American Folklore*. New York: Crown Publishers, Inc., 1944.

COHEN, MIKE (ed.). *101 Plus 5 Folksongs for Camp*. New York: Oak Publications, 1966.

EBERHARD, WOLFRAM (ed. and trans.). *Chinese Fairy Tales and Folk Tales*. New York: E. P. Dutton & Co., 1938.

FAST, HOWARD. *Patrick Henry and the Frigate's Keel*. New York: World Publishing Co., 1946.

HUGHES, LANGSTON, and BONTEMPS, ARNA (eds.). *The Poetry of the Negro, 1746–1949*. New York: Doubleday and Co., Ltd., 1949.

LEE, FRANK HAROLD (ed.). *Folk Tales of All Nations*. New York: Coward-McCann, Inc., 1930.

SANDBURG, CARL. *American Songbag*. New York: Harcourt, Brace and Co., 1927.

SIKS, GERALDINE B. (ed.). *Children's Literature for Dramatization: An Anthology*. New York, Evanston and London: Harper & Row, Publishers, Inc., 1964.

VAN DOREN, MARK (ed.). *An Anthology of World Poetry*. New York: Albert & Charles Boni, Inc., 1928.

Index